Language development and individual differences

LANGUAGE DEVELOPMENT AND INDIVIDUAL DIFFERENCES

A STUDY OF AUXILIARY VERB LEARNING

BRIAN J. RICHARDS

UNIVERSITY OF READING
FACULTY OF EDUCATION
AND COMMUNITY STUDIES

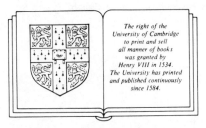

The right of the
University of Cambridge
to print and sell
all manner of books
was granted by
Henry VIII in 1534.
The University has printed
and published continuously
since 1584.

CAMBRIDGE UNIVERSITY PRESS

CAMBRIDGE

NEW YORK   PORT CHESTER

MELBOURNE   SYDNEY

Published by the Press Syndicate of the University of Cambridge
The Pitt Building, Trumpington Street, Cambridge CB2 1RP
40 West 20th Street, New York, NY 10011, USA
10 Stamford Road, Oakleigh, Melbourne 3166, Australia

First published 1990

Printed in Great Britain by The Bath Press, Avon

British Library cataloguing in publication data

Richards, Brian J.
Language development and individual differences: a
study of auxiliary verb learning.
1. Children. Language skills. Development
I. Title
401'.9

Library of Congress cataloguing in publication data
Richards, Brian J.
Language development and individual differences: a study of
auxiliary verb learning/Brian J. Richards.
    p. ca.
Includes bibliographical references.
ISBN 0 521 36253 9
1. Language acquisition.   2. Grammar, Comparative and general –
Auxiliaries.   3. Individual differences in children.   4. English
language – Auxiliary verbs.   I. Title.
P118.R495   1990
401'.93 – dc20   89–22198   CIP

To Mair and Fiona

Contents

PART III: ENVIRONMENTAL INFLUENCES AND INDIVI-
DUAL DIFFERENCES IN AUXILIARY VERB LEARNING

Figures

Tables

Preface

This book is based on research funded by the Economic and Social Research Council (ESRC) (reference number: C00428325005) and by a grant from Bristol University. I should also like to thank the following for their help and support during the preparation of this volume: Peter Robinson and Gordon Wells for advice during the planning and execution of the research; Sally Barnes, Mary Gutfreund, David Satterly, and Gordon Wells for giving me access to their data and documentation, and for answering innumerable queries about the fine details of their study; Dorothy Gibbs, Elena Lieven, Sara Meadows, Peter Robinson, and especially Lynette Dunn for their comments on earlier drafts; my parents, parents-in-law, and my wife Mair for their painstaking help with the tedious task of checking and correcting the manuscript; finally, the children themselves – Catherine Evans, David Gabica, Hannah Gillard, Helen Gordon, Siân Hewlett, Lawrence Humphries, Sophie Lane, Rachel Smith and David Trudgeon, who provided the material for Part II of the book, and, of course, their parents who suffered the inconvenience of a stranger entering their homes at regular intervals for a period of nine months.

Symbols used in transcription
(Adapted from Wells, 1981, pp. 277–8)

[　] Contextual information, interpretations of utterances and descriptions of tone of voice.

⟨　⟩ Utterances or parts of utterances which are in doubt are enclosed in angular brackets. Where two interpretations are possible, these are separated by an oblique line (/).

? Used at the end of any utterance where an interrogative meaning is considered to have been intended.

! Used at the end of an utterance considered to have exclamatory force.

* Used to indicate an ungrammatical sentence.

⟨?⟩ Used to indicate an unintelligible word.

... Stops indicate pauses. One stop indicates a short pause. Thereafter, the number of stops corresponds with the estimated length of the pause in seconds.

(v) Indicates that the preceding word was used as a vocative, to call or hold the attention of the addressee.

\# Used to indicate that a sentence has been invented for the purpose of illustration.

Stress (adapted from Quirk et al., 1985):

′ Indicates primary stress.

ˈ Indicates secondary stress.

″ Indicates very heavy, or contrastive stress.

Pronunciation table

| | CONSONANTS | | | | VOWELS | |
	Voiceless			Voiced		
/p/	pig	/b/	big		/iː/	sheep
/t/	ten	/d/	den		/ɪ/	ship
/k/	cot	/g/	got		/e/	bed
/f/	fat	/v/	vat		/æ/	bad
/θ/	thin	/ð/	then		/ɑː/	calm
/s/	soon	/z/	zero		/ɒ/	pot
/ʃ/	fish	/ʒ/	pleasure		/ɔː/	caught
/tʃ/	cheap	/dʒ/	jeep		/ʊ/	put
/h/	hot	/m/	sum		/uː/	boot
		/n/	sun		/ʌ/	cut
		/ŋ/	sung		/ɜːʳ/	bird
		/l/	led		/ə/	above
		/r/	red		/eɪ/	day
		/j/	yet		/əʊ/	coal
		/w/	wet		/aɪ/	lie
					/aʊ/	now
					/ɔɪ/	boy
					/ɪəʳ/	here
					/eəʳ/	there
					/ʊəʳ/	poor
					/eɪəʳ/	player
					/əʊəʳ/	lower
					/aɪəʳ/	tire
					/aʊəʳ/	tower
					/ɔɪəʳ/	employer

Syllabic consonants are indicated thus: n̩, l̩
/ ʳ/ denotes the possibility (e.g. in AmE) of 'postvocalic r'.

Source: Quirk et al., 1985, p. viii.

PART I

Introductory sections

Introduction

Why should a book about individual differences choose to focus on auxiliary verb learning?

When I was first attached to the Bristol Longitudinal Study of Language Development in the autumn of 1983, I had no clear idea of the direction in which an investigation into individual differences would take me. Nevertheless, a survey of the existing child language literature highlighted the auxiliary system as a feature on which children varied in a number of ways which might possibly be related.

The auxiliary seemed to be of particular interest in three ways. Firstly, it appeared that a high frequency of auxiliaries at a certain stage might be associated with a distinctive 'style' or 'route' of language development, or with strategies to communicate at a level beyond the child's current stage of linguistic competence. Secondly, Gordon Wells' paper 'Learning and using the auxiliary verb in English' (Wells, 1979a) showed extensive variation in the rate of emergence of auxiliaries which he interpreted as evidence of children's differing analytical abilities in the development of form classes. Thirdly, evidence from experimental and naturalistic studies suggested that the auxiliary and the structures in which it participated were particularly sensitive to environmental influences. A statistical relationship between the frequency of Yes/No questions (Y/Ns) heard by children and subsequent rate of auxiliary verb growth emerged as the most stable finding from correlational studies of the effects of input on rate of language development.

Since the publication of Newport, Gleitman and Gleitman's (1977) study of 'motherese' effects, the view has gained currency that children learn auxiliaries via the analytic route of hearing noncontracted, stressed forms in initial position in Y/N inversions but first using them in medial position in declaratives. This soon became the accepted wisdom among child language researchers and theorists working from widely divergent perspectives. Yet an examination of the fine details of the published research revealed a number of discrepancies and gave rise to some puzzling questions. These were both theoretical and methodological in nature, and raised issues which were equally relevant to studying variation in the sequence and style of auxiliary verb learning as to investigating predictors of accelerated development. How, for example, do we define the auxiliary? Is the set of verbs included in child language research compatible with accounts of the processes involved in their acquisition? How do we measure rate of development? Is a faster rate of auxiliary learning as measured in previous research truly indicative of rule-based performance – or are there other explanations? How do we know whether usage reflects linguistic competence? Is the concept of 'acquisition' at all appropriate in the context of the auxiliary and, if so, how do we define it? Above all, why had input studies which subdivided Y/Ns found that it was not inverted Y/Ns which predicted auxiliary gains, but a category which tended to drop the auxiliary altogether?

In the research reported below these questions were addressed by analysing data from three sources. The recordings and transcripts of thirty-three Bristol children in Wells' (1979a) study were reanalysed in order to test alternative explanations for the differences in rate of development and to assess the effect of varying the set of verbs classified as 'auxiliary'. Data from thirty-two Bristol children in Barnes, Gutfreund, Satterly and Wells' (1983) study of environmental influences were also analysed in greater depth to test specific hypotheses about the relationship between input and auxiliary learning. Finally, using a combination of an elicitation task and home recordings of spontaneous speech, seven children from South Wales were monitored over a period of nine months in a more fine-grained study of variation in style, sequence and rate of development.

1 The auxiliary and the young language learner

1.1 The importance of the auxiliary in the child's linguistic development

Auxiliary verbs are an essential component of most well-formed interrogatives, negation, ellipsis, positive emphasis, and the negative imperative. They convey temporal and aspectual meanings and, in the case of the modal verbs, meanings of possibility, ability, permission, volition, obligation and necessity. The modals also form the basis of hypothetical reference and, through variation on dimensions such as type of modality and tense, convey requests of differing degrees of politeness (Perkins, 1983a).

In the sequence of child language learning, analysis of emergence data (Wells, 1985) shows the importance of auxiliaries and the meanings they express in successive levels of development. Elaboration of the verb phrase is particularly dependent on the inclusion, co-occurrence and manipulation of the auxiliary element (see Wells, 1985, p. 269). It is also evident that children in the early stages of language learning are able to realise certain of the meanings and functions associated with the auxiliary by other means. Yes/No questions (Y/Ns) marked by intonation, and continuous and perfect aspect, for example, generally appear before the co-occurrence of the appropriate auxiliary and a main verb. Despite the possibility of alternative strategies to express auxiliary meanings, however, an increasing mastery of the syntax, semantics and pragmatics of auxiliary usage is an inextricable part of language development from an early stage.

1.2 Auxiliary verb learning

1.2.1 Studies of the auxiliary verb in young children

Studies which concentrate exclusively on the full range of auxiliary verbs or even a significant subset are relatively few in number. Much of our knowledge of early auxiliary verb learning comes from investigations into general linguistic development or into areas in which the auxiliary was not usually the primary focus of attention. These include studies of negation, types of question, ellipsis, and continuous and perfect aspect.

Modal verbs have frequently been treated separately from the rest of the auxiliary class. Subjects in these studies embrace a wider age range (up to 12 years) than those referred to above (usually 2–4 years). Modal verb studies tend to concentrate on either syntax or semantics. Major's (1974) cross-sectional study of children's syntactic competence with modals is an example of the former type. Highly complex combinations of modal and primary auxiliaries were elicited in sentences which varied according to mood, tense, and polarity. The development of modal meanings in English is investigated in naturalistic studies by Perkins (1983a) and Shields (1974), and in experimental work by Hirst and Weil (1982).

Three pieces of research set out to investigate the auxiliary class without omitting any subcategory. Kypriotaki (1974) used an imitation test with thirty children aged between 2;1 and 5;1. Grammatical competence with fifteen possible types of auxiliary verb string was tested in declarative sentences, and affirmative and negative questions. Items therefore vary in complexity from 'NP + can see me on the floor', to some of marginal acceptability such as 'The new supermarket should have been being built slowly' (Kypriotaki, 1974, p. 89). In observational studies, Park (1971) analysed the auxiliary verb development in two German speaking children from 2;1 and 2;4 to 3;2 and 3;5 respectively, and Wells (1979a) followed the progress of the sixty younger children in the Bristol study of language development between 1;6 and 3;6. In the most comprehensive investigation into early auxiliary development to date, Wells examined the emergence and rate of development of auxiliary forms and meanings. Distribution of forms in the language of the children and in the speech addressed to them was compared, and relationships between rate of development and demographic variables such as sex and social class were examined. This influential piece of research, which is supplemented by further analyses in Wells (1985) to include data from older children, provided the initial impetus for the work described below.

1.2.2 Key aspects of auxiliary verb development

The change in perspective on auxiliary verb development during the years spanned by the above research mirrors shifts in the interpretation of language development in general. Gradually we have seen a movement away from an emphasis on the apparent ease and rapidity of language learning, characterised by 'across the board' progress (Chomsky, 1964, p. 39). More finely-grained analyses have given rise to a more gradual account of how specific knowledge and 'limited scope patterns' (Peters, 1986) become integrated as a more broadly based rule system, possibly after undergoing a series of minor, closely spaced reorganisations (Peters, 1986). If sampling is infrequent, however, these can be wrongly interpreted as sudden, major developmental shifts.

With regard to the auxiliary, an example of the former approach is provided by Ervin-Tripp:

> Complex patterns such as the auxiliary system in English ... are acquired in a relatively short period of time, obviously on the basis of transfer of patterns between items which do not share semantic features. I think it will be very hard to find any semantic commonality between *can*, *will*, and *do*, which would be adequate to the rapid acquisition of the system by 2 year olds. (Ervin-Tripp, 1973, p. 282)

A more recent perspective on the auxiliary results from research which shows the gradual extension of highly specific knowledge of auxiliaries to a wider range of linguistic contexts and syntactic frames before the various auxiliaries and their subforms (or allomorphs) are related and integrated across the contexts in which they occur. Such processes have been identified in learning auxiliary HAVE[1] (Fletcher, 1982), copula and auxiliary BE (Kuczaj, 1981b), and auxiliary inversion in Wh-questions (Kuczaj and Brannick, 1979). One result can be the existence of intermediate stages during which the child has a mixture of general and specific knowledge of the system being acquired. This can be seen in Kuczaj and Maratsos' (1983) analysis of auxiliary usage in Y/Ns in sixteen children aged 1;11 to 5;6. Evidence from patterns in inverted and non-inverted questions suggested that while children had a general rule requiring an auxiliary in initial position in Y/Ns (as evidenced by the absence of non-inverted Y/Ns), it was only applied to specific auxiliaries, even though other auxiliaries occurred in declarative sentences. On the other hand, it is acknowledged that across-the-board developments can also take place (Kuczaj and Maratsos, 1983), though these are the exception rather than the rule (Kuczaj and Brannick, 1979). This is an area of individual differences which will be explored below.

There has also been a growing appreciation that the earliest auxiliary verb usage tends to be not just syntactically unanalysed (e.g. Ervin, 1964; Klima and Bellugi, 1966; Menyuk, 1971) but also highly restricted semantically. The modal auxiliaries, for example, tend to be used first as pure performatives (Fletcher, 1979) for which emergence is piecemeal (Stephany, 1986). The further development of modal and primary auxiliaries then unfolds in a sequence which corresponds to a combination of grammatical and semantic complexity (Wells, 1979a, 1985).

1.3 Individual differences and auxiliary verb learning

Problems associated with learning auxiliaries lead one to suspect that this would be an area of pronounced variation. Difficulties come under two headings: the phonological and the syntactic/semantic. Phonologically, the difficulty is that, unless used for contrastive stress, as operators in main verb ellipsis, or possibly in initial position in subject-auxiliary inversion, auxiliaries are most commonly unstressed. Since lack of stress is also frequently accompanied by phonological reduction and contraction, most auxiliaries have weak forms which occur in unstressed positions (Palmer, 1965). These may be syllabic forms such as /kən/ or nonsyllabic /kn/, or contracted forms (e.g. 'he's'). In addition, Fletcher (1983) has shown that, even in the language addressed to young children, there is variation in the degree of reduction of auxiliary forms. With regard to contraction, the auxiliary is both reduced, and enclitic to the previous morpheme, usually a noun or pronoun. As a result, the child is faced with both a segmentation task, and the difficulty of attending to non-salient items in the incoming stream of speech.

In addition to the phonological features of auxiliaries, they belong to the closed classes of lexical items. In contrast with the open classes, such as nouns, lexical verbs, and adjectives, which have high semantic content and characterise Stage I telegraphic speech (Brown, 1973), auxiliaries comprise a small, closed set of grammatical words, or functors, which have low semantic content. By one analysis, auxiliaries are not part of the propositional content of a sentence, but may co-occur with any proposition as a means of modulating the meaning according to time, modality and aspect. As a small set of items with such extensive applications, their meanings will be broad and polysemous, and not easily interpretable from aspects of the situational context (Woisetschlaeger, 1985).

1.3.1 Rate of development
Given the features outlined above, it is not surprising that considerable differences are evident in normally developing children in both age of emergence and rate of development of auxiliaries. The period from first emergence among sixty children to a criterion of mastery can range from less than three months to more than twelve (Wells, 1979a). Variation in the rate of learning auxiliaries has been found to be related to the frequency of auxiliaries in input (K. E. Nelson[2], Denninger, Bonvillian, Kaplan and Baker, 1984) or more usually

to an interaction between the quality and frequency of auxiliaries. In particular, Y/Ns with certain functions or syntactic features predict rate of development (Barnes et al., 1983; Furrow, Nelson and Benedict, 1979; Gleitman, Newport and Gleitman, 1984; Hoff-Ginsberg, 1985, 1986; Yoder and Kaiser, 1989). Further evidence of the auxiliary's susceptibility to environmental effects is provided by the experimental studies of K. E. Nelson and colleagues (Baker and Nelson, 1984; Nelson, 1977; Nelson, Carskaddon and Bonvillian, 1973). This issue will be pursued in Chapter 10 where the role of Y/Ns in clarifying the auxiliary for the child will be explored in detail.

1.3.2 Children with language learning difficulties

It can also be predicted that, despite its indispensability in making the transition to a more adult linguistic style, some of the essential features of auxiliaries are hurdles which some children only overcome with difficulty, and results of several studies suggest that anomalies in auxiliary verb development result from more than just a general language delay. Blind children, for example, are delayed in auxiliary development while normal in other respects (Landau and Gleitman, 1985). One child, described as a bright, slow language learner (Weeks, 1974), shows a delay in using auxiliary DO which places it well outside the expected sequence of development. Teenage prelingually deaf children make a large number of errors in structures which would usually contain an auxiliary, including errors both of omission and anomalous usage (e.g. 'I have been take my friend to park', Dawson, 1981, p. 69). The status of 'deafisms' is controversial (see Dawson, 1981), but there is some consensus that the prelingually deaf make considerable use of stereotyped expressions (Dawson, 1981; Moores, 1970), and it seems likely that many such errors are the result of rote-learning strategies.

Language-impaired children have particular difficulty in dealing with the type of structure in which the auxiliary participates (Haber, 1981, 1982) and one particularly illuminating study is reported by Fletcher (1983) in which the syntax of normally developing 5-year-olds was compared with that of a language-impaired group. The interesting aspect of this research is not simply that the normal children used more auxiliaries, nor that the delayed group made more errors of auxiliary omission. What is particularly thought provoking is that while the frequency of *full* auxiliaries, modals, DO-support, and other auxiliaries discriminate significantly between the two groups, the frequency of *catenatives* and *contracted* auxiliaries do not. One explanation would be that the language-impaired group had not been able to relate the contracted and noncontracted forms, but did have the capacity to learn Pronoun + Contracted Auxiliary as unanalysed, unsegmented single morphemes.

1.3.3 Variation in style[3] of development

Several studies suggest qualitative differences between normally developing children learning structures containing auxiliaries. It will be shown in Chapter 7, for example, that the literature on tag questions shows highly varied patterns relating to error and the stage and rate of development.

Kuczaj links differences in the age at which two children (Abe and Ben) acquire auxiliary forms in declaratives and Y/Ns (Kuczaj and Maratsos, 1983) and in the acquisition of auxiliary and copula BE (Kuczaj, 1981b) to differences in the children's language learning style. The children are characterised as follows: 'Abe was a much more reflective language learner than Ben and appeared to consolidate much of his linguistic knowledge prior to employing it in his spontaneous speech... On the other hand, Ben appeared to be a much more impulsive language learner, frequently using forms and structures on the basis of fragmentary (and sometimes incorrect) analyses' (Kuczaj and Maratsos, 1983, p. 442). When we look at Kuczaj and Maratsos' results (pp. 442 and 443) it appears that Ben is actually the faster developer. In nearly every case, Ben acquired the target forms in declarative and Y/N contexts at an earlier age than Abe. On the other hand, Kuczaj notes elsewhere that in the acquisition of BE forms, 'Ben exhibited a constant lack of integration of allomorphs' (Kuczaj, 1981b, p. 80). Abe, by contrast, showed greater evidence of simultaneous acquisitions, which Kuczaj takes as evidence of the existence of a more integrated system.

If Kuczaj's interpretation is correct, children differ on two, possibly correlated dimensions: firstly, a willingness to use, and develop piecemeal, parts of a system which is relatively poorly understood; secondly, 'how quickly and on what basis children attempt to generalize' (Kuczaj, 1981b, p. 82). Evidence from children learning auxiliaries to form the compound past tense in German also suggests differences in the extent to which children proceed by piecemeal learning or by making generalisations (Mills, 1985). Mills' analysis, however, does not tally perfectly with the data from Abe and Ben. Essentially, the difference is that for Mills, some children are learning, context by context, which of two auxiliaries co-occurs with certain lexical verbs. These children, therefore, make no errors in auxiliary verb choice. The children who make the errors will be those who overgeneralise on the basis of the form heard most frequently. Ben, on the other hand, learns forms piecemeal, but makes errors because he is prepared to attempt generalisations from too little evidence. Abe's data contain fewer errors because his more reflective approach allows more secure rules to be extracted from a wider range of linguistic experience.

This contrast between data from two aspects of learning auxiliaries suggests that the various continua on which children differ may at times appear to be poorly correlated. A common approach to learning different areas of a linguistic system, such as the development of the auxiliary class, as opposed to learning to apply an auxiliary selection rule to existing form-classes, may give rise to quite different features in children's utterances.

1.3.4 The analytic–holistic, referential–expressive, and nominal–pronominal dichotomies: relevance for the auxiliary

Since the early 1970s a body of research has emerged which suggests that a number of variables on which children differ during early language development are associated in such a way that two distinct styles of language learning can be hypothesised. These variables, which have been reviewed in detail by Bates, Bretherton and Snyder (1988), Bretherton, McNew, Snyder and Bates (1983), Richards (1987a), Nelson (1985), Wells (1986) are summarised in Table 1.1.

At one extreme, some children appear to emphasise learning and using nouns and noun phrases, use language for representational rather than personal–social functions, articulate clearly, and apply an analytic or 'bottom-up' (Peters, 1986) approach to processing language associated with a predictable sequence of grammatical and phonological development. This style has attracted the labels 'referential' (Nelson, 1973), 'nominal' (Bloom, Lightbown and Hood, 1975), or 'analytic' (Peters, 1983).

By contrast, other children use a higher proportion of pronouns and other function words, learn stereotyped phrases, and lengthy unanalysed units, display advanced intonation but speak less clearly, use language for personal–social functions and use a 'top-down' (Peters, 1986) approach to language learning. Such children have been referred to as 'expressive' (Nelson, 1973), 'pronominal' (Bloom et al., 1975), and 'gestalt' or 'holistic' (Peters, 1983).

Before discussing the relevance of these studies to the auxiliary, it is important to emphasise that the dichotomy which has been created is to be regarded as a useful conceptual tool rather than two discrete categories to which all, or even some, language learners can be unequivocally allocated (Barnes, 1984). Each 'style' is therefore a collection of variables, each of which has been shown to be related to at least one other variable in the group, and

Table 1.1 *Characteristics associated with contrasting styles of early language development*

Referential/Nominal/Analytic	Expressive/Pronominal/Holistic
Function and focus	
representational functions	personal–social functions
	wider range of speech acts
object oriented	person oriented
Syntactic/semantic features	
emphasis on general nominals/nouns/ noun phrases	higher proportion of functors, especially pronouns
telegraphic style	pivot constructions
	unanalysed routines
	formulae
wider range of constituent combinations	
Strategies	
risk-takers	
	use of dummy forms
imitation of object names	general imitation
Rate of development	
faster syntax development	
larger vocabulary	
Phonology	
clear articulation	less clear segmentation
	advanced intonation
	filler sounds
	faster speech rate
Demographic variables	
educated parents	
girls	
first-born children	

some of which can be shown to cluster in statistically related groups (Bretherton et al., 1983). These linguistic variables are continua, but a variable in Style 1 (e.g. frequency of nominals), and its corresponding variable in Style 2 (e.g. frequency of pronominals) have to be seen as two separate continua rather than as a single dimension. Recently, Bates et al. (1988) have identified comprehension, analysed production, and rote production as three partially separable strands of variance in their study of twenty-seven children from

10 months to 28 months. The relative importance of each mechanism varies at different stages of development; distinct style results from an undue emphasis on one mechanism.

While it is possible to demonstrate statistically that a number of variables in each group do form clusters, the groupings and interrelationships are far more complex than the above dichotomy would suggest, and Bretherton et al. (1983) found several variables (sex, position in the family, imitation, and pivot constructions) not to be associated with the expected clusters. The authors also pointed out that while making reference is highly dependent on nominals, their use for personal–social functions is in no way precluded. In addition, several authors draw attention to the influence of context on within-child variation; nominal or pronominal tendency varies according to situation (Nelson, 1985) just as a tendency to use analytic or holistic strategies depends on the functional demands of the context (Peters, 1977). Nelson points out the formulaic nature of much social speech, and the tendency for utterances addressed to children in contexts of social control to be multiword sequences which present difficulties of segmentation. Differential exposure to this type of context or to labelling contexts, in which sentence constituents tend to be presented separately, may, according to Nelson, influence both the child's approach to processing speech, as well as the child's conception of what language is most useful for.

The relevance of the exposition above for the auxiliary is as follows. Auxiliaries were found by Bretherton et al. (1983) to be associated with a 'multiword grammatical morpheme cluster'. This group of measures, which included various functors, pronouns, and inflections, most closely resembled a pronominal/expressive style. Since Bretherton et al. attribute the similarity of the expressive and pronominal styles to an underlying tendency to acquire phrases or sentences holistically, it is possible that some children more than others develop the auxiliary in unanalysed or partially analysed units of several morphemes. It is also possible, therefore, given the influence of context and function, that these will be associated with contexts in which the function of utterances is personal–social.

When considered in the light of other factors identified above – variation in age of emergence and rate at which the auxiliary develops, piecemeal emergence in contrast with across-the-board developments, early unanalysed usage, restricted use of modals as performatives, variation in the amount of evidence from which children develop rules, the use of holistic strategies by children with language learning difficulties, and environmental effects related to analytic rule-learning – the analytic and holistic dimensions provide a useful frame of reference for investigating individual differences in auxiliary verb learning.

1.4 Summary of sources of variation in rate and style of auxiliary verb development

The evidence outlined above suggests the following sources of variation in auxiliary verb learning:

1. The ability to attend to and encode unstressed elements. The ability to encode and exploit features of input which facilitate segmentation of the auxiliary constituent. The ability to encode consistencies in form/meaning relationships.
2. The ability to perceive regularities in the syntactic behaviour of auxiliaries and to apply this knowledge in developing the auxiliary as a form-class.
3. Variation in the degree to which children acquire unanalysed structures containing auxiliary forms.
4. Relative caution or impulsiveness in using a system which is only partially understood.
5. Environmental influences on rate, and possibly on style of development. Features of input may be facilitative if they a) increase the salience of unstressed auxiliaries, b) demonstrate the relationship between contracted and full forms, c) lessen variation in the degree of reduction of auxiliary forms, d) clarify the boundaries between auxiliaries and other constituents, and e) illustrate consistent relationships between situational context and the linguistic context of the auxiliary.

1.5 Definition of the auxiliary

Chapter 10 will demonstrate the extent of variation in the group of verbs classified as auxiliaries in child language research. However, it is important for any research which investigates the development of a form-class to adopt a definition which is consistent with the researcher's hypotheses about a) how the child acquires exemplars from the linguistic environment, and b) the common ground shared by those exemplars which is sufficiently salient for the child to perceive. This may seem an obvious point, but where the approach to child language has been empirical rather than theoretical, assumptions underlying the investigators' choice of auxiliaries have rarely been made explicit.

Although the status of the auxiliary is controversial (see papers in Heny and Richards, 1983), the view is taken here that a subgroup of verbs can be defined on the basis of a common set of distributional characteristics which are likely to be perceived by the child, and which are relevant to hypotheses about the role of input in clarification and segmentation. Some of the criteria outlined in the literature (e.g. the 'voice transformation' criterion of Quirk, Greenbaum, Leech and Svartvik, 1972) have no obvious relevance for the early development of a form-class in young children and the diversity of meanings conveyed by the various auxiliaries makes a grouping on semantic grounds difficult to justify. While it is possible to regard the modal auxiliaries as a more cohesive group, since they subject propositions to varying types and degrees of potential and constraint, it is difficult to see how the child could possibly relate these to the aspectual meanings conveyed by HAVE and BE, or the semantically empty DO. It is more likely to be syntactic operations these verbs have in common which would be salient for the child, and allow the development of a form-class based on a distributional analysis (see, for example, Maratsos, 1982; Maratsos and Chalkley, 1980).

Apart from their ability to co-occur with lexical verbs and their participles without the infinitive particle 'to', the most salient syntactic features of auxiliaries are Palmer's (1965, 1979) NICE properties (Negation, Interrogation, Code, Emphatic Affirmation). Negation of the auxiliary is accomplished by the addition of the negative particle 'not', particularly its contracted form '-n't' (has/hasn't). Y/N questions and most Wh- questions can be formed by subject–auxiliary inversion (#'Can I...?'). In 'code', auxiliaries act as operator for main verb ellipsis (#'I can't do this but you *can*') while 'emphatic affirmation' refers to the use of the stressed auxiliary for contrastive emphasis, or contradiction ('I 'have done it'). These processes are, of course, not available to verbs other than auxiliaries and copula BE (#*'Plays he for United?', etc.) and in all other cases an appropriate form of DO is introduced (#'Does he play for United?').

In the research to be described in Chapters 2 to 11, it is these four properties which will be regarded as the defining characteristics of the auxiliary. It will be noticed, however, that this criterion automatically excludes several auxiliary forms which elsewhere have been included in child language studies. Using Quirk, Greenbaum, Leech and Svartvik's (1985, p. 137) classification of verbs, 'marginal modals' (e.g. used to, dare), 'modal idioms' (had better, got to), 'semi-auxiliaries' (going to, have to), and Main Verb + Infinitive constructions (want to) will be omitted from the analysis *unless children are found to use them for the NICE operations*. One effect of varying membership of the auxiliary class will be examined in the next chapter but the main justification is that a definition of the auxiliary is being adopted which limits the verbs studied to those whose syntactic behaviour is most consistent, and also most relevant to hypotheses about how members of the auxiliary class are acquired: inversion, stress, and ellipsis have the potential to increase the salience and facilitate the segmentation of unstressed, reduced and contracted forms addressed to the child.

The set of verbs to be analysed is therefore the primary auxiliaries (DO, HAVE, BE) and the central modals (CAN, COULD, MAY, MIGHT, SHALL, SHOULD, WILL, WOULD, MUST).

2 Rate of auxiliary verb learning in thirty-three children

2.1 Introduction

Perhaps the most dramatic demonstration of variation in the development of the auxiliary is to be found in Wells (1979a). Using the Bristol child language corpus, Wells studied sixty children's emerging auxiliary forms and meanings between the ages 1;6 and 3;6. For each child the transcripts of nine recordings made at three-monthly intervals were analysed. The children had been selected to provide a representative sample balanced for family background, sex, and season of birth, and naturalistic data were obtained using radio-microphones and tape recorders pre-programmed to record 24 × 90 second samples between 9am and 6pm.

Wells attempted to distinguish between piecemeal development and syntactic rule learning by measuring the interval between the first emergence of auxiliaries (defined as the occurrence of a single form, but excluding negative imperative 'don't') and evidence of rule-based auxiliary use (defined as the occurrence of five different major forms). For most children (forty), the figure obtained is the equivalent of one or two recording intervals (i.e. three or six months). Four children, however, attain the criterion on a single occasion (in less than three months), while a further three take at least four occasions (twelve months or more). The fact that over a third of the sample reach the criterion in three months or less is taken by Wells as evidence of rapid rule learning. For the remainder, a more piecemeal approach was indicated.

If variation in the time which elapses between first emergence of auxiliaries and a criterion of mastery really does reflect a single dimension of piecemeal versus analytic learning, this would clearly be of considerable interest to an investigation into individual differences. On the other hand, Wells' results are also open to quite different interpretations, and the methodology raises further important questions which need to be addressed before moving on to the more intensive study described in Part II of this volume.

2.2 Alternative interpretations of variation in 'emergence to criterion' scores

Richards (1987a) replicated and then systematically varied Wells' procedure on a subsample of thirty-three of the original subjects in order to consider the possible contribution of five factors: transcription and sampling error, the set of verbs defined as 'auxiliary', the validity of Wells' criterion of acquisition, variation in time of first emergence, and the possibility that fast developers were rapid piecemeal learners with little knowledge of the syntax of auxiliaries. These five factors will be considered below.

2.2.1 Transcription and sampling error

Because emergence is defined as the recorded usage of any one auxiliary form, a single error can result in a large difference to a child's emergence to criterion score. Suppose, for example, a child was wrongly attributed a form in Recording 2, and produced no further forms until Recording 10 when five different forms were sampled. This would mean that a 'true' score of zero (i.e. less than three months) would incorrectly rate as a score of twenty-four months. Errors of equal magnitude can arise from failing to credit a child with an auxiliary.

Richards (1987a) retranscribed recordings from thirty-three children in order to estimate the effect of transcription error, and found the correlation between emergence to criterion scores before and after retranscription to be .78. It was found that although there was an overall agreement of just over 80% on the transcription of auxiliary forms, the retranscription caused the scores of eleven out of the thirty-three children to be revised. For one child the emergence to criterion score had to be reduced from eighteen months to three months. In all other cases, however, the difference was no greater than plus or minus one recording interval (three months). As one might predict from the properties of auxiliaries discussed in Section 1.3 it was those auxiliaries which are capable of contraction (HAVE, BE, WILL) which were associated with the highest incidence of transcription error. Nevertheless, the amount of variation in emergence to criterion scores was not reduced as a result of retranscription. The apparent variation in rate of syntactic rule learning cannot therefore be regarded as an artefact of transcription error.

2.2.2 The set of verbs defined as 'auxiliary'

Wells included the following twenty major forms: DO, HAVE+EN, BE+ING, BE (Passive), CAN, COULD, WILL, WOULD, SHALL, SHOULD,

MUST, MAY, MIGHT , BE GOING TO, HAVE GOT TO, HAVE TO, HAD BETTER, WOULD LIKE TO, BE ABLE TO, OUGHT. Minor variations on Wells' procedure in the treatment of forms with doubtful auxiliary status such as /s/ and /z/ + 'gone' or the truncated passive led to only negligible changes in emergence to criterion scores. However, Wells' set of auxiliaries is a heterogeneous group and it was possible that variation in rate of learning would be substantially reduced if the analysis were confined to a group whose syntactic behaviour was more similar. The procedure was therefore repeated using only the primary auxiliaries and central modals listed in Section 1.5 above.

Changing the definition of the auxiliary in this way results in a reduction of available major forms from twenty to twelve. Since Wells' criterion of five forms is now more difficult to attain and has become inappropriate, a new criterion of fifteen subforms was introduced (see Section 2.2.3). The new procedure made little difference to the values given to each of the thirty-three children for age of auxiliary emergence ($r = .96$) because it was rarely the marginal auxiliaries which were recorded first. The interval between emergence and criterion still shows considerable variation (Mean = 9.6 months; $SD = 5.0$ months; Range = 3–21 months).

2.2.3 The criterion of acquisition

What sort of evidence would we need from a spontaneous speech sample in order to claim that a child had 'acquired' an auxiliary? This question operates at several levels. At the most basic level is the question of whether individual subforms are analysed as discrete units in the linguistic context in which they are embedded – is their inclusion rule based? At another level is the question of whether the emergence of a major form (e.g. BE) implies knowledge of all or any of the other related subforms (e.g. 'am', 'is', 'are') and, if so, whether the relationships between these subforms are understood. At yet another level, there is the question of whether the child is aware that the major forms belong to a group of verbs with a common set of syntactic behaviours.

Elsewhere in child language research acquisition has been defined in relation to criteria such as percentage inclusion in obligatory contexts, or the over-generalisation of a rule. However, obligatory contexts cannot be reliably identified for most forms of the auxiliary, and although there is anecdotal evidence that children sometimes overgeneralise the NICE properties to the marginal auxiliaries, producing utterances such as 'bettern't I?', there was no evidence of this in the transcripts analysed here. In order to demonstrate productive usage evidence would be needed that forms are used in a range of linguistic contexts (with different grammatical subjects, and co-occurring with different lexical verbs) and in order to demonstrate that they are integrated as a form-class we would also have to show that the various subforms occur as an operator in the various syntactic frames which are the defining properties of the auxiliary. One of the strongest pieces of evidence would be the occurrence of a range of auxiliary forms in tag questions, particularly tags which reverse the polarity of the verb in the previous clause (#'He can swim, can't he?'). After all, utterances of this type combine three of the NICE properties in one syntactic unit. A range of auxiliaries used as tags can therefore be regarded as a more than sufficient criterion.

Unfortunately, because of the small size of samples and the three-month intervals between them, it is difficult to demonstrate productivity in the way described above. It is even more difficult to judge from the occurrences of separate subforms whether they are integrated as a syntactic class. Tag questions cannot be used to evaluate Wells' criterion because only a third of the children have produced a tag containing an auxiliary when they reach it. It was possible, however, to examine the range of subforms which have emerged by Wells' criterion and the syntactic frames in which they occur.

The following subforms of the primary auxiliaries and central modals were taken as the unit of analysis:

> DO: do, does, don't, doesn't, did, didn't
> HAVE + EN: have, 've, has, /s/ and /z/, haven't, hasn't, ain't, had, hadn't
> BE + ING: be, am, 'm, are, 're, is, /s/ and /z/, aren't, isn't, ain't, was, were, wasn't, weren't
> BE (Passive): be, am, 'm, are, 're, is, /s/ and /z/, aren't, isn't, ain't, was, were, wasn't, weren't
> CAN: can, can't, could, couldn't
> WILL: will, 'll, won't, would, 'd, wouldn't
> SHALL: shall, shan't, should, shouldn't
> MUST: must, mustn't
> MAY: may, might, mightn't

The number of subforms to have emerged by the time each child had reached Wells' criterion, and the syntactic frames (declarative, inversion, negation, ellipsis, and emphatic affirmation) in which they had occurred was noted.

The result of this analysis demonstrated the wide range of competence with auxiliaries at Wells' criterion of five major forms. The number of subforms to have emerged ranges from 4[1] to 21 (mean = 10.8; $SD = 3.9$) and the number of subforms sampled in the five syntactic frames also varies considerably (Table 2.1).

Table 2.1 *Number of auxiliary subforms used in five syntactic frames for thirty-three children*

	Number of subforms		
Frame	Mean	*SD*	Range
Declarative	8.8	3.4	3–17
Negation	3.0	1.5	1–7
Inversion	3.0	2.5	0–9
Ellipsis	2.9	2.7	0–9
Emphatic	1.1	1.4	0–5

Less than half the children (fifteen) have used an auxiliary in each frame, but twenty-seven have produced a token in at least four. Only seven children have used at least two subforms in each frame, and only eighteen have used two subforms in at least four of the frames. It seems that, although a few children are using a broad set of subforms across a variety of syntactic contexts, other children show little knowledge of related subforms, nor of the distributional characteristics of auxiliaries.

In order to replicate the emergence to criterion analysis with the more homogeneous set of auxiliaries, an alternative criterion was required which would be more appropriate for a smaller group of major forms. Unfortunately any objective measure is likely to embrace a different range of competences for different subjects. Nevertheless, a new criterion was chosen which was based on the emergence of fifteen subforms. This was found to be the stage by which three-quarters of the children had begun to use auxiliaries in all five syntactic frames. It is, however, a more stringent criterion than the original (the mean number of subforms to have emerged by Wells' criterion is 10.8) and six children who failed to reach it by their last recording at 3;6 had to be omitted from the analysis. The median age of the remaining twenty-seven children at the new criterion is 2;9 compared with 2;6 on the original. There were no children for whom emergence to fifteen subforms occurred in a single recording.

As indicated in Section 2.2.2, the combination of changing the definition of the auxiliary and the new criterion did not remove variation between children in emergence to criterion scores. There were, however, important consequences of these new procedures which will be outlined below.

2.2.4 Variation in age of emergence

That children differ in the age at which auxiliaries first appear is well documented, and the ages of the thirty-three children studied here ranged from 1;6 to 3;3 when the first form was sampled. What has been less clear is whether this results from variation in general linguistic development or whether the effect can be specific to the auxiliary (Stephany, 1986). In Chapter 1 it was suggested that children may differ in their tendency to rote-learn utterances containing auxiliaries or to use auxiliaries whose syntactic properties are poorly understood. The effect of this would be to increase emergence to criterion scores for premature auxiliary users. By contrast the more 'reflective' learner who delays usage until a more detailed analysis has taken place would appear, on Wells' procedure, to be a faster auxiliary learner. If this is correct, one would expect a *negative* correlation between time of first usage and emergence to criterion scores.

This hypothesis was tested first of all on the figures obtained from using Wells' original procedure. The correlation between age of emergence and number of months between emergence and criterion was computed. However, although the correlation was in the expected direction it fell short of significance ($r = -.22$). The problem with this approach is that it tests a hypothesis relating to the degree of analysis of early auxiliary usage purely by reference to age. The concept of 'early' would be better defined in terms of the child's stage of syntactic development. It was therefore predicted that MLU at emergence would be negatively correlated with a) the time interval between emergence and the criterion, and b) the MLU increment between these two points.

Following Wells (1985), mean length of structured utterances (MLUS) at emergence and criterion were obtained and the increment in MLUS between these two points was calculated for each child. Results show considerable variation in the MLUS at which auxiliaries emerge (range: 1.41–4.79, mean = 2.36, $SD = .75$). In fact the figures suggest that children vary as much on MLUS at emergence as on MLUS at the criterion (range: 1.43–4.79 (*sic*), mean = 3.33, $SD = .74$). Not surprisingly therefore both correlations proved significant: MLUS at emergence predicts both time from emergence to criterion ($r = -.43$; $p < .01$; $df = 31$; one-tailed) and the increase in MLUS between emergence and criterion ($r = -.53$; $p < .005$; $df = 31$; one-tailed).

This procedure was then repeated using the revised set of auxiliaries and the new criterion. This time all three correlations were significant: early emergence ($r = -.34$; $p < .05$; $df = 25$) and MLUS at emergence ($r = -.43$; $p < .025$; $df = 25$) predict a longer period between emergence and the new criterion, and there is a negative correlation between MLUS at emergence and MLUS increments ($r = -.81$; $p < .0005$; $df = 25$; one-tailed).

The final correlation ($-.81$) is stronger than the corresponding coefficient ($-.53$) derived from Wells' procedure, despite the fact that the children's MLUS at emergence is almost identical. Clearly the revised procedure has resulted in less variation in children's MLUS at the new criterion. The extent of this can be seen from Table 2.2.

Table 2.2 *Number of children in MLUS bands at two criteria*

MLUS band (Middle of interval)	Criterion	
	Wells' 5 forms	15 subforms
1.5	1	0
2.0	1	0
2.5	4	0
3.0	9	1
3.5	7	1
4.0	8	14
4.5	2	8
5.0	1	2
5.5	0	1
Totals	33	27

2.2.5 Fast developers as rapid piecemeal learners

Wells regards children who progress rapidly from emergence to criterion as showing evidence of syntactic rule learning, but it is also possible that some have little syntactic knowledge and are rapid piecemeal learners. Children most easily identified as falling into this category would be fast auxiliary learners whose first auxiliary emerges at a low MLUS. On Wells' procedure only one child (Jonathan) is below the mean for both MLUS at emergence and the emergence to criterion score. For Jonathan, the five forms appear in a single recording, but his MLUS at emergence (1.43 morphemes) is 1.24 standard deviations below the mean for the group. In Jonathan's case at least it seems likely that attaining the criterion of five forms within three months is not evidence of a rule for introducing the auxiliary constituent into the sentence.

2.3 Conclusion

The hypothesis was tested that the extensive variation in rate of auxiliary verb learning as measured by emergence to criterion scores was at least partially brought about by differences in children's willingness or ability to use unanalysed or partially analysed auxiliaries at an early age or low MLU. The results are entirely consistent with such a hypothesis. Variation in MLUS at emergence was extensive, and when the analysis was repeated using data obtained from a revised criterion and a revised set of auxiliaries, it was this variation which predicted most of the variance in the MLUS increment between emergence and criterion.

It was shown that variation in MLUS at criterion was reduced by using the revised procedures. One interpretation of this would be that restricting the analysis to a more homogeneous group of auxiliaries narrows down the stage during which they develop as an integrated class. That this should be the case is not surprising. In Chapter 1 it was claimed that successive levels of language development are at least partially dependent on a developing knowledge of auxiliaries. The relationship between auxiliaries and other aspects of language development is, however, a reciprocal one. Auxiliaries modulate the meanings of propositions and perform syntactic functions. In order to be used productively, therefore, the linguistic units on which they operate must already be under control.

It is possible to think of the relationship between age, or stage, of emergence and subsequent rate of development as a four-cell model (Fig. 2.1). The demonstrated effect of age/stage of emergence means that children will tend to cluster in Cells (a) and (d).

	Early emergence	Late emergence
Apparent slow learners	(a)	(b)
Apparent fast learners	(c)	(d)

Fig. 2.1 Emergence and rate of development – four possibilities

Children in Cell (a) are those who are most likely to be rote-learners or early users of partially analysed auxiliaries. Cell (d) contains children who appear to have more analytical ability because rule-based usage quickly follows the first form sampled. On the other hand, they may simply be more reflective and spend longer analysing and internalising the relevant features of their input. One additional difference between the children in Cells (a) and (d) might be the extent to which they analyse the language they hear (Cell d), or (Cell a) gradually segment their own output by processes such as those outlined by Peters (1983) or Wong Fillmore (1979).

While most children fall into Cells (a) and (d), scattergrams produced for the six correlations reported above show that if a division is made according to the median on each variable, there can also be children in Cells (b) and (c). It has already been suggested that one child (Jonathan) engages in rapid piecemeal learning, and this would fall into Cell (c). This cell may also include those characterised elsewhere as risk-takers. The late slow learners in Cell (b) are more difficult to characterise, but they may be children whose linguistic environment does less to facilitate learning auxiliaries, or who are less able to infer the rules governing their syntactic behaviour.

Issues which have been raised in this chapter – measuring rate of auxiliary verb development, the identification of rule-based and unanalysed usage, the problems of sampling and transcription error – will be addressed in the next chapter where their contribution to the design of the main study will be discussed.

PART II

Individual differences
and auxiliary verb learning
in seven children

3   Research design

3.1 Rationale

Chapter 2 showed that the rate at which children developed rule-based usage
of the auxiliary was not independent of other aspects of syntactic development
and that measures of rate of learning could be unduly influenced by children's
learning styles, sampling and transcription error, and the set of verbs included.
The work also demonstrated the difficulties of identifying rule-based usage,
especially in relatively small language samples recorded at infrequent intervals.

In this section a more intensive longitudinal study of auxiliary verb learning
in seven children is described. The study combines larger samples of spontaneous speech collected at shorter intervals and is supplemented by an elicitation task which attempts to overcome the problem of sampling less commonly
used verb forms. The rationale for identifying unanalysed units is based on
MacWhinney (1982, pp. 76–83). From an extensive survey of the literature,
MacWhinney evaluates fourteen types of evidence that can indicate rote-learning. Those most relevant to the current investigation are the following:

1. Dual- or multimorpheme structures with a single intonational unit (to
   this we will add the condition that the intonation pattern is invariable).
2. Producing the whole phrase before the separate components.
3. Producing contracted forms before full forms.
4. The production of 'precocious strings'.
5. Redundancy errors, such as # 'What's is it?'.

Of MacWhinney's indicators, items 2, 3 and 4 all derive from the relationship between complexity and sequence. If other factors are held constant,
acquisition proceeds in a sequence which corresponds with syntactic complexity (Block and Kessel, 1980; Brown, 1973; Brown and Hanlon, 1970;
Pinker, 1981; De Villiers and De Villiers, 1973). This will be referred to
as the Complexity Principle and will be applied to the order in which auxiliary
subforms emerge in contexts of differing complexity. Violations of the prin-

ciple will occur where an auxiliary appears in a complex context such as a tag question before, say, a simple declarative, and will be taken to be indicative of a holistic strategy.

Evidence of rule learning and 'simultaneous acquisition', on the other hand, will be obtained by analysing changes in frequency of usage, in the range of subforms used, and in the variety of main verbs with which they co-occur. The extent to which auxiliaries participate in the syntactic operations which are taken to be their defining features will also be examined, and for two appropriate subforms the rate at which children proceed from non-inclusion to inclusion in obligatory contexts will be measured. An elicited imitation task will be used to test how rapidly children will be able to process sentences containing a wide range of auxiliary forms.

In addition, two auxiliary verb systems (DO and CAN) will be analysed for indications of holistic and analytic strategies and, because the use of different auxiliaries in tag questions is a more than sufficient criterion of acquisition, the development of tags will also be studied in detail.

3.2 Data collection

The aims of the investigation required longitudinal data from the earliest stages of auxiliary verb usage until the development of tag questions. Speech samples needed to be large enough to gain insights into productivity, and frequent enough to detect fairly small changes in children's rule systems. On the basis of a pilot study with two children, Zoe (2;5) and Wayne (2;7), the decision was made to record 45 minutes of spontaneous speech and administer an imitation battery at three-weekly intervals. It was found that 45 minutes of unstructured play with the researcher yielded 250 to 300 child utterances.

The study took place in Newport, South Wales, an industrial town with a population of approximately 110,000. All seven children in the final sample lived in the town or its immediate environs and were growing up in a monolingual environment.

3.2.1 The subjects
The children selected for the study were taken from a larger group of thirty-one whose parents had responded to an advertisement. Subjects had to fulfil two criteria: to demonstrate sufficient sociability to co-operate on an elicitation task, and to be at a stage of development during which auxiliaries only occurred in rare stereotyped phrases. Preliminary home visits were used for assessment

but were also useful to set the pattern for future visits and to develop a relationship with the children in the final group.

Eight children were finally selected, but one boy was withdrawn soon after the programme of recording had begun. The ages of the remaining two boys and five girls at the beginning of the study ranged from 1;10 to 2;7. As can be seen from Table 3.1 the family background of the subjects varied considerably.

Table 3.1 *Education and occupation (or previous occupation) of children's parents*

	Mother		Father	
Child	Education	Occupation	Education	Occupation
Alex	Minimal	Shop manageress	Further	Youth training tutor
Betty	Further	Clerk	Further	Carpenter
Clare	Further	Technician in pharmacy	Further	Technical manager
Daisy	Minimal	Telephonist	Minimal	Docker
Eric	Higher	Tax officer	Further	Merchant Navy officer
Fleur	Further	Local government officer	Further	Local government officer
Gemma	Further	Nurse	Higher	Hospital consultant

Key to levels of education:
Minimal: No formal national qualifications *and* minimal years of schooling.
Further: Formal national qualifications *or* educated beyond the minimal school leaving age.
Higher: Degree level or beyond.

3.3 Spontaneous speech samples

3.3.1 Recording

All tape-recordings were made in the child's home and although mothers were present they were not usually directly involved. The early recordings of Gemma were an exception to this because she was very wary of strangers. Fortunately this did not inhibit her talkativeness and gradually a relationship developed in which the researcher became more and more involved in her play.

A standard set of toys, books and activities was used for all children. Particularly useful were materials supplied by the Humpty Dumpty Club (published by Hamlyn). These included animal flashcards, zoo dominoes, and sets of simple funny face and animal jigsaws. However, the items which did most to stimulate spontaneous conversation were a magnetic fishing game and, perversely, a broken, one-eyed doll with a dummy which could be inserted into the mouth or empty eye socket.

The planned intervals of three weeks between recordings were kept to as closely as possible, but inevitably there were some variations resulting from illness and holidays. Sometimes there were shorter intervals during the early stages to check that children had been correctly assessed during preliminary visits. Consequently there is not an equal number of recordings for each child (see Table 3.2). In addition, extra sessions were arranged for Betty because her tag questions had reached a particularly interesting stage of development when the study was due to finish (see Chapter 7).

Table 3.2 *Ages of the children during the period of the study*

| Subject | Age | | Interval | No. of recs. |
	First rec.	Final rec.		
Alex	2;7.6	3;3.20	256 days	13
Betty	2;4.8	3;1.2	267 days	14
Clare	2;4.3	3;0.1	240 days	12
Daisy	2;3.17	2;11.21	247 days	12
Eric	2;2.8	2;10.19	251 days	13
Fleur	2;1.23	2;9.22	244 days	12
Gemma	1;10.6	2;6.26	264 days	12

Key: Rec. = recording.

3.3.2 Transcription
Standard orthographic transcription was used following the conventions in Wells (1981, pp. 277–8). A key to these is given on page xvii. In addition, intonation of tag questions was indicated as rising or falling, and contrastive stress in emphatic affirmation and negation was also marked. Nonstandard

pronunciation of auxiliaries and, especially where there was contraction and reduction, their surrounding context was transcribed using the symbols in Quirk et al. (1985). A pronunciation table can be found on page xviii.

It was pointed out in Chapter 2 that the auxiliary verb is an area where there are specific problems of transcription reliability. For this reason, the assessment of reliability below is based only on figures for utterances containing auxiliary verbs, or which are obligatory contexts for auxiliary verbs. In order to do this 4 × 15 minute sections of recording were randomly selected for each child and retranscribed. The percentage agreement obtained was 83.5%.

The transcripts and taped recordings have subsequently been used as part of the validation procedures for the Bristol Language Development Scales (Gutfreund, Harrison and Wells, 1989).

3.3.3 Coding

Auxiliaries
Initially all auxiliary forms, including marginal members (NEED, GOING TO, GOT TO, HAVE TO, BETTER), were coded. However, in the absence of any evidence that the seven children overgeneralised the properties of the primary auxiliaries and central modals to the marginal forms, the latter were excluded from further analysis. The final set of forms and subforms is therefore identical to those in Section 2.2.3.

The following instances were also omitted:

1. /s/ and /z/ + 'gone' and obligatory contexts containing 'gone'; it is rarely clear whether 'gone' functions as a description of state (# 'It *is* gone') or as a perfective (# 'It *has* gone').
2. Utterances where the presence of the auxiliary was in doubt.
3. Auxiliaries contained in nursery rhymes and songs.
4. Auxiliaries contained in elicited imitation.
5. Auxiliaries contained in spontaneous imitations of the *previous* utterance of another speaker.
6. BE forms which precede a main verb uninflected for progressive aspect (# 'He's play football').
7. Utterances such as # 'It is broken' which have the surface structure of truncated passives (BE + past participle) but which may be processed as Copula + Adjectival Complement. Only Quirk et al.'s (1985) category of 'true passives' is included, that is to say those which have 'a clear correspondence with an active verb phrase or active clause'.

Obligatory contexts

As a result of the work of Roger Brown and his associates (Brown, 1973; Cazden, 1968) the term 'obligatory context' has been applied to utterances or parts of utterances which lack a specified morpheme. Sources of evidence for identifying obligatory contexts and coding their mood and polarity are adapted from Brown (1973, p. 255):

1. Linguistic context: Brown's criterion is extended by insisting that the linguistic context surrounding the omission is intact. This makes it less likely that children who have developed rules for ellipsis and reduction are attributed with empty obligatory contexts. It also removes some of the unreliability of attributing aspectual and modal meanings on the basis of external context alone. While # 'I going out' could therefore be coded as an obligatory context, # 'going out' and # 'I go out' could not.
2. Nonlinguistic context: current activity, physical setting, shared knowledge of the topic, and accompanying gestures and facial expression.
3. Prior linguistic context: utterances by the child and others.
4. Subsequent linguistic context (where applicable): expansion of the syntax or extension of the meaning of the utterance by the child or others.

Linguistic context

HAVE + GOT, and HAVE + GOT TO were given a separate coding from perfective HAVE + EN meanings. Semantically these are very different. HAVE + GOT TO expresses meanings of Epistemic Modality and Dynamic Necessity; HAVE + GOT, which indicates current possession, is also quite distinct from perfective HAVE + EN (Cazden, 1968; Fletcher, 1981; Gathercole, 1986). Similarly, BE + GOING TO was distinguished from the BE + ING of progressive aspect.

Mood

All utterances containing auxiliaries were allocated to one of the following categories:

Imperative:	# *Don't* do that!
Declarative:	# I *can* see you.
Y/N inversion:	# *Can* I go out?
Y/N non-inverted:	# He's going out?
Wh- inversion:	# Why *can't* I do it?
Wh- non-inverted:	# Who *can* do that?
Wh- inversion error:	# Why I *can't* do it?
Declarative Tag:	# I've got a dog I *have*.
Tag question:	# You like it *don't* you?

(See Chapter 7 for the coding of intonation and polarity in tag questions.)

Ellipsis, emphasis and negation
The mood coding was supplemented for main verb ellipsis and/or contrastive stress, and for negation achieved by the noncontracted negative particle.

Ellipsis:	*#Don't.*
	#I can't.
Contrastive stress:	# You can't do that.
	Yes, I *" can!*
External negation:	#I *am not* going out.

Reliability
Each auxiliary and obligatory context which had been consistently retranscribed during the assessment of transcription reliability was also recoded. Percentage agreement was 93.4%.

3.3.4 Indices of development
MLU and auxiliary frequency were calculated from structured utterances only, the distinction between structured and unstructured being based on Wells' criteria (Wells, 1975). Unstructured utterances are defined as those which have 'no explicitly mentioned topic' (p. 65). They include single word or idiomatic affirmative and negative responses ('O.K.', 'No'), other idiomatic utterances ('Come on!', 'There, there'), rote-learned songs and rhymes, exclamations, routine formulae ('Good-bye', 'Pardon'), and vocatives occurring alone.

For the seven children in this study the mean number of utterances per recording (excluding elicited imitation) was 323. Of these 10.5% were not sufficiently intelligible to give an accurate morpheme count. Of the remainder, 74.6% were structured and 25.4% were unstructured. A check was made to see whether children became more voluble as they became less inhibited in the presence of the observer. No significant trends were found.

Mean Length of Structured Utterances (MLUS)
As a rule-of-thumb index of language development MLU is generally considered to be valid for children of the age and stage of those studied here. Following Wells (1985) mean utterance length in morphemes was calculated from structured utterances only. There are two reasons for this. Firstly, it

is believed that MLUs calculated from structured utterances (MLUS) discriminate more validly between children because values are not depressed in contexts which tend to elicit single word social or polar responses (Wells, 1978). Secondly, using Wells' MLUS allows comparisons to be made with the Bristol children at a comparable age.

Mean length of the children's longest utterances

Brown (1973) recorded the 'upper bound' (length in morphemes of the longest utterance in a sample) for the three Harvard children. In a refinement of this measure, Wells (1978; 1985) has found mean length of the three longest utterances (MLUL) to be highly correlated with other syntactic and semantic indices. The current study attempts a further refinement by weighting the values obtained to compensate for variations in sample size. Measures such as MLU and MLUS are not *systematically* related to sample size because they measure the central tendency of the whole sample. A larger corpus of utterances simply tends to distribute more evenly any random errors of sampling and morpheme counting, thus increasing reliability. Wells' MLUL, by contrast, measures not the central tendency of the whole sample but the central tendency of only one extreme end of the distribution of utterances. If utterance length follows the normal distribution it can be predicted that the larger the speech sample, the more likely it is that utterances at the extremes of length will occur. One would therefore expect a measure derived from a *constant number* of longest utterances to be positively correlated with sample size. To compensate for this effect, MLUL in the present study was always calculated from a *constant proportion* (.05) of the utterances in the sample. The disadvantage is that the values obtained are no longer comparable with those of the Bristol children. However, they will be referred to when an indication of maximum processing ability is necessary for the interpretation of results.

Auxiliary frequency

For each sample the number of auxiliaries was expressed as a percentage of the number of structured utterances. Growth spurts in auxiliary learning are expected to be reflected in rises in proportional frequencies. However, increases in frequency are no guarantee of developments in rule learning, and further indices described below are used to ensure that high frequencies reflect more than repetitive usage of a limited number of auxiliaries.

Range of auxiliary forms

The number of different auxiliary subforms per occasion was adjusted for variation in size of speech sample by expressing the range as a percentage of the total number of structured utterances. The resulting measure estimates the range of auxiliary subforms per 100 structured utterances.

Cumulative range of auxiliary subforms

The number of different subforms sampled up to and including each session was recorded. A maximum of sixty-five subforms was possible (see p. 20).

Type/Token Ratios (TTRS)

TTRS are most frequently used as a measure of vocabulary diversity. They are calculated by dividing the number of different words in a language sample (Types) by the total number of words in that sample (Tokens). It ought to be possible, therefore, to produce a similar ratio for auxiliaries only (different forms divided by total number of auxiliaries) as an index of stereotyped versus diverse usage. Unfortunately small numbers of tokens and variation in the frequency of auxiliaries made comparisons of TTRS between children, and between samples within children, invalid. Further investigation (Richards, 1987b) showed TTRS to be negatively correlated with sample size. Instead of reporting ratios, therefore, raw figures for auxiliary types and tokens will be quoted.

3.4 Eliciting auxiliary verbs from 2-year-olds

An imitation test was devised in order to judge how quickly a child would be able to apply a rule for introducing the auxiliary across a range of major forms. In addition to freeing the research from the chance element of naturalistic sampling it was expected that children's responses would also give valuable insights into a) sequence of acquisition of auxiliary forms, b) the relative order of appearance in spontaneous and elicited speech, c) knowledge of forms and structures which are rare in normal speech, and d) the child's current rule system from 'recoded' responses (Slobin and Welsh, 1973).

3.4.1 Previous work

The largest and most comprehensive experimental studies of the syntax of auxiliaries in general, or modals in particular, are, respectively, those of Kypriotaki (1974) and Major (1974). Major succeeded in eliciting negated modals, inverted modals in Wh-, Y/N and tag questions, and modals in sequences of tenses. In each case the stimulus was a declarative (usually affirmative) sentence. In order to elicit declarative modals Major administered a battery of fifty sentences to be imitated. Details of the techniques used to motivate the children during the six batteries of tests are not described but since the children were rather older than the 2-year-olds to be studied here (the youngest were at Kindergarten), co-operation may have been willingly given. Kypriotaki (1974) tested thirty children aged 2;1 to 5;1 on sentences containing all fifteen possibilities for the co-occurrence of auxiliaries which can be generated by Chomsky's auxiliary expansion rule. Subjects were required to imitate statements, and affirmative and negative questions. There were some problems in gaining the co-operation of the youngest children.

Elsewhere, imitation tasks have been used to elicit various parts or functions of the auxiliary system (Bellugi, 1971; Kuczaj and Brannick, 1979; Menyuk, 1969; Kuczaj and Maratsos, 1975). In the majority of cases, however, where children have successfully participated, they have usually been considerably older than the children to be studied here. The child language literature contains many references to the problems of using experimental procedures with young children. For subjects under the age of 3 or 4 it is extremely difficult to construct tests which tap linguistic competence rather than the child's understanding of the task (Menyuk, 1969, 1971) and there are many documented failures with children below this age, the most famous being Adam's 'Pop goes the weasel' response to a request for a grammatical judgement (Brown and Bellugi, 1964, p. 135). Even an apparently straightforward procedure such as imitation has foundered with younger children (see, for example, Kypriotaki, 1974; K. E. Nelson et al., 1973; Park, 1981), or failed because of task difficulty (Kuczaj, 1979b). The experience of the Bristol imitation test (Treder Barr-Smith, 1980) shows that even in a longitudinal study where children have more opportunity to get to know the experimenter and understand the demands of the task, co-operation cannot be taken for granted.

Nevertheless, it is comparatively easy to construct contexts in which the act of repetition makes sense to children. Kuczaj and Brannick's (1979) game in which the child's puppet has to imitate the experimenter's puppet is an example, and some successes for elicited imitation as a test of the grammatical competence of 2-year-olds have been recorded (e.g. Brown and Fraser, 1963; Cazden, 1965; Menyuk, 1969; Nelson, 1973; Slobin, 1982; Slobin and Welsh, 1973).

3.4.2 Imitation tests: their rationale
Studies which have successfully used elicited imitation (especially Jordan and Robinson, 1972; Menyuk, 1969; Slobin and Welsh, 1973) suggest that provided models are sufficiently long to exceed short-term memory capacity,

responses will reflect the subject's current grammatical competence; the propositional content of the item is decoded, stored in long-term memory and re-encoded via the child's productive rule system. In Piagetian terms the process is one of assimilation. This principle forms the rationale for the use of imitation tests in the studies referred to above. Nevertheless, there are some crucial lessons on the construction and administration of imitation tests to be gleaned from the literature:

1. The length of the stimulus may determine whether the child even attempts a response (Scholes, cited in Menyuk, 1971).
2. Words in final position are more likely to be included (Brown and Fraser, 1963).
3. A child may fail to imitate a structure or an utterance which had previously been produced spontaneously (Bloom, 1974; Slobin and Welsh, 1973). This points to the importance of contextual support and motivation to convey meaning, which are frequently absent from the experimental situation (Donaldson, 1978).
4. Other factors which may affect the correctness of responses may be lexical content, the semantic relationships expressed in the model, and the phonological structure (Menyuk, 1971).
5. Two-year-olds will only attempt a small number of items in one session (Treder Barr-Smith, 1980).
6. Imitations are more likely to be successful if models are presented with normal, rather than flat intonation, and at normal speed, rather than faster or slower than normal (Bonvillian, Raeburn and Horan, 1979).
7. If functors are stressed they are more likely to be retained (Brown and Bellugi, 1964; Brown and Fraser, 1963; Slobin and Welsh, 1973).
8. Children may imitate items which are very slightly ahead of their current stage of production (Kuczaj and Maratsos, 1975; Menyuk, 1969). This phenomenon has been referred to as 'preanalysis' or 'preorganization' (Kuczaj and Maratsos, 1975).

3.4.3 The design and administration of the imitation test

The final version of the imitation test (Fig 3.1) resulted from the literature review described above and extensive piloting with Wayne and Zoe. The following features were incorporated:

1. Contextual support and order of presentation: children were told that they were helping to tell a 'farm story'. An eighteen-page loose-leaf booklet was made up containing coloured pictures of animals with a text printed underneath. Each page usually held just one sentence containing the target auxiliary or auxiliaries and any necessary additional sentences to provide links with the rest of the 'story'. There were twenty-two target auxiliaries and semi-auxiliaries contained in twenty sentences. Each page was given a code number and before each visit the numbers were placed in random

1. He *is* going out.
   He *is* going out to play.
2. He *has* got a tail.
   He *has* got a nice long tail.
3. She *can* give us milk.
   She *can* give us lots of milk.
4. It *doesn't* eat grass.
   It *doesn't* eat grass at all.
5. You *can't* play here.
   Puppies *can't* play in here.
6. She *will* come and play.
   She *will* come and play with us.
7. He *has to* be careful.
   The boy *has to* be very careful.
8. His mummy *is* calling.
   His mummy *is* calling him in.
9. He *has got to* hurry.
   She says he *has got to* hurry.
10. Now she *has* come home.
    Now she *has* found her way home.
11. She *is going to* swim.
    She *is going to* have a swim.
12. We *must* let her in.
    We *must* give the cat some milk.
13. The goat *may* say 'hello'.
    The goat *may* come and see us.
14. He *should* be at home.
    The pig *should* really be at home.
15. *Can* you see the pig?
    Can you see the pig over there?
16. She *could* give us wool.
    She *could* give us lots of wool.
17. The donkey *would* carry us.
    The donkey *would* carry one of us.
18. He *might* take us home.
    The horse *might* take us home too.
19. *Does* he live here?
    We ask, *Does* he live here?
20. Of course he *doesn't*.
    That's silly. Of course he *doesn't*.

Figure 3.1 Final set of five and seven morpheme imitation items (excluding link sentences)

order. Apart from the title page and any linking pages the remainder of the booklet was placed in the order which corresponded with the obtained random sequence.

2. Construction of items: since the study began with a broad definition of the auxiliary, three semi-auxiliaries ('has to', 'going to' and 'got to') were included. This meant that two sentences contained both an auxiliary and a semi-auxiliary. Each sentence in the battery was constructed to sound as natural as possible, and checks were made to ensure that the vocabulary in each item was known to the children. Difficult blends of consonants were avoided. In every case, the auxiliary was presented in its uncontracted form in order to avoid the possibility of Subject + Auxiliary (e.g. 'he's') being processed as a single unit.

   Nineteen auxiliaries were unstressed declaratives in medial position. There were also two Y/N inversions and one ellipsed emphatic negation. These demonstrated functions of auxiliary DO.

3. Length of the model: after the pilot study model sentences were initially set at a standard five morphemes. Following Kuczaj and Maratsos (1975) who gradually lengthened sentences during the period of their study, the length was increased to seven morphemes approximately half way through the research. The intention was to prevent 'parrotting' as short-term memory increased.

4. Presentation: Telling the story consisted of relaying the target sentences to a cuddly animal of the child's choice. At first two telephones were used, one for the child to speak into, and one with the receiver attached to the animal's ear. This scenario seemed to make sense to the children and helped to define the nature of the task. Once this had been established, it was possible to vary the procedure to motivate children when they refused to co-operate. One method which worked with Clare and Daisy was to use a set of toy animals, and place them on the appropriate picture in the booklet as the sentence was repeated. Usually, however, Daisy preferred to tell the story to a Basil Brush puppet without the telephone, and Gemma eventually relayed it directly to her mother. Betty, on the other hand, soon tired of the booklet, but was prepared to tell the story holding each toy animal in turn. Alex was the most difficult child to motivate, but he provided his own solution by shooting each animal picture with his toy gun while repeating the sentence. Clare also developed a more enjoyable variation. On one occasion she responded to each item by pushing a toy car full of Lego people across the floor, refusing to say anything. The experimenter pushed the car back, saying the sentence again. This time, as she returned the car she repeated the model. This set the pattern for the rest of the session.

3.4.4 *Problems with the imitation test*

A potential problem of repeated administrations is that children might gradually memorise the items. It was hoped that randomising the order of the pages before each session, and lengthening the model, would make this less likely. Varying the linguistic context of the auxiliary was also considered, but rejected on the grounds that this would introduce an additional source of variation and might influence the subject's understanding of the sentence in unforeseen ways. In fact there is no evidence of rote-learning, and children never commented on the fact that the order of the pictures varied from visit to visit.

Despite careful planning, however, there were some worrying problems, the most serious being that it was not possible to carry out the first administration of the test on the same occasion for all children. It simply took longer with some children than others to establish what was required and to provide the necessary motivation. In addition, it was rarely possible to administer more than a small proportion of items during early sessions (see Chapter 4, Table 4.6). Once the breakthrough had been made, however, there followed for all children a 'honeymoon period' during which most, if not all, the sentences were attempted on each occasion. At this stage children looked forward to the story and eagerly searched the toy bag for the booklet. Inevitably, however, the novelty wore off and for the final occasions items were omitted if they had already been 'acquired', that is to say, if the auxiliary had been correctly included on the previous two occasions.

The transition from five to seven morpheme items ran smoothly in all cases except one. Alex and Gemma were successfully promoted to the longer version after only two attempts because they were coping so easily. Betty, Clare, Daisy, and Eric made the transition as planned after the third attempt. For Fleur, on the other hand, five morphemes seemed to be the limit of her capacity even though she was producing some responses which included the auxiliary. The longer sentences were therefore delayed until Recording 7 (2;6.6). Unfortunately, even this proved to be a mistake. Fleur refused to continue after four sentences and on the following occasion the five morpheme version was tried again. This time only ten items could be presented and responses to these were mumbled or consisted of nonsense words and filler sounds. No more attempts were made to use the longer version, and although Fleur reverted to normal responses in Recording 9 (2;7.17) the proportion retaining the auxiliary never recovered.

Less serious because it was only a transitory phase was an early tendency of Betty and Alex to respond to sentences rather than repeat them. Clare, however, discovered during Recording 6 that it made the game much more interesting to comment on, or contradict the proposition in the model sentence. These responses were quite deliberate and were accompanied by a quizzical glance followed by hysterical laughter. Fortunately this was also only a temporary phase and, despite such problems, data obtained from the elicitation task were a valuable supplement to the samples of spontaneous speech.

4 Rate of development

4.1 Profile of children at recording 1

4.1.1 Auxiliary verbs

All children demonstrate some usage of auxiliaries at the beginning of the study (Table 4.1), though for three of the younger children, Daisy, Eric, and Gemma, this is restricted to one subform and is relatively infrequent. Fleur, on the other hand, and despite her age, has the highest proportional frequency of auxiliaries with seven subforms per 100 structured utterances rising to 16.1 in her second recording. However, Fleur's range of subforms for these first two recordings is only three, while the number of auxiliary tokens is thirty-six. An inspection of the first two transcripts shows that stereo-

Table 4.1 *Children's scores on the five auxiliary measures at the first recording*

Subject	Age	MLUS	Auxiliary measures				
			1	2	3	4	5
Alex	2;7.6	2.6	9	5.5	6	3.7	6/9
Betty	2;4.8	3.3	10	5.2	6	3.1	6/10
Clare	2;4.3	2.8	6	3.2	6	3.2	6/6
Daisy	2;3.17	2.3	3	0.9	1	0.3	1/3
Eric	2;2.8	2.6	1	0.5	1	0.5	1/1
Fleur	2;1.23	2.8	9	7.0	3	2.3	3/9
Gemma	1;10.6	2.9	1	0.8	1	0.8	1/1

Key—1: Number of subforms (tokens).
    2: Subforms per 100 structured utterances.
    3: Range (types).
    4: Range per 100 structured utterances.
    5: Range/number of subforms (types/tokens).

typed usage of 'can't' accounts for thirty-two of the thirty-nine tokens. The others are /dənəʊ/ ('don't know') which has the prosodic features of a single unit, and two anomalous tokens of ellipsed 'I do':

> F: I got one [playing the magnetic fishing game]
> R: I've caught another one
> F: uh uh I do (= so have I)   *(Fleur, Rec. 2, 2;2.14)*

The three oldest children (Alex, Betty, and Clare) show more diverse usage in the first sample. But evidence will be presented below that for Alex and Clare some of these early utterances which ostensibly contain auxiliaries are at best only partially analysed syntactically and semantically. For both children at this stage auxiliaries occur in complex structures even before affirmative declarative usage has been established. Thus in the first recording Clare's six auxiliary tokens include ellipsis, emphatic contrast, and inversion in two tag questions. Similarly, of Alex's nine tokens, only two are non-ellipsed declaratives. Others include contracted allomorphs of BE + ING in Wh- questions, and one tag question. By contrast, Betty, whose syntactic development will be seen to conform more to the *simple→complex* sequence, uses all nine of her auxiliary tokens in Recording 1 in non-ellipsed declarative frames. While this might be indicative of a developing mastery of a limited range of auxiliaries in declarative mood, there is evidence of context-restricted usage. Utterances containing 'can't', for example, are exclusively 'can't find it' until the third sample.

It is true to say that for all children, and particularly the four youngest, auxiliaries are rare at the beginning of the study and that the range of forms which occur is limited. Even the older children, whose range is slightly more extensive, appear to use forms in a restricted range of linguistic contexts or show little evidence that the more complex utterances in which they occur are analysed.

4.1.2 *MLUS*

Table 4.1 also shows that MLUS for the first recording extends from Daisy's 2.3 morphemes to 3.3 for Betty, with the remaining children forming a cluster within a range of 2.6 to 2.9 morphemes. In order to put these figures in perspective, Table 4.2 quotes the mean MLUS and mean MLU (Brown's criteria) for the sixty younger Bristol children at comparable ages (see Wells, 1985, p. 123). The table also gives an idea of how Wells' MLUS compares with Brown's MLU. As would be expected, the result of confining morphemes to those in structured utterances produces figures which are consistently higher.

Table 4.2 *Mean MLUS and MLU of the sixty younger Bristol children between 1;9 and 2;9*

	Wells' MLUS		Brown's MLU	
Age	MLUS	*SD*	MLU	*SD*
1;9	1.5	0.55	1.3	0.34
2;0	2.1	0.68	1.6	0.54
2;3	2.5	0.92	1.9	0.65
2;6	3.1	0.95	2.4	0.74
2;9	3.6	0.90	2.8	0.68

When comparing the seven children with the Bristol sample, it must be borne in mind that the contexts in which data were collected were quite different. On the other hand, we can at least obtain a rough idea of how the seven children compare with a much larger, more representative sample of the population. From the very first visits there had been a strong feeling that Gemma was linguistically advanced for her age, but the general level of the group was unknown.

Comparisons with the Bristol children were made as follows: the MLUS was taken for the first recording at which the age of each child corresponded closely with the age of Bristol children in their recordings. For example, Gemma's third recording (age 1;11.23) was closest to the age of Bristol children at their fourth recording. At this age her MLUS was 3.1. As Table 4.2 shows, the mean MLUS for the Bristol sample at 2;0 is 2.1, with a standard deviation of .68. An MLUS equal to Gemma's at this age would therefore be 1.47 standard deviations above the mean for the Bristol sample. However, while three other children (Betty, Fleur, and Eric) also appear to be above the average for the Bristol sample, none are more than one standard deviation above the mean, and Betty at 2;6.7 scores only .1 morphemes higher than the Bristol average at 2;6. Three children (Alex, Clare, and Daisy) fall below the Bristol averages, though again all are within one standard deviation, and one of these (Clare) is within .1 morphemes of the average.

4.2 Individual differences in the development of MLUS

It can be seen from Table 4.3 that the development of MLUS over the period of the study is by no means linear for most children. The general trend is a series of gradually rising peaks and troughs.

Table 4.3 *Children's MLUS for each recording*

	Recording													
Child	1	2	3	4	5	6	7	8	9	10	11	12	13	14
Alex	2.6	2.9	2.8	3.0	3.5	3.5	3.5	3.6	3.8	3.8	3.5	3.9	4.4	
Betty	3.3	2.8	3.7	3.5	3.2	3.7	4.0	3.6	4.2	4.4	4.6	4.9	4.9	4.4
Clare	2.8	2.7	3.0	3.4	3.2	3.3	3.6	3.8	3.7	4.1	4.0	4.8		
Daisy	2.3	2.4	2.6	2.8	2.8	3.2	3.2	3.4	3.7	3.5	3.9	3.9		
Eric	2.6	2.8	2.6	3.1	3.1	3.6	3.0	3.8	3.6	3.7	4.0	3.9	3.9	
Fleur	2.8	2.9	2.8	2.7	2.8	3.3	3.0	3.0	2.7	2.8	4.0	3.1		
Gemma	2.9	2.7	3.1	3.6	5.0	3.9	4.7	4.9	5.2	5.0	4.4	5.1		

Given the close match on MLUS at Recording 1 for five of the seven children, their rate of development is relatively easy to compare. By the time data collection was complete, Eric and Fleur had attained an overall maximum MLUS of 4.0 in their eleventh recording. Their pattern of development was very different, however. For Eric an MLUS of 4.0 in Recording 11 represents a plateau which had been gradually and steadily achieved over the period of the study. For Fleur, by contrast, this was an exceptional peak which followed a long period during which little progress had been observed, and which was marked by frequent regressions, sometimes (for example during Recordings 9 and 10) to a value lower than that of the first sample.

One child who was less advanced on MLUS during the first recordings was Daisy. By her last two recordings, however, she had an MLUS which was comparable with Eric and Fleur (3.9 morphemes). Two children whose initial status was comparable with Eric and Fleur are Clare and Gemma. They had made rather more progress by their last recording (MLUS = 4.8 and 5.2 morphemes respectively), and in Gemma's case this is all the more significant because she was three and a half months younger than any other child when the study began. Nevertheless, the picture is not quite as clear as it might seem because of variations in the interval between the first and last recordings. These differences (see Table 3.2) range from 240 days (Clare) to 267 (Betty). In order to make comparisons of rate of development easier, gains in MLUS from the mean of the first two recordings to the sample closest to Clare's minimum interval of 240 days were calculated. This reduced the range to 16 days (mean interval = 239 days; SD = 5.8; range = 231–247).

Table 4.4 *MLUS increments, and intervals in days between the first recording and the recording closest to an interval of 240 days*

Subject	Interval (days)	Rec. no.	MLUS gain
Alex	231	12	1.1
Betty	241	13	1.8
Clare	240	12	2.0
Daisy	247	12	1.5
Eric	233	12	1.3
Fleur	244	12	1.1
Gemma	236	11	2.4

While acknowledging that the gain scores in Table 4.4 are crude measures, both in the sense that MLUS can only be a rough index and is prone to sampling error, and in the sense that they have not been adjusted for differences in initial scores, they can still be useful to indicate gross differences. Using a terminology similar to Ellis and Wells (1980) to relate age and rate of development, it is possible to classify the two children at the extremes as: Early Fast Developer (Gemma) and Late Slow Developer (Alex).

4.3 Rate of auxiliary verb development in spontaneous speech

To compare children on rate of auxiliary development it was decided to follow Wells (1978, 1979a, 1985) and examine the range of auxiliary forms to have emerged. The procedure is comparable with Wells' (1979a) emergence to criterion analysis (see Chapter 2), but here the measure is based on cumulative range of subforms. As a measure of rate of emergence it was decided to use the number of days from the appearance of six forms (the maximum at Recording 1) to the emergence of twenty-two forms (the minimum to have emerged by the last recording). One immediate problem was that extra recordings of some children had been made during the earliest stages as a diagnostic aid. In order to give children more equal opportunity to contribute types over a given period, therefore, the data for the second recording of Alex and Betty were omitted. Results are presented in Table 4.5.

Table 4.5 *Time in days from the emergence
of six subforms to twenty-two subforms*

Subject	Interval (days)
Alex	119
Betty	107
Clare	112
Daisy	83
Eric	133
Fleur	153
Gemma	60

The degree of variation in these intervals is quite considerable. Even allowing that sampling error could make a difference of the equivalent of one recording interval (approximately 21 days), there can be no doubt that the variation identified by Wells (1979a) is a very real phenomenon. The range is from 60 days (Gemma) to 153 days (Fleur), the equivalent of over four recording intervals. It is also clear that there is a similarity between the scores on rate of auxiliary emergence and rate of MLUS development (Table 4.4). Gemma and Fleur emerge as the fastest and slowest respectively on both measures. A comparison of the rank orders of all seven children shows a statistically significant relationship ($rho = 0.79$; $N = 7$; $p < .025$).

4.4 Rate of development in elicited imitation

4.4.1 Scoring
Rules for scoring auxiliaries were as follows:

1. Because there is no evidence that the semi-auxiliaries function for any child at any stage as full auxiliaries, the forms 'going to', 'got to', and 'has to' have been omitted from further analysis. The number of target forms is now nineteen.
2. Responses were scored for the presence or absence of the target auxiliary.
3. Contractions of a noncontracted auxiliary in the stimulus were counted as inclusions.
4. Responses where presence of the auxiliary was indeterminate were counted as omissions.

4.4.2 Children's response rate

Table 4.6 shows the number of items on each occasion which produced a response, compared with the number of responses which retained the auxiliary. Because of variation in co-operation, and consequently the number of items both presented and responded to, raw figures rather than proportions are given.

The figures for responses in Table 4.6 reflect an increasing degree of co-operation over time, usually resulting in several sessions when the majority of items could be presented. Subsequently, however, children were more difficult to motivate. At this point items which had been 'acquired' (see Section 3.4.5) were omitted. This accounts for the lower response rate during the last recordings. The only exception to this sequence is Fleur, who was unable to make the transition to the seven morpheme models (Recording 7).

4.4.3 Cumulative range of forms imitated

Cumulative range was used to indicate rate of auxiliary learning, and a single occurrence of a form in an imitated response was taken to be sufficient for that form to be included in the child's range. The progress of each child is presented in Table 4.7.

By the end of the study, five children have included all (Betty, Eric, Gemma) or most (Alex, Clare) of the nineteen forms. Daisy and Fleur on the other hand fall conspicuously behind, having produced only thirteen and twelve forms respectively. Surprisingly, one auxiliary which was never included by either of these children was declarative 'can' in its ability meaning. This is all the more unexpected because apparently more complex uses of CAN (Y/N and negative) are correctly imitated by both children (see Fig. 3.1 for the full models). 'Can't' is known to be an auxiliary which emerges as an unanalysed unit before the occurrence of the corresponding affirmative form (Bloom, 1970; Ervin, 1964; Fletcher, 1979; Klima and Bellugi, 1966), and this is reflected in the imitation responses of the remaining five children who all include 'can't' before 'can'. However, this does nothing to explain the emergence of polar interrogative CAN (Y) before CAN (D), not just in the data from Daisy and Fleur, but, on inspection, in the responses of all children. Based on Brown and Hanlon's (1970) findings on sequence of acquisition and syntactic complexity (SAAD→N→Q→NQ), one would expect the auxiliary to occur in the Simple Active Affirmative Declarative item before being included in the Interrogative sentence.

One possible explanation is the position of the target auxiliary in the model.

Table 4.6 *Number of imitated responses which retain the auxiliary, compared with total responses for each occasion*

Child	Recording													
	1	2	3	4	5	6	7	8	9	10	11	12	13	14
Alex	000	2/6	4/6	0/2	6/13	7/17	8/15	7/16	2/2	XXX	11/12	3/6	XXX	
Betty	000	XXX	0/3	3/5	3/6	4/9	7/13	10/17	6/7	6/10	1/3	6/8	1/1	4/6
Clare	2/3	XXX	4/16	3/10	7/14	7/17	10/18	2/11	2/11	0/11	1/10	1/6		
Daisy	1/3	0/6	0/4	1/5	4/9	4/18	4/15	5/17	1/13	0/1	3/6	6/12		
Eric	000	0/1	1/2	2/4	9/17	8/17	14/18	8/13	4/6	3/10	11/14	8/10	6/6	
Fleur	0/1	2/6	2/17	4/18	6/14	8/16	0/3	2/8	4/16	4/14	5/14	1/11		
Gemma	000	000	000	7/17	8/16	15/18	17/18	1/2	1/4	2/4	3/3	000		

Key – 000: No test administered.
XXX: Test attempted but no co-operation.

Table 4.7 *The development of cumulative range of auxiliary forms in elicited imitation*

	Recording													
Child	1	2	3	4	5	6	7	8	9	10	11	12	13	14
Alex	000	2	6	6	10	12	13	15	15	XXX	18	18	XXX	
Betty	000	XXX	0	3	5	8	12	17	17	17	18	19	19	19
Clare	2	XXX	6	7	10	13	15	15	15	15	16	17		
Daisy	0	0	0	1	4	6	6	7	8	8	9	13		
Eric	000	0	1	3	10	12	14	14	14	14	16	18	19	
Fleur	0	2	4	6	8	11	11	11	11	12	12	12		
Gemma	000	000	000	7	10	16	18	18	18	18	19	000		

Key—000:   No test administered.
XXX: Test attempted but no co-operation.

In the Y/N sentence the auxiliary form is in initial position, whereas in the declarative sentence it occurs medially. Position is clearly important, as shown by the work of Brown and Fraser (1963). They found that morphemes in final position are more likely to be included in elicited imitations than those in medial position. Morphemes in initial position were also retained in more cases than those in medial position, though this effect was not statistically significant. More specifically, research into the effects of input on auxiliary verb learning (Gleitman et al., 1984; Newport et al., 1977; this volume, Chapter 11) suggests that the auxiliary in initial position is more salient for the child. One explanation would therefore be that it is the position of the form in the *model* which makes it easier to reproduce. A second, but related explanation would be that children approach the imitation task with more knowledge of CAN in initial position because of its greater salience in that position in the *input* to the child.

The second of these explanations can be tested by comparing order of emergence in the test with order of emergence in spontaneous speech. If children imitate CAN (Y) before CAN (D) because they have more knowledge of the inverted form from properties of their input, then one would expect the same order of emergence in spontaneous production. Trends for the emergence of CAN in affirmative declarative, negative declarative, affirmative Y/N inversion, and negative Y/N inversion were therefore examined for each child. Rank orders for the emergence of CAN in each syntactic frame were summed over the seven subjects and the significance of the trend was tested using Page's *L* statistic (Hollander and Wolfe, 1973). The procedure reveals the sequence below ($L = 204.5$; Subjects $= 7$; Conditions $= 4$; $p < .001$):

> can't (D) → can (D) → can (Y) → can't (Y)

Except for 'can't', which can be expected to emerge early in an unanalysed form, order of emergence corresponds with Brown and Hanlon's (1970) predictions based on cumulative syntactic complexity. However, the relative positions of CAN (D) and CAN (Y) do not correspond with the sequence of emergence in the imitation test. There is no evidence therefore to support the hypothesis that knowledge of CAN in Y/N inversions accounts for the sequence in the test.

This restores the burden of explanation to the test items themselves. If this result is caused by the position of the auxiliary in the item, then a similar result should be obtained when the relative time of emergence of other inverted/non-inverted auxiliary pairs is examined. Unfortunately, there is no precisely comparable pair of items in the test. Since there is no item containing affirmative declarative DO, only 'doesn't' (D) and 'does' (Y) can be compared. In this case it is not the inverted form which emerges first. In fact the reverse is true. 'Doesn't' is included first for five children. For the remaining two (Alex and Betty) the sequence is unknown since both forms were repeated during the first administration of the test.

If no explanation can be found in the position of the auxiliary in the model sentence, perhaps the reason lies in the context, linguistic and visual, in which the form is embedded. This interpretation receives support from a comparison between age of emergence of CAN (D) in spontaneous and elicited speech. Research into elicited imitation and modal verbs (Kuczaj and Maratsos, 1975) suggests that if syntactic development is not concurrent in elicited and spontaneous speech, then advances will first become apparent through elicitation. In our study, however, the reverse happens – all seven children use CAN (D) in spontaneous speech at least two recordings before its inclusion in an imitated response. This is also true of Daisy and Fleur, the two children who never succeeded on this item even though they both attempted it.

The wording of the item in question was: 'She can give us milk', later extended to: 'She can give us lots of milk'. The accompanying picture showed in profile a brown and white cow standing in a green field. All children except Gemma reproduced the surrounding linguistic context of the item ('She give us milk') before including the auxiliary. In five cases (Alex, Clare, Daisy, Eric and Fleur) the interval between reproducing the context and supplying the auxiliary was from four to eight recording sessions. This suggests that the difficulty of the item lies in the interaction between the auxiliary and its context, rather than in specific features of the context itself such as the personal pronoun 'us' which is normally relatively late to emerge (Wells, 1985). An inspection of the responses to this item, however, shows some interesting patterns of recording. Four children responded at some stage by substituting a main verb inflection for the auxiliary:

> she gives us the milk   (*Clare, Rec. 4, 2;6.12*)

The result is a response which contains a number of morphemes equal to or greater than the number in the model.

Another response strategy was to include a filler sound or different auxiliary in the slot reserved for CAN. This type of response was recorded at some stage for all children except Alex and Gemma. Imitations such as these could be difficult to transcribe accurately because it was sometimes impossible to distinguish fillers from sounds which approached those of certain auxiliary forms. This lack of precision in articulation may reflect children's uncertainty. It is as though they are aware of the need to include an additional morpheme, aware that an auxiliary fits the context but are unable to re-encode the meaning of the original model:

> you ⟨must⟩ give her the milk   (*Eric, Rec. 6, 2;5.21*)
> Yeh he ⟨/di/⟩ give us the milk   (*Clare, Rec.5, 2;7.2*)

One potentially illuminating feature is that Daisy and Fleur, the two children who never include 'can', both recode the sentence towards the end of the study to include COULD as a substitute. This occurs in the last recording for Daisy, and in the last two recordings for Fleur. Together with the fact that CAN (D) has been present in spontaneous speech for a considerable period, this suggests even more strongly that the modal meaning of ability which the item was intended to communicate, was not the meaning perceived by the child. Since there are no clear instances of children recoding the item into the past tense it can probably be assumed that 'could' is to be associated here with a meaning of Tentative Possibility (Wells, 1979a) rather than the past tense of ability or permission. Wells has shown that such meanings emerge later than those of ability, permission or the performative meanings of CAN. It is also worth noting therefore that the items containing 'can' (Y) and 'can't', which ostensibly have modal meanings of ability and permission, also have a performative interpretation which may have facilitated imitation. It seems likely that the sentences 'You can't play here' and 'Can you see the pig?' were interpreted as deontic utterances functioning to regulate behaviour. The child's understanding would then have been equivalent to 'Don't play here' and 'Look at the pig'. In this way sentences could be decoded and re-encoded without assimilation to any schema of degrees and types of modal meaning.

One can only speculate about the reasons which may prevent children interpreting this item as ability. The problem may lie in a lack of real-world knowledge about cows and milk production. Whatever the reason, however, there is a salutary lesson here concerning test construction and the attribution of adult meanings to sentences to be presented to children.

4.4.4 Variation in rate of emergence in elicited imitation

As Tables 4.6 and 4.7 indicated, there is little evidence of simultaneous acquisition. In general, additions to a child's range are piecemeal, though there is clear variation in the rate at which this takes place. Two children (Betty, Recs. 6–8; Gemma, Recs. 5–7) go through a period of more rapid development, but exact comparisons are difficult because of variation in the number of items presented and responded to. Nevertheless, if the recording by which seventeen forms have been included is taken as the criterion which discriminates most effectively (see Table 4.7), then the children fall roughly into three groups with Gemma and Betty as the fastest developers, followed by an intermediate group consisting of Alex, Clare, and Eric, and finally Daisy and Fleur who lag well behind.

Although there is no clear correspondence for most children between their performance on the imitation test and rate of development measured by MLUS and spontaneous use of auxiliaries (rank order correlations are nonsignificant), a clearer profile of a few children is beginning to emerge. Fleur's rate of development is relatively slow on all three analyses and there is a suggestion that her early auxiliary usage consists of the stereotyped repetition of a small repertoire of forms. Alex and Clare appear to be breaking into the auxiliary system using more complex utterances which are probably only partially analysed. Gemma, despite being the youngest child, is consistently and substantially the fastest developer in the group.

5 Indicators of analytic and piecemeal learning

5.1 General developments for the combined auxiliary class

The analyses to be described here treat growth spurts in auxiliary frequency as suggesting developments in the child's rule system. Frequency is considered from three different perspectives: auxiliary tokens and auxiliary types per 100 structured utterances, and the rate of inclusion of certain forms in obligatory contexts.

Figures 5.1, 5.2, and 5.3 plot the frequency, range, and cumulative range of auxiliary forms over successive recordings. By comparing curves for frequency and range it is possible to develop hypotheses about distinctive styles of learning during those periods when the two do not develop in parallel.

5.1.1 Frequency of auxiliaries

The maximum frequency ranges from 16 (Daisy) to 38 (Betty) auxiliaries/100 structured utterances. To put such figures into perspective, an estimate for adult–adult conversation was obtained using the Bristol corpus. Eight transcripts of the younger Bristol children at 1;3 were taken at random and analysed for number of auxiliaries/100 structured adult–adult utterances. The mean value obtained was 50.8, well above the maximum figure for the Welsh children.

Figure 5.1 shows that while there is a clear increase in frequency over time, development is usually not linear, though Clare and Eric's progress is less marked by regressions than the remaining children. It is also difficult to identify single points at which there are sharp increases in the steepness of curves which might be indicative of changes in rule systems. However, six children show fairly rapid increases at some stage, the exception being Daisy whose maximum of 16.0 auxiliaries/100 structured utterances is considerably lower than for other children. In particular, the frequency for Clare rises from a previous highest of 13.4 to 24.4 auxiliaries/100 structured utterances (Recordings 9 to 10), and for Eric from a previous highest

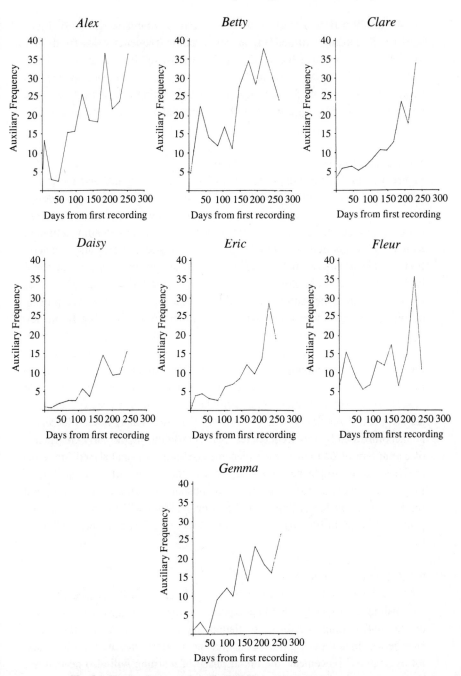

Fig. 5.1 The development of auxiliaries/100 structured utterances

of 14.1 to 29.4 (Recordings 11 to 12). The most dramatic rise is for Fleur between Recordings 10 and 11, at which point frequency rises from 18.1 to 36.4, an increase which coincides with her most significant gain in MLUS (see Table 4.3 above). Gemma also shows a sudden increase in MLUS (from 3.6 in Recording 5 to 5.0 in Recording 6) but in her case this precedes, rather than coincides with the largest rise in auxiliary frequency (Recording 7).

5.1.2 Range of auxiliaries per recording

Figure 5.2 confirms that the range of subforms in each sample also increases, and a comparison with frequency in Figure 5.1 shows a correspondence between the two variables. Increases in frequency, therefore, usually represent more than greater usage of a constant number of forms, or extending a limited number of forms across a wider range of linguistic contexts and syntactic frames. The relationship between range and frequency is most consistent in the data from Alex. However, it is equally informative to examine cases where trends in range conflict with trends in frequency, or where developments on one index are more rapid than on the other. A faster rising frequency can be seen most clearly in Fleur's first four recordings, a further indication of her stereotyped usage. At times the opposite tendency can be discerned: range rising more rapidly than frequency. This trend is more difficult to interpret. Increases in range can be a useful indication that a syntactic rule or set of rules which characterise a form-class or subclass has been generalised across a set of members of that class. On the other hand, if such increases are accompanied by low frequencies, particularly during the early emergence of exemplars of that class, then piecemeal addition of unanalysed, or semi-analysed forms might be indicated. This is the pattern of development of range and frequency for Clare during a substantial period of the study, and for Eric between Recordings 2 and 5. Further light will be thrown on this phenomenon in an investigation into indicators of holistic learning (Chapter 6).

5.1.3 Cumulative range

Since auxiliary subforms are a closed set of sixty-five items (see p.20), a diminishing returns effect is to be expected in the later stages causing curves of cumulative range of forms to flatten out after a period of more rapid emergence. In addition, if the earliest tokens of auxiliaries are semi-analysed forms acquired piecemeal, the initial phase of learning will also be realised by a more gently rising curve.

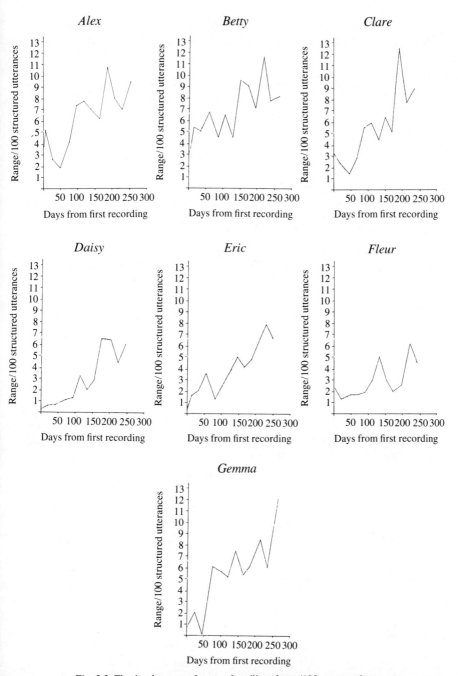

Fig. 5.2 The development of range of auxiliary forms/100 structured utterances

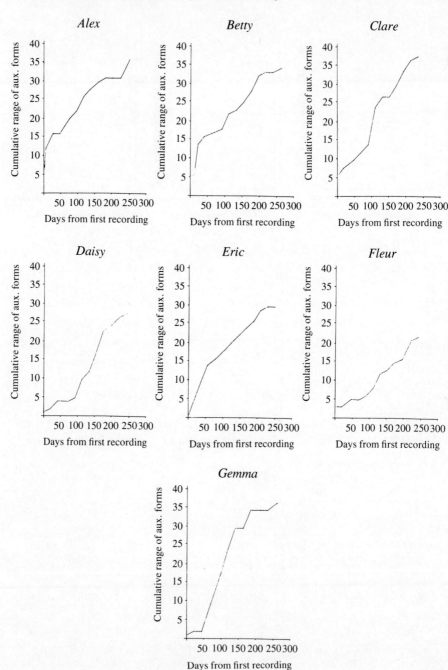

Fig. 5.3 The development of cumulative range of auxiliary forms

Graphs of the development of cumulative range are shown in Figure 5.3. While there is indeed a tendency for curves to be 'S'-shaped, this is not the case for all the children. Eric, for example, shows an initial steep rise from Recording 1 to Recording 4. This marks the fastest rate of emergence for Eric. Alex shows sharp rises at both the beginning and end of the study, an effect which is partially accounted for by the sudden emergence of past tense forms of BE + ING in Sample 13.

The purest example of the predicted curve is Gemma. Rapid development between Recordings 3 and 9 is flanked by periods of slower rate of emergence at the beginning and end of the study. But the most dramatic increase between recordings is for Clare. Between Recordings 5 and 6 her cumulative range increases by ten. Since these forms belong to several different verbs (four HAVE + EN forms, three BE + ING forms, one DO form, 'can', and 'shouldn't') and since they represent *new* forms which are not accompanied by substantial rises in auxiliary frequency or range per occasion (noncumulative) (see Figs. 5.1 and 5.2), it is difficult to know whether these advances are developments of an integrated form-class system or whether this marks a period of rapid piecemeal learning. Evidence will be found below in Chapter 6 which is consistent with the latter interpretation.

5.1.4 Summary

Comparisons of the three sets of curves suggest different learning styles both within and between children. The most rapid development in frequency occurs for Fleur, but it does so after a lengthy period of relative stagnation in her general linguistic development and is not accompanied by a corresponding increase in range. This is consistent with earlier observations which suggested stereotyped usage. Similarly, there is further evidence here of piecemeal learning for Clare in particular, and also for Eric.

5.2 Variation in the rate at which obligatory contexts are filled

The analysis reported in this section is founded on the expectation that variation in the rate of increase in the proportion of auxiliaries supplied in obligatory contexts will reflect different styles of syntactic development. In a similar analysis Kuczaj and Maratsos (1983) identified 'impulsive' and 'reflective' styles in two children (see Section 1.3.3 above), but here an alternative explanation will be considered – that rate of inclusion of auxiliaries in obligatory contexts reflects syntactic-rule learning ability. If children can be shown to vary in the manner anticipated, an error analysis can determine whether impulsiveness or analytical ability is the correct interpretation for rapid increases in the proportion of forms included.

5.2.1 Introduction

In a study of the order of acquisition of fourteen morphemes, Brown (1973) analysed the development of contractible and noncontractible auxiliary BE in obligatory contexts. The criterion of acquisition was taken to be 90% presence. Before continuing, however, the contractible/noncontractible distinction needs some clarification, because it refers to the context of the auxiliary rather than its form. It is important therefore to distinguish between a contract*ible* context and a contract*ible* auxiliary, and between a contract*ible* auxiliary and a contract*ed* auxiliary. In other words, there are linguistic contexts where the auxiliary can contract, such as medial position in declarative sentences, and there are other contexts where it may not contract, such as initial position in Y/N questions (see Brown, 1973). There are also auxiliary forms which can contract ('is', 'am', etc.) and there are those which can't ('was', 'be', etc.). Considerable difficulties exist, however, in putting these distinctions into operation (Kuczaj, 1979a). Noncontracted and noncontractible forms can occur in contractible positions, but contractible forms in contractible positions must occur in full when they are used emphatically. Kuczaj draws attention to the problem of how to treat non-inverted Y/Ns, but it is also unclear how Brown treats Wh- questions. The only examples he gives are for the copula, e.g. 'Who is it?' (p. 266). Obviously this is uncontractible, but most Wh- questions, whether inverted or not, are contractible contexts. Problems such as these, and differences in the frequency of empty contractible and uncontractible contexts may be of some consequence if the objective is to determine order of acquisition of the auxiliary or copula in contractible and uncontractible contexts. Kuczaj (1979a) attributes discrepancies between the findings of Brown (1973) and De Villiers and De Villiers (1973) as to whether acquisition first occurs in contractible or uncontractible contexts to such scoring difficulties, and also to possible variations in sampling. Another factor has been given less attention. This is the differential redundancy of the auxiliary in contractible and noncontractible contexts. Present tense BE has low *semantic* content in both types of context but in the uncontractible contexts it is usually performing a *syntactic* function in Y/N inversion, main verb ellipsis, and emphasis. It is therefore more difficult to identify empty contexts where the auxiliary verb would normally be such an essential part of a syntactic operation. It is hardly possible to envisage empty obligatory contexts for ellipsis and emphasis. With ellipsis, one would presumably be looking for utterances like some of Betty's first tags ('we got ⟨?⟩ book we got', Rec.2, 2;4.15), and with emphasis, for abnormal stress patterns, in particular, heavy stress on main verbs in what appear to be contractible contexts. Problems such as these produce a bias in favour of a higher percentage of inclusion, and consequently earlier acquisition, in *uncontractible* contexts. As far as Y/Ns are concerned, if the auxiliary is absent (# 'you going out?'), it is not clear whether the obligatory context is in medial position – as a non-inverted, intonation only Y/N (hence a contractible context), or whether the context is in initial position – as a Y/N inversion (hence an uncontractible context).

5.2.2 Method

Since the current aim is to look at the rate at which children proceed from a low proportion of auxiliaries in obligatory contexts to a criterion of acquisition, it was not necessary to duplicate Brown's procedure. On the other hand, it was essential to confine the analysis to a fairly uniform set of contexts to avoid confounding the effects of contractible and noncontractible contexts. Originally, the intention had been to carry out separate analyses of auxiliary inclusion in these two areas. However, it soon became evident that a large proportion of uncontractibles either involved ellipsis, were emphatic, or were tag questions. The total number of empty obligatory contexts for these was minuscule. Empty contexts in Y/Ns were also rare, regardless of the problem of classifying them as contractible or noncontractible. Possibly, the reason for this was that the criterion for an obligatory context (that the surrounding linguistic context had to be complete) may have been more stringent than that employed elsewhere. The result of this scarcity of empty uncontractible contexts is that a replication of Brown's analyses on the two auxiliaries to be considered below would, without doubt, show the development of the uncontractible auxiliary to be in advance of the contractible auxiliary. This would be consistent with Brown (1973) but would conflict with the findings of De Villiers and De Villiers (1973). Unfortunately there are simply too few tokens, too few empty contexts, and too little variation in the ratio of empty to filled contexts to make any assessment of rate of acquisition of the uncontractible auxiliary.

The only auxiliaries for which obligatory contexts can be identified reliably and in sufficient numbers are BE and HAVE. Because of its high frequency for all children, the analysis of HAVE is confined to the Possession meaning of HAVE + 'got'. This has the additional advantage of reducing variation due to co-occurrence with different lexical verbs.

In line with the decision to use contractible contexts only, the following were excluded: questions, main verb ellipsis, stressed auxiliaries, and, for BE + ING, the forms 'be' and 'been'.

5.2.3 Results (BE + ING)

Table 5.1 shows the number of auxiliaries present compared with the number of obligatory contexts. Two things immediately become clear. Firstly, frequencies for individual speech samples are in most cases too small to justify the calculation of percentages. Secondly, the presence of the auxiliary is inconsistent; there is no obvious developmental trend for any child except Clare. Fluctuations are almost random and there are few single occasions where there are sufficient auxiliaries to suggest more than chance inclusion. A 90% criterion of acquisition for three consecutive samples (Brown's criterion) is unattainable during the period under study. The only children who on any occasion include the auxiliary at a level which suggests a non-random effect ($p < .05$ on a sign test), are Clare (Rec. 12), Eric (Rec. 9), and Gemma (Recs. 5 and 12), and only Eric uses the auxiliary at above the 50% level over a sustained period (Recs. 7 to 13).

Pooling the data from groups of occasions fails to clarify the picture (see Richards, 1987a). Development is still far from linear for individual children and it is only Clare, Eric, and Gemma who at any time include the auxiliary at a level greater than chance. Even the combined data from all children fail to show a clear trend, the inclusion rate remaining at approximately 50% for the last three groups of three recordings.

Table 5.1 *Proportion of auxiliary BE forms present in obligatory contexts*

Child	Recording													
	1	2	3	4	5	6	7	8	9	10	11	12	13	14
Alex	0/1	3/14	2/6	1/7	1/14	3/4	4/8	9/13	0/5	4/10	2/5	1/10	3/7	
Betty	1/4	1/1	3/11	0/4	1/3	3/5	2/4	4/5	2/5	1/2	4/7	4/8	1/3	3/4
Clare	0/3	0/3	0/0	1/1	1/7	3/7	2/10	2/8	4/10	1/2	5/8	13/16		
Daisy	0/1	0/0	1/1	0/0	0/2	2/3	1/2	2/8	5/10	2/4	3/9	1/2		
Eric	0/3	1/7	7/19	1/3	0/2	1/2	5/6	5/7	14/18	4/5	3/7	6/11	2/2	
Fleur	0/0	0/0	0/1	0/2	0/2	0/1	1/1	3/3	2/3	0/1	7/9	0/5		
Gemma	0/1	0/3	1/4	3/7	19/27	2/2	7/10	6/14	4/13	8/17	1/3	7/7		

5.2.4 Results (HAVE + got)

Table 5.2 shows a similar picture of fluctuating presence of the auxiliary, though there is a discernible upward trend for Alex when groups of three occasions are pooled. There is a suggestion that Gemma may have begun an upward trend by Recording 12, but without subsequent data this is impossible to confirm. Levels of inclusion are generally lower than for BE + ING; only Betty has more than a 50% inclusion rate over more than one recording. If the data for all children and all samples are pooled, it can be seen that there are more obligatory contexts for HAVE (768 compared with 515 for BE), but fewer which contain the auxiliary (117 compared with 232). Overall inclusion is therefore 15.2% for HAVE and 45% for BE.

Table 5.2 *Proportion of auxiliary HAVE + got forms present in obligatory contexts*

Child	Recording

Child	1	2	3	4	5	6	7	8	9	10	11	12	13	14
Alex	1/3	0/8	0/5	0/3	3/10	0/7	0/4	2/5	3/16	1/6	3/6	6/10	3/8	
Betty	2/24	2/12	0/28	3/18	1/11	2/8	1/23	2/13	1/3	6/8	2/3	4/11	2/6	3/18
Clare	0/7	0/4	0/22	0/3	2/4	5/17	1/5	0/4	1/10	3/11	5/10	4/13		
Daisy	0/6	0/4	0/1	0/4	0/4	0/2	1/3	3/11	2/9	0/3	1/13	1/13		
Eric	0/0	0/0	2/5	0/2	0/6	0/19	0/5	0/10	0/9	0/5	3/8	1/11	0/4	
Fleur	0/8	0/7	0/4	0/8	0/16	3/10	0/3	0/1	0/5	0/0	2/8	2/4		
Gemma	0/3	0/1	0/2	0/2	0/1	6/30	1/18	1/34	2/25	2/10	1/10	9/14		

5.2.5 Conclusion

From the point of view of individual differences this analysis has been largely uninformative. The lack of clear developmental trends and the low frequency of contexts for some children make comparisons of the rate of acquisition extremely difficult at this stage of development. Brown (1973) produces evidence that the pattern of acquisition varies for different forms of auxiliary and copula BE, and Kuczaj (1981b) shows that these forms initially develop independently, reaching the 90% criterion at different times. There is a good case therefore for analysing the various subforms separately. Unfortunately there are insufficient data in the available speech samples to make this possible.

From a broader perspective on auxiliary verb learning these results are of more interest. Brown (1973) also found the behaviour of copula and auxiliary BE to be highly erratic, even when analysed separately and by separate subforms. For Adam and Eve the presence of the auxiliary or copula was unpredictable for a period of two years. One factor was the status of contracted forms with regard to their segmentation from the previous constituent. 'It's', for example, functioned as a single morpheme for Adam (though not for Eve and Sarah). This issue has been addressed by Brown, Cazden and Bellugi (1969) and more recently by Kuczaj (1976, 1979a; Maratsos and Kuczaj, 1978). Another explanation therefore in addition to variation by subform for the inconsistent behaviour of these two auxiliaries is that if the contracted morpheme is not segmented from its context, an initially high rate of inclusion may be followed by a drop as analysis takes place. A subsequent period of doubt may then ensue during which either form (e.g. 'it' or 'it's') will be supplied. The question of unanalysed contractions will be considered in the next chapter, but it is also worth bearing in mind that the absence of an auxiliary from an obligatory context need not signify lack of grammatical knowledge, either of the form itself or its relationship with the context. This point will be taken up in the discussion of tag questions in Chapter 7.

6 The complexity principle as an indicator of holistic learning

The Complexity Principle which was introduced in Section 3.1 assumes that analytic learning proceeds from the syntactically less complex to the syntactically more complex. If in the emergence of syntactic structures this principle appears to be violated, it can be taken as an indication that the complex structures have been acquired holistically. In this chapter four syntactic processes will be considered in relation to base forms: negation, ellipsis, formation of questions, and contraction. In addition, where obligatory contexts can be identified, the transcripts will be examined for instances of early auxiliary inclusion which precede unfilled obligatory contexts. Finally, the development of tags will be analysed as a system which in its mature form depends among other things on a knowledge of all four processes listed above.

The results of these analyses will then be combined to test whether tendencies to use unanalysed structures are consistent across different domains. In all cases the analysis rests on Emergence rather than Acquisition, emergence being defined as the sampling of a single token, and the characteristic sequence of emergence for all seven children will be established before violations of the principle 'simple precedes complex' are considered. In doing so, any areas where apparently more complex structures emerge first can be identified.

6.1 Principle 1: affirmative forms precede negated forms

Negation of the auxiliary was usually achieved by the contracted negative particle '-n't'. There are only twelve tokens of auxiliaries followed by uncontracted 'not' in the whole database, and a further seven tokens in unfilled obligatory contexts (# 'it not going').

A total of eighteen Affirmative/Contracted Negative pairs can be identified for the auxiliaries which were sampled in the study. BE forms are BE + ING only:

do/don't	does/doesn't	did/didn't
have/haven't	has/hasn't	had/hadn't

can/can't	are/aren't	is/isn't
was/wasn't	were/weren't	will/won't
shall/shan't	could/couldn't	might/mightn't
should/shouldn't	would/wouldn't	must/mustn't

It will be noticed that the above list includes the three affirmative DO forms. These have fewer privileges of occurrence than their negative counterparts in standard English, because they do not occur unstressed in declarative sentences. Nevertheless, they do occur in certain dialects and are included here because they were present in the speech of the children (see Chapter 8).

For each child the affirmative/negative pairs were coded in one of four ways:

1. The affirmative form emerges before the negative form.
2. The negative form emerges before the affirmative form.
3. The affirmative and negative forms emerge in the same sample.
4. Neither form occurs in any sample.

Table 6.1 shows how many of the eighteen pairs were in the first three of these categories.

Table 6.1 *Relative time of emergence of affirmative and negative auxiliaries*

	No. of cases		
Subject	S < C	C < S	S = C
Alex	7	3	3
Betty	10	3	2
Clare	7	8	1
Daisy	7	5	0
Eric	8	5	1
Fleur	5	2	3
Gemma	12	3	2
Totals	56	29	12

Key: S: simple form.   C: complex form.
     < : precedes.   = : co-emerges with.

The number of cases supporting the complexity prediction exceeds the number of disconfirmatory cases and the statistical significance of this finding can be tested using a sign test. In accordance with Siegel (1956) ties (co-emergent cases) are omitted and the N reduced correspondingly. If the total number of cases exceeds 25 a z-score is calculated using the formula:

$$z = \frac{x - \tfrac{1}{2}N}{\tfrac{1}{2}\sqrt{N}}$$

where N is the total number of cases and x is the number of exceptions. Corrected for continuity:

$$z = \frac{(x + .5) - \tfrac{1}{2}N}{\tfrac{1}{2}\sqrt{N}}$$

(Siegel, 1956, p. 72)

From Table 6.1 it can be seen that $N = 85$ ($56 + 29$) and $x = 29$. Therefore $z = -2.82$ ($p < .005$). The overall tendency for affirmative forms to precede corresponding negative forms is therefore statistically significant.

The only areas where negative forms tend to emerge first for the majority of children are: do/don't (for six out of seven children), does/doesn't (for five out of seven children), and can/can't (for five out of seven children). In view of the restricted role played by DO in affirmative declarative sentences, and the common observation of the early emergence of 'can't', these exceptions come as no surprise.

As far as individual children are concerned Clare is the only exception to the general trend: for her, less than half of the cases support the complexity prediction. While the other children all provide more confirmatory than disconfirmatory cases, Betty ($p < .05$) and Gemma ($p < .02$) are the only individuals for whom this is statistically significant.

6.2 Principle 2: co-occurrence with main verbs precedes ellipsis

All major forms which are included under the working definition of auxiliary for this research can function as residual operators in main verb ellipsis. This applies to:

(a) Declarative sentences:
   R: can you do it? [solve a Mr. Men puzzle]
   Eric: I can't *(Eric, Rec. 12, 2;9.29)*

(b) Declarative sentences with contrastive stress:
   M: you didn't even finish your breakfast this morning did you?
   M: no
   Eric: I ″did *(Eric, Rec. 9, 2;7.26)*

(c) Wh-, Y/N and tag questions:
Eric: I haven't got one of these have I? [Lego car]   (*Eric, Rec. 13, 2;10.19*)

(d) Imperative sentences containing 'don't'.

Like the previous analysis, this section relates the data for the group as a whole and for individual children to the prediction that emergence will take place in less complex (non-ellipsed) syntactic frames before more complex (ellipsed) syntactic frames. Unfortunately, this apparently simple procedure is problematic. Ellipsis is in Brown's (1973) terminology an uncontractible context. That is to say, the auxiliary (or copula) retains its uncontracted and unreduced form when functioning as a residual operator. This rule is obligatory and invariable, and the data contain no errors of the type:

> * # I've got a new book I've
> * # he won't go 'll he?

In full declarative sentences, on the other hand, both full and contracted forms are grammatical:

> Bonny's going to the vet's [Eric's dog is ill]   (*Eric, Rec.8, 2;7.4*)
> My friend is playing out   (*Eric, Rec.12, 2;9.29*)

Because a smaller range of auxiliary subforms can occur in ellipsed contexts than in non-ellipsed contexts, the probability is increased that non-elliptical usage will be the first to be sampled. In order to remove this bias, the analysis is restricted to those auxiliary forms which are invariable whether the context is contractible or noncontractible. This means that while, for example, 'don't', 'can', and 'was' are retained, ''ve' and 'have', $/z/ +$ EN and 'has', ''m' and 'am', etc. are omitted.

The remaining forms recorded for each child were allocated to one of four categories corresponding to those outlined in Section 6.1 above. Results are presented in Table 6.2.

Using the sign test appropriate for samples where $N > 25$ (see above) we can confirm the complexity prediction for the group as a whole: $N = 105$; $x = 24$; $z = 5.47$; $p < .0005$. For all children the number of confirmatory cases exceeds exceptions. This is statistically significant on a conventional sign test ($N < 26$) for Betty ($p < .002$), Eric ($p < .002$), and Gemma ($p < .001$).

The analysis so far has considered all cases of ellipsis, regardless of other syntactic features of the utterance. As pointed out above, however, the auxiliary can function simultaneously as an operator for interrogation and ellipsis. Since interrogation is also to be analysed with regard to the complexity principle, it is important to avoid confounding interrogation and ellipsis if rank

Table 6.2 *Relative time of emergence of forms used with main verbs and in ellipsis*

Subject	No. of cases		
	S < C	C < S	S = C
Alex	11	7	1
Betty	15	1	2
Clare	10	7	1
Daisy	8	3	1
Eric	14	2	0
Fleur	8	2	1
Gemma	15	2	4
Totals	81	24	10

Key: S: simple form.   C: complex form.
         < : precedes.   = : co-emerges with.

orders of children on each of these syntactic dimensions are eventually to be compared. The procedure was therefore repeated so that instances of ellipsis were included only if they did not occur in questions. Correspondingly revised figures for declaratives and imperatives only are set out in Table 6.3.

Again, ellipsis clearly emerges later than auxiliary + main verb: $N = 95$; $x = 20$; $z = -5.64$; $p < .0005$. For all children, the number of confirmatory instances exceeds the number of exceptions. This is statistically significant for four children: Betty $(p < .002)$, Eric $(p < .01)$, Fleur $(p < .05)$, and Gemma $(p < .002)$.

6.3 Principle 3: declaratives precede inversion in questions

In Standard English, Y/N interrogatives invert the grammatical subject and an auxiliary or copula verb. Wh- questions require the same transformation unless the Wh- word is also the subject of the sentence. It has been observed (Bellugi, 1971; Menyuk, 1971) that one stage in the development of questions, particularly Wh- questions, is the presence of a non-inverted operator, interrogative mood being marked by rising intonation. Our samples were not analysed for the development of copula BE, but of those questions which contained an auxiliary, nearly all were inversions. In total there were just three intonation only Y/Ns which retained the auxiliary (e.g. 'you haven't got name?': Daisy, to a cuddly toy, Rec. 9, 2;9.12). Wh- questions where non-inversion was

Table 6.3 *Relative time of emergence of forms used with main verbs and in ellipsis: questions omitted*

Subject	No. of cases		
	S < C	C < S	S = C
Alex	8	6	2
Betty	14	2	2
Clare	10	4	1
Daisy	8	2	0
Eric	12	2	0
Fleur	7	1	2
Gemma	16	3	1
Totals	75	20	8

Key: S: simple form.   C: complex form.
         < : precedes.   = : co-emerges with.

an error were also rare – ten tokens (e.g. 'what he's doin'?': Eric, looking at a book, Rec. 3, 2;3.12), and Wh- questions where no inversion is required because the Wh- word is the subject of an auxiliary, were even rarer – three tokens (e.g. 'what's happening here?': Betty, looking at a book, Rec. 11, 2;10.24). Although the analysis here is restricted to questions with subject/ auxiliary inversion, it is clear therefore that these represent the vast majority of questions which contain an auxiliary.

The procedure follows that outlined above for negation and ellipsis. Since inversion, like ellipsis, is a noncontractible context, contractible and contracted auxiliary subforms have again been omitted. Relative times of emergence of the remaining auxiliary forms as declaratives and in inverted questions are shown in Table 6.4.

Once again, the complexity prediction is confirmed: $N = 111$; $x = 25$; $z = -5.69$; $p < .0005$. Auxiliaries emerge in declaratives before they emerge in inverted questions. For all children the forms supporting the prediction are in the majority. This tendency is significant for Betty ($p < .001$), Daisy ($p < .025$), Eric ($p < .05$), Fleur ($p < .05$), and Gemma ($p < .002$).

There are some fairly obvious similarities between these results and those for ellipsis (Table 6.2), particularly if children are placed in rank order according to the percentage of forms supporting the complexity principle (see Table 6.9). However, it was pointed out above that some utterances contributed to both categories. The analysis of inversions was therefore repeated to exclude

Table 6.4 *Relative time of emergence of forms used as declaratives and in inverted questions*

	No. of cases		
Subject	S < C	C < S	S = C
Alex	10	8	0
Betty	16	1	1
Clare	11	7	1
Daisy	10	2	0
Eric	12	4	0
Fleur	9	2	1
Gemma	18	1	1
Totals	86	25	4

Key: S: simple form.   C: complex form.
        < : precedes.   = : co-emerges with.

Table 6.5 *Relative time of emergence of forms in declaratives and inverted questions: ellipsis omitted*

	No. of cases		
Subject	S < C	C < S	S = C
Alex	11	3	0
Betty	15	2	0
Clare	14	1	0
Daisy	10	2	0
Eric	13	3	0
Fleur	9	0	0
Gemma	17	3	0
Totals	89	14	0

Key: S: simple form.   C: complex form.
        < : precedes.   = : co-emerges with.

all tokens which involved main verb ellipsis, either in declaratives or inverted questions. The results are presented in Table 6.5.

When elliptical usage is excluded, the tendency for declarative forms to emerge first is even stronger ($N = 103$; $x = 14$; $z = -7.39$; $p < .0005$) and is now also independently significant for all seven children.

Interestingly, the proportion of disconfirmatory cases decreased both in the analysis of ellipsis and in the analysis of inversion when they were reanalysed as mutually exclusive categories. The differences were particularly marked for Clare (cf. Tables 6.2 and 6.3, and Tables 6.4 and 6.5). The most common feature which combines both inversion and ellipsis is the tag question and although the rules for producing tag questions are complex, it is not inconceivable that some children could have developed strategies for producing tags at a relatively early stage of their auxiliary verb development based on a limited understanding of the syntactic processes involved. The relative time of emergence of auxiliaries in tag questions and other syntactic frames will be examined as Principle 6 (see Section 6.6 below).

6.4 Principle 4: full forms precede contracted forms

Seven auxiliary forms used by the children are contractible in certain contexts:

have	've
has	/s/, /z/
am	'm
are	're
is	/s/, /z/
will, shall	'll
would	'd

Since the status of ''ll' is usually unclear, 'will' and 'shall' have arbitrarily been treated as a single form.

Once again, since privileges of occurrence for contracted and full forms are not equal, it is appropriate to confine the analysis to declarative contractible contexts.

Table 6.6 shows that for this analysis the complexity prediction has to be rejected. Less than a quarter of cases provide support. In fact the reverse appears to be true, contracted forms emerge before full forms: $N = 38$; $x = 9$; $z = -3.08$; $p < .002$; two-tailed. Numbers are too small to discriminate between children, even if substantial individual differences exist on this variable. Nor are the numbers large enough to attain statistical significance for individuals. It is interesting, however, that Gemma should be the only child for whom the majority of auxiliaries first emerge in a noncontracted form.

The unexpected rejection of Principle 4 conflicts with widely held views on the development of the auxiliary (e.g. Gleitman et al., 1984) and suggests

Table 6.6 *Relative time of emergence of contracted and full forms in declaratives*

Subject	No. of cases		
	S < C	C < S	S = C
Alex	2	4	0
Betty	1	4	1
Clare	1	5	1
Daisy	1	4	1
Eric	0	5	1
Fleur	0	4	1
Gemma	4	3	0
Totals	9	29	5

Key: S: simple form.   C: complex form.
         <: precedes.   =: co-emerges with.

that the extent of early unanalysed usage is greater than is generally assumed. The significance of this finding will be discussed in Chapters 11 and 12.

6.5 Principle 5: empty obligatory contexts precede filled obligatory contexts

Although it is frequently possible to identify contexts where an auxiliary seems to be necessary for syntactic completeness, it is not always possible to specify which verb is lacking. This is particularly true of performative utterances where CAN or SHALL would fit the context equally well: 'we do it together?' (Alex, wanting to do a jigsaw, Rec. 1, 2;7.6). Similarly, requests for help such as, 'where this one go?' (Alex, trying to do the jigsaw, Rec. 1, 2;7.6), while appearing to be an obligatory context for 'does', would equally make sense with the insertion of 'can', 'might', 'should', 'must', or 'will'. Obligatory contexts can be identified more reliably for BE + ING, HAVE + EN, and possibly WILL expressing intention. Even for these, however, noncontractible contexts are problematic (see Section 5.2.1). There can be no unfilled obligatory context for auxiliaries in tag questions, for example, since the auxiliary is the kernel of the tag. For these reasons, and the finding in Section 6.4 that contracted forms tend to be sampled first, the analysis which follows is limited to declarative contractible contexts and the nonstressed contracted forms listed below:

've + EN   've + got   've + got to
/z/ + EN   /z/ + got   /z/ + got to
/s/ + EN   /s/ + got   /s/ + got to
'm + ING   'm + going to
're + ING   're + going to
/z/ + ING   /z/ + going to
/s/ + ING   /s/ + going to
'll

Table 6.7 shows the results of this analysis to be consistent with the complexity principle: $N = 102$; $x = 34$; $z = -3.27$; $p < .0006$. For all children, the proportion of confirmatory cases exceeds 50%, though this only reaches a significant level for Clare ($p = .002$).

Table 6.7 *Relative time of emergence of empty and filled obligatory contexts*

	No. of cases		
Subject	S < C	C < S	S = C
Alex	9	5	3
Betty	10	7	1
Clare	14	2	0
Daisy	9	5	1
Eric	7	5	2
Fleur	9	5	0
Gemma	10	5	1
Totals	68	34	8

Key: S: simple form.   C: complex form.
          <: precedes.   =: co-emerges with.

6.6 Principle 6: combinations of inversion and ellipsis emerge later than other syntactic frames

Analyses 6.2 and 6.3 suggested that auxiliary verb usage which combines inversion and ellipsis was responsible for a high proportion of violations of the complexity principle. Tag questions are the feature which most frequently fall into this category, and an inspection of the transcripts shows that there are indeed cases where a form was first sampled in a tag question. Wh- questions can also combine inversion and main verb ellipsis (# 'Why can't I?') but no examples were found. On the other hand, Y/Ns combining inversion and main verb ellipsis were present (#'Can I?'), though unlike tags there are no cases of an auxiliary form first being sampled in one of these.

Before proceeding it is important to explain how it is possible for an auxiliary to be present in a tag before that auxiliary has occurred elsewhere. There are two reasons why this is counterintuitive. Firstly, the tag frame is syntactically the most complex syntactic frame in which a single auxiliary can occur (see Chapter 7). On complexity alone tags would be expected to emerge late. Secondly, unless the operator is DO, the auxiliary in the tag normally matches a corresponding auxiliary in the previous matrix clause. It would be a reasonable assumption, therefore, that the auxiliary in the tag is usually derived in some way (syntactically or semantically) from an auxiliary in the matrix. A classic transformational treatment would assume a Copying Rule to place the auxiliary in the tag. However, the type of early tag discussed here either supplies an inappropriate auxiliary in the tag ('I know him aren't I?': Alex, Rec. 2, 2;7.13), or appropriately tags an *empty* auxiliary context in the matrix ('Got a mellow (a Ford car) /æntʃuː/ (haven't you?)' : Alex, Rec. 1, 2;7.6). If a T-G account is pursued, in the latter example we must posit an auxiliary deletion transformation at a stage when Alex is not yet producing the auxiliary in declarative frames. This is clearly less satisfactory than an explanation which focuses on the productivity of the auxiliary in the tag itself.

Table 6.8 compares time of emergence of auxiliaries in tags and in any other syntactic frame. Because tag questions usually reverse the polarity of the matrix clause and are noncontractible contexts, corresponding affirmatives and negatives, and contracted and noncontracted forms (e.g. ''ll', 'will' and 'won't'), are treated as one form. It can be seen from the table that most forms emerge in a less complex structure before they emerge in inversion plus ellipsis ($N = 47$; $x = 9$; $z = -4.08$; $p < .0005$).

All disconfirmatory cases are tag questions and are supplied by Alex or Clare. In fact more than half of the forms which Clare uses in tag questions do not appear until a later occasion in a different syntactic frame. Given the number and complexity of the rules of tag production, it is also noteworthy that for Clare the majority, and for Alex all of these exceptions to the complexity hypothesis occur during the first two speech samples, at a stage when in all other respects auxiliary verb development was at a primitive stage. What is also interesting is that Gemma, who by the end of the study was more advanced than the other children on several indices of development

Table 6.8 *Relative time of emergence of auxiliaries in*
inversion + ellipsis and other syntactic frames

	No. of cases		
Subject	S < C	C < S	S = C
Alex	9	3	0
Betty	13	0	0
Clare	5	6	2
Daisy	1	0	0
Eric	8	0	0
Fleur	2	0	1
Gemma	0	0	0
Totals	38	9	3

Key: S: simple form.   C: complex form.
        <: precedes.   =: co-emerges with.

(see Chapter 4), never learnt to use tags. This surprising aspect of Gemma's
development will be followed up in Chapter 7.

6.7 Indicators of holistic learning: summary

It would be unrealistic to expect a count of exceptions to the six complexity
principles to discriminate finely between the seven children in each case.
For one thing, the number of auxiliary forms available for the six analyses
was generally fairly small, and the violations usually represented a low proportion of the total number of cases. The possibility that at least some of these
can be accounted for by sampling error cannot be ruled out. Tables 6.9 and
6.10 show that if the children are placed in rank order according to the
percentage of cases in each analysis which support the complexity hypothesis,
there is no clear relationship between the rank orders beyond what might
be expected by chance alone. Nevertheless, these figures are still capable
of indicating gross differences between children with regard to any tendency
(or lack of tendency) to use partially analysed complex structures at an earlier
stage than would be expected. That Gemma should score lowest is entirely
consistent with previous analyses and contributes to a developing profile of
a young fast analytic learner. At the other extreme Alex, as the oldest child,
will be shown to use holistic strategies to function conversationally at a level
beyond his grammatical competence. Similarly, the relatively high scores

Table 6.9 *Rank orders on indicators of holistic learning*

			Indicator				
Subject	Neg.	Ellip.	Inv.	Contr.	Obl. Con.	Inv. + Ellip.	Total
Alex	4	7	7	2	4	6	30
Betty	2	1.5	3	3.5	7	3	20
Clare	7	6	2	5	1	7	28
Daisy	6	5	5	3.5	4	3	26.5
Eric	5	3	6	6.5	6	3	29.5
Fleur	3	1.5	1	6.5	4	3	19
Gemma	1	4	4	1	2	3	15

Table 6.10 *Intercorrelations between rank orders on indicators of holistic learning[a]*

	2	3	4	5
1. Negation	.52	.11	.44	−.26
2. Ellipsis		.49	−.44	−.58
3. Inversion			−.38	.26
4. Contraction				.23
5. Oblig. Contexts				

[a] Figures are for the Spearman rank order correlation, and have been corrected for tied ranks (see Siegel, 1956). All are n.s.; $N = 7$; one-tailed.

for Clare and Eric support the tentative conclusions about piecemeal learning reached in Chapter 5.

At a general level this chapter confirms the view that auxiliaries tend to emerge in simple contexts first. However, there is also evidence that it is unanalysed contracted forms which first occupy previously empty obligatory contexts. This is a theme which will be explored in later chapters.

7 Individual differences and the development of auxiliaries in tag questions[1]

7.1 Introduction

Tags can combine Negation, Inversion and Code (ellipsis), three of the defining characteristics of the auxiliary, and it was suggested in Section 2.2.3 that evidence of a range of auxiliaries in tag questions, particularly if they reverse the polarity of an auxiliary in the matrix clause, could be used as a criterion of acquisition. However, we have seen in Chapter 6 that two children (Alex and Clare) use auxiliary forms in tags before their recorded emergence in less complex contexts. On the other hand, another child (Gemma), who by the end of the study has shown the most evidence of rapid advances in auxiliary verb learning, produced no tags at any stage.

The possibility that apparent contraventions of the Complexity Principle are the result of sampling error was mooted above. Initially, therefore, this chapter addresses the issue of whether the first occurrence of tags for Clare and Alex is genuinely early in relation to other aspects of their development, and whether the features of these tags support the interpretation that they are produced as unanalysed wholes. Secondly, the non-occurrence of tag questions for Gemma will be related to general syntactic and auxiliary verb development to discover whether she has sufficient mastery of the separate grammatical processes involved in tag production to make their emergence possible. Two other preconditions for tag production will also be considered: the availability of tags in the speech addressed to her, and her ability to process utterances of comparable length and complexity. It will be shown that traditional analyses of the place of tags in the sequence of language development are unable to account for their non-appearance in Gemma's speech and an explanation will be considered which goes beyond syntax and input to a theoretical account of the meaning and function of tags.

Thirdly, the hypothesis will be tested that among the seven children it will be possible to identify two contrasting styles of tag development: a 'holistic' style for those whose tag emergence is premature, and an 'analytic' style for children who independently master the components of tags in a sequence which corresponds with syntactic complexity.

Fourthly, it will be shown that for Betty one step in the development of tags is never completed. As a result, errors persist to the end of the investigation. By drawing on the available literature and analysing antecedents of these errors, an attempt will be made to explain them.

7.2 The features of tag questions

The description and theoretical discussion which follow serve to demonstrate the complexity of the system being learned in terms of syntax, meaning and function. Tag questions are defined here as structures which contain an inverted auxiliary or copula verb (an operator) and a pronoun, and which are appended to a statement (the matrix clause) made by the same speaker.

The first type to emerge (Fletcher, 1985; Mills, 1981), and the most common in the language of young children (Berninger and Garvey, 1982), has falling intonation and reverses the polarity of the matrix clause. This type, which will be referred to as the Standard Model, can be illustrated by Eric's 'it won't come in the bath will it' (Rec. 9, 2;9.29) on seeing a picture of a shark.

7.2.1 The syntax of tags

While acknowledging work on tags from a transformational-generative perspective (e.g. Armagost, 1972), and analyses which consider the complexities of tagging multiple clause sentences (Cattell, 1973; Lakoff, 1969), the surface characteristics of the Standard Model will simply be treated as a set of six rules:

1. Match the copula or auxiliary in the matrix with a corresponding operator in the tag. If the matrix contains no operator, insert an appropriate form of DO. The matching rule also extends to verbs where there is asymmetry between the meanings of affirmative and negative forms. *'He must come, needn't he?' (Palmer, 1979, p. 29) is therefore unacceptable. Nevertheless, there are exceptions. Where 'may' appears in the matrix, speakers tend to substitute modals such as 'mightn't', 'can't', or 'won't' (Quirk et al., 1985). Presumably this is because of the rarity of 'mayn't' in everyday speech.
2. Pronominalisation is obligatory (* # 'John can come, can't John?'). Pronouns must be correct for person, number and gender.
3. Inversion is obligatory. Only informal tags (see below) mark interrogation by intonation only.
4. In the Standard Model an affirmative matrix produces a negative tag, and *vice versa* (Polarity Reversal).
5. Main verb ellipsis is obligatory, but ellipsis of nonfinite auxiliary elements

in complex verb phrases is optional: 'John shouldn't have been smoking, should he have been?' (Schachter, 1983, p. 150).
6. The operator carries the nuclear tone (Quirk et al., 1985). Standard Model tags have falling intonation.

Figure 7.1 illustrates possible patterns of intonation and polarity in the matrix and its tag. The Standard Model is represented by Cell 1. Other options are:

Cell 2: tags with reversed polarity and rising intonation (# 'John can come, can't he?').
Cell 3a: affirmative tags with rising intonation following an affirmative matrix (# 'You've got a new car, have you?').
Cell 3b: negative tags with rising intonation following a negative matrix. The tone of these is disapproving, sarcastic or threatening (# 'You're not going to do it, aren't you?')

	Reversed polarity		Matched polarity	
Falling Intonation	1. + −	− +	4. Non- grammatical	
Rising Intonation	2. + −	− +	3. + −	+ −

Key: Polarity of matrix and tag are indicated by + (affirmative), and − (negative).

Fig. 7.1 Combinations of intonation and polarity in matrix and tag

A combination of falling intonation and matched polarity (Cell 4) is ungrammatical in standard English but occurs as a temporary phase for some children.
The following can also occur:

1. Tags in medial position in the matrix clause (# 'He went to the doctor's, didn't he, yesterday morning?')
2. Tagged imperatives containing a restricted set of subject-oriented modals (Perkins, 1983a): CAN, COULD, WILL, WOULD. # 'Close the door, can you! (. . .can't you!)', # 'Don't close the door, will you!' SHALL can follow the first person plural imperative marker 'let's': # 'Let's have tea, shall we?' Polarity and intonation vary according to the forcefulness of the request (Quirk et al., 1985) but there are restrictions – a negative tag following a negative matrix (* # 'Don't close the door, won't you?') or a negative tag following 'let's' (* # 'Let's have tea, shan't we?') are ungrammatical (Hudson, 1975).

3. Informal tags (Lakoff, 1973) such as 'right?', 'huh?', 'okay?'. These always have rising intonation and are invariable, regardless of the polarity of the matrix.
4. Declarative Tags (Armagost, 1972): 'I see – I see Mary Poppins last night I did' (*Alex, Rec. 5, 2;9.22*).

Like some tag questions, especially those with falling intonation, declarative tags appear to function to reinforce the truth of a proposition. It is possible therefore that the syntactically and conversationally less complex declarative tag forms an intermediate stage on the route to formal tag questions. This will be investigated below.

7.2.2 Meaning and function of tags

Lakoff (1972, 1973) has described tag questions as occupying an intermediate position between statements and questions. Their function, she says, is to ask for agreement, but at the same time to acknowledge the possibility that it might not be forthcoming. They differ from most other Y/Ns, therefore, in two important respects. Firstly, they are biased towards responses of a certain polarity. This is known as Conduciveness. When Eric says, 'it won't come in the bath will it', he surely expects a negative answer, though, he may be sufficiently anxious about sharks to need reassurance. Secondly, tags vary in the extent to which they require a response from an addressee. This seems to be linked with the force of the tagged statement or the speaker's commitment to its truth. It will be noticed that both the tagged imperatives in Section 7.2.1 as well as tagged declaratives and some Y/Ns can serve as exclamations. The greater their force the smaller the expectation of a verbal response:

> # Isn't it a lovely day!
> # It's a magnificent present, isn't it!

Hudson (1975) analyses sentences such as these and tagged imperatives in terms of their sincerity conditions. Semantically, declarative plus tag is the equivalent of statement plus question. According to Hudson the sincerity condition for a statement is that, 'The speaker believes that the proposition is true' (p. 24). For *any* Y/N to be asked felicitously, the speaker must believe 'that the hearer knows at least as well as he himself does whether the proposition is true or false' (p. 12). The sincerity condition for exclamations is that, 'The speaker is impressed by the degree to which a property defined in the proposition is present' (p. 10).

Usually, in affirmative Y/Ns the sincerity condition applies to a situation where the speaker's orientation towards the truth of the proposition is neutral. The speaker doesn't know the answer. Such questions are therefore nonconducive. Tagged exclamations or statements, on the other hand, combine the sincerity condition of the statement or exclamation with that of the question. The speaker believes in the proposition and believes that the addressee has the same insight into its truth. Tag questions are therefore conducive, but a null response can be taken as acquiescence. However, one type of tag question which functions to inform the addressee (Hudson, 1975) does not appear to fit this analysis. This is a reversed polarity falling intonation tag which seems to be peculiar to certain dialects of British English. As Hudson points out, they violate the sincerity condition relating to questions. Tags in sentences such as # 'I went to town, didn't I?' where relevant knowledge is not shared by the addressee, serve to impress the truth of the proposition on the hearer, rather than to seek confirmation or even an acknowledgement. Perhaps it is for this reason that such tags often have an aggressive ring, and to reply in the affirmative or negative would be inappropriate. Tags like these, which we will refer to as Emphatic Tags, have more in common functionally with directives than with questions, though they differ from tags which follow imperatives because it is the imperative matrix which has directive force, not the tag itself.

Thus far, the discussion has been about falling intonation tags. If we accept Lakoff's assertion that tag questions lie somewhere between statements and questions, it would seem that the latter are more like statements. Others, those with rising intonation, are more like questions. According to Hudson, rising intonation indicates that 'the speaker DEFERS to the hearer with respect to the truth of the proposition' (Hudson, 1975, p. 15). It seems likely, then, that rising intonation in tags reflects a lower degree of commitment to the truth of the proposition with a more neutral expectation of confirmation from the addressee (Quirk et al., 1985) and a higher probability of a response.

The idea that tags reflect the speaker's attitude towards the propositional content of the matrix would make them candidates for inclusion in the system of epistemic modality which is normally regarded as the province of modal verbs and modal expressions such as 'perhaps' and 'surely'. Perkins has tentatively suggested that all questions express modality: 'Since questions qualify the truth of a proposition by making it relative to the speaker's uncertainty, they may be regarded as expressing epistemic modality, and in particular, "addressee-oriented" epistemic modality' (Perkins, 1983a, p. 111). However, as Perkins points out, there are problems with such an analysis at the pragmatic level, since questions generally function as a means of eliciting a response, whether verbal or nonverbal. They are not primarily a means of expressing one's doubt or ignorance. Nevertheless, a stronger case can be made for tag questions being expressions of epistemic modality. It can be argued that, unlike most other questions whose felicity conditions require lack of knowledge on the part of the speaker, and most Y/Ns which require a neutral orientation towards the truth of the proposition, tags can show either a positive or negative orientation. This becomes clearer when we include in the analysis the two types of tag whose polarity matches that of the matrix (Cell 3, Fig. 7.1). Both of these have rising intonation. Firstly there is the affirmative matrix with the affirmative tag (# 'That's your car, is it?'), and secondly the negative matrix with the negative tag (# 'It isn't your car, isn't it?'). These have several features in common. Just as the affirmative type can express surprise, disbelief (Palmer, 1965), or sarcasm (Quirk et al., 1985), and function as a threat (Palmer, 1965), so can the negative type. # 'That's your car, is it?' conveys any of these meanings depending on the prosodic features of the matrix, and the situational context. The sentence takes on one meaning when addressed to the proud owner of a new car, a different meaning for the driver parked illegally, and yet another for the joyrider stopped by a patrol car.

Another feature of matched polarity tags is that the matrix is derived from the context, linguistic or extralinguistic. It either repeats the proposition of an interlocutor (hence their frequency as contingent responses in the 'mother-ese' register) or is a conclusion drawn from the proposition of an interlocutor, or a conclusion drawn from other aspects of the context and the speaker's background knowledge. In one of the Bristol transcripts Gerald's mother responds to his noises of protest with the following mildly disapproving inter-pretation: 'You don't want to do that do you not?' If the matrices of rising intonation tags refer to elements of the situation, rather than express the speaker's own knowledge or beliefs, it might be claimed that the speaker's commitment to the truth of these propositions is weaker than to those which are self-initiated and followed by reversed polarity tags. This is consistent with Hudson's (1975) claim that matched polarity tags express shared beliefs rather than communicate new information. However, when such utterances are sarcastic, or cast doubt on the truth of a proposition, the speaker merely pretends to accept the truth of the other's statement. In a classroom scenario, for example, a denial such as # 'It wasn't me, Sir!' might elicit, # 'It wasn't you, wasn't it?'

What the above outline serves to illustrate is that there are two main interact-ing semantic and interpersonal continua which correlate with the syntax and intonation of sentences containing tags, and with the broader situational and linguistic context. Firstly, there is the speaker's own commitment to the truth of the proposition. Tagged statements can vary in strength from the strong commitment of falling intonation emphatic tags and tagged exclamations, through varying degrees of doubt to the downright disbelief expressed by certain rising intonation matched polarity tags. The second dimension appears to be negatively correlated with the first. This is the degree of obligation placed on the addressee to respond, and ranges from the strong obligation of the matched polarity tag to the weak obligation of the more rhetorical emphatic and exclamation tags. It might also be claimed that there is a third variable – the degree of expectation that the addressee will agree with the proposition – but, unless the speaker is deliberately provoking disagreement by uttering statements which are known to be anathema to the hearer, this seems to be closely associated with epistemic modality.

7.3 Tags and child language research

The previous section showed the complexities which the child has to master. These complexities clearly extend far beyond the syntactic processes involved in producing the Standard Model of tag. Even so, child language research has paid most attention to the place of tags in the sequence of syntactic develop-ment (e.g. Brown, 1973; Brown and Hanlon, 1970; Fletcher, 1985; Wells, 1985), to the transformations required for their production (Major, 1974), and to explaining persistent patterns of error (Todd, 1982). Nevertheless, Mills (1981) has also examined form and function relationships for a bilingual child, and functions and discourse role in effecting turn transfers between children have been studied by Berninger and Garvey (1982).

7.3.1 Age and stage of emergence of tags

Brown and Hanlon (1970) correctly predicted that for the three children in the Harvard study, tags would appear later than the separate processes of negation, interrogation and ellipsis. This study is frequently taken as evidence of the importance of derivational cumulative complexity in predicting sequence of acquisition or emergence (Brown and Hanlon used a 'threshold of emergence' criterion consisting of the presence of a minimum of six tokens in a sample). For tags, this evidence is thought to be particularly strong because it is assumed that the functions they perform are identical to those carried out by informal tags (Brown and Hanlon, 1970; Brown, 1973; De Villiers and De Villiers, 1978; Berninger and Garvey, 1982), and informal tags appear at a much earlier stage of development – Brown's Stage I, as opposed to after Stage V for formal tags. Brown concludes, 'It seems, then, that in this case the long-deferred appearance of well-formed tags must be attributed to grammatical complexity in its own right' (Brown, 1973, p. 408). This view appears consistent with Berninger and Garvey's (1982) study of thirty-six child dyads between 2;10 and 5;7. Informal tags as a proportion of all tags decreased as the children got older, and as syntactic competence increased apparently identical functions were taken over by more complex forms.

For Adam, the period during which formal tags developed in the Brown and Hanlon study was between approximately 4;0 and 4;7. This is relatively late compared with most of the children in the current study, none of whom was older than 3;4 by the completion of the research, but other British studies also find tags emerging comparatively early. Fletcher (1985) notes that his subject was producing tags at 3;5 with a similar frequency to Brown and Hanlon's Adam at 4;7, and at an earlier stage of development. Mills (1981) reports similar findings: sporadic usage at 3;6 but regular production at 3;9. Wells (1985) found that declarative plus formal tag, despite its low frequency of occurrence, had been recorded for 50% of the Bristol children by 3;3, for 75% by 3;9, and for 90% by 4;3.

Wells attributes the discrepancy in age of emergence between the British and American studies to differences in frequency of tag usage in British and American English. Although input frequencies appear to be a less powerful predictor of sequence of emergence or acquisition than measures of complexity (Brown, 1973; De Villiers and De Villiers, 1973; Block and Kessel, 1980), it is possible that a higher input frequency could account for an accelerated emergence within a given sequence. K. E. Nelson (1977), for example, has shown, using the technique of 'recasting', that the developing of tags in 3-year-olds can be accelerated by increasing the frequency of tag questions which are contingent on a previous child utterance. Claims for frequency differences between British and American English are, however, unsupported by evidence (e.g. De Villiers and De Villiers, 1979). One way to resolve this is to compare frequencies of tags in British and American input studies. Unpublished figures from Barnes et al. (1983) show that 2.8% of utterances addressed to thirty-two children with an MLU of 1.5 were declarative plus tag. Of American studies of children at a roughly similar age and stage, Hoff-Ginsberg (1985) obtains a mean figure of 0.6% ($N = 22$), and Broen 1.9% ($N = 10$) (Broen, 1972: combined data from Tables 12 and 17). This gives some support for the claim, but the picture is still confused because Gleason and Weintraub (1978) recorded frequencies as high as 8% for American mothers and 4% for fathers.

In addition, not all American research shows a delay in the emergence of tags in comparison with British children. One study (Todd, 1982) shows tags emerging by 3;2. It is probably fair to say, therefore, that the case for both earlier tag learning and the higher frequency of tags in British English still needs to be substantiated. What we do know, however, is that there is broad individual variation in the age at which formal tags emerge, and that these differences are not predicted by input frequency (Wells, 1985). Wells' data also show variation in the interval between learning Y/Ns and the onset of tag production.

7.3.2 Subsequent development

Individual differences are also evident in the time from regular usage to complete mastery. For Sophie (Fletcher, 1985) a range of eleven auxiliary subforms in tags emerged quickly and almost entirely correctly, and errors were only a temporary phenomenon for Adam and Sarah (Brown and Hanlon, 1970). Mills (1981), on the other hand, found that it took at least six months from the emergence of formal tags until there were no polarity errors, and at least a further two and a half months before all modal verbs in the matrix were correctly matched in the tag. In a more extreme case (Todd, 1982) polarity errors persisted for nearly two years.

Even older children have difficulties, especially in a testing situation. Major (1974) elicited tags containing modals from first- to third-graders and from kindergarteners. The task was difficult for the whole age range despite their skill with modals in other areas. Major describes responses as 'generally too scattered and dissimilar to reveal any patterns in the children's processing of the task...' (Major, 1974, p. 101). A large part of the problem undoubtedly lay in the task itself. If the claim that tags reflect commitment to the truth of propositions is correct, then tagging a proposition devised by an experimenter makes no sense. And the difficulty is even greater when marginal modals are included in sentences such as 'Jim dare touch a grasshopper' (Major, 1974, p. 116).

Perkins (1983a) reports that even children between the ages of 6 and 12 failed to match the modal verb in the matrix. He interprets this as evidence that the children wrongly believed the two modal verbs in question to correspond in meaning. However the 'errors' he quotes would possibly not be uncommon in mature speakers: 'There ought to be a little window by here, shouldn't there?' (Perkins, 1983a, p. 149). It is worth remembering, in the light of the findings of Major and Perkins, that an experiment by Langendoen (1970) with forty-six teachers of English showed that there was often considerable confusion about polarity, and supplying the correct auxiliary and pronoun. It is particularly interesting that nineteen out of the forty-six subjects tagged 'You ought to smoke' with 'Shouldn't you?', a very similar, though not identical, 'error' to those made by Perkins' younger subjects.

A fair summary of these studies is to say that once the basic syntactic operations necessary for tag production have been mastered, there is variation in the time which elapses before tags emerge. Subsequent development may proceed effortlessly, tags being supplied in a wide range of contexts fairly quickly. Otherwise there may be a period of varying length during which polarity, pronoun, and verb matching errors continue. The latter errors may then persist while a semantic matching strategy overrides the syntactic rule that the same auxiliary appears in matrix and tag. The known sequence of development can be summarised as follows:

1. Informal tags precede other tag questions (Brown, 1973).
2. Within the mood system, polar interrogatives precede tags (Brown and Hanlon, 1970; Wells, 1985)
3. The first tag questions have falling intonation (Fletcher, 1985; Mills, 1981).
4. The first tag questions are negative, following an affirmative matrix (Fletcher, 1985). Evidence is relatively weak here, originating from a single child. Berninger and Garvey (1982) found that the $+ \rightarrow -$ pattern outnumbers $- \rightarrow +$ by two to one, so the apparent prior emergence of negative tags could simply be a frequency effect. This item will be tested against the data from the seven children.
5. Wells' (1985) analysis of order of emergence in 125 children found Declarative + Tag to precede Tag Alone. In a few cases, Tag Alone means separation from the matrix by an intervening utterance or a time interval. Here it is feasible that memory constraints could account for its later emergence. In most cases, however, Tag Alone is a response to another person's utterance (# 'I'm not going out.' 'Aren't you?') (Wells, p.c.), and for these explanations are more difficult to find. In fact, in the research described in this volume similar utterances would have been coded as Y/N + Ellipsis, not as tags.
6. Imperative + Tag emerges later than either Declarative + Tag or Tag Alone (Wells, 1985).
7. In the two studies which publish major sections of their corpus of tags (Fletcher, 1985; Todd, 1982), there is no evidence of a sequence of auxiliaries. Neither is there clear ordering between copula and auxiliary tags.

7.4 The development of tags in seven children

Although tokens of 'see?', 'right?', 'O.K.?', or 'all right?' were recorded for all children except Eric and Gemma, informal tags have been omitted from the study. There are a number of reasons for this. Firstly, their occurrence was surprisingly rare. Secondly, the focus of the investigation is the use of verbs which act as operators. Thirdly, despite the claims of researchers referred to above, it has never been satisfactorily demonstrated that the functions and meanings of early informal and formal tags are identical. That informal tags have rising intonation and invariable polarity, while the first formal tags have falling tone and reverse polarity, leads one to suspect that they may not be. Only Berninger and Garvey (1982) attempt to demonstrate that the two types of tag are used for similar purposes, but the six function categories to which tags are allocated fail to account fully for intonation and polarity patterns in formal tags. In addition, their youngest children were aged between 2;10 and 3;3 and were already producing formal and informal types. There is no evidence therefore that informal tags are used for identical functions *before* the emergence of formal tags and it is possible that factors additional to syntactic complexity influence the place of tags in the overall sequence of development. Certainly the impression from our children is that early informal tags fall into Berninger and Garvey's Attention Request, Verbal Response Request, Compliance Request, and Permission Request categories, rather than the Information Request and Agreement Request of the first formal tags. However, confirmation of this would require a separate and more detailed coding.

One type of tag is included here which, as far as can be ascertained, has received no attention in the literature. This is the non-inverted, non-interrogative, matched polarity Declarative Tag:

I see – I see Mary Poppins last night I did (*Alex, Rec.5, 2;9.22*)

These might be expected to precede formal tag questions on grounds of their relative syntactic and functional simplicity. Like the standard model tag they reinforce the truth of a proposition, but unlike many tag questions they do not overtly invite a response.

7.4.1 Preliminary results
Table 7.1 shows the number of tags recorded for each child expressed as a raw total and as a percentage of structured utterances. Table 7.2 then breaks down these figures to show the separate development of tag questions containing copula and auxiliary verbs. There is no evidence of ordering with respect to auxiliary and copula tags.

Table 7.2 also clearly demonstrates the extent to which Alex and Clare, children for whom some auxiliaries had been found first to emerge in tags,

Table 7.1 *Total frequency of tag*
questions pooled for all recordings

Subject	N	%
Alex	106	3.42
Betty	47	1.73
Clare	54	2.10
Daisy	0	0.00
Eric	35	1.13
Fleur	4	0.18
Gemma	0	0.00

use tag questions from their earliest recordings. Clare shows a low but fairly constant frequency throughout the study, while for Alex there is a more obvious increase over time and a conspicuous peak at Recording 9. As would be expected of the children who use tags over the longest period, Alex and Clare have the highest frequency for the pooled data for all recordings.

The development of tags for Clare and Alex contrasts sharply with that of the remaining children, who either fail to develop tag questions at all (Daisy and Gemma), or presumably require time to lay the necessary syntactic, semantic, and pragmatic foundations (Betty, Eric, and Fleur). This latter assumption, in as far as it relates to syntax, will be tested below. However, it is to be expected that the ability to derive a tag from a matrix clause, and to produce both clauses as a single utterance, will be constrained by the child's processing capacity. Figures are presented in Table 7.3 to show the MLUS at which tags first emerge, and at which three auxiliary subforms have occurred in tags. For children who never produced tags, their maximum recorded MLUS is given as an indication of whether they were capable of processing utterances of comparable length in morphemes. Because MLU may tell us more about situational constraints on utterance length, or even the child's preference for certain utterance types, than about potential for producing complex utterances, figures for longest utterances (MLUL) are also given.

The values obtained support the view that Alex and Clare's tag production is premature. On both criteria of tag emergence they have by far the lowest MLUS and MLUL. By contrast, figures for Gemma give no indication of possible constraints on the development of tags.

Table 7.4 shows increases in the range of auxiliary subforms used in tag

Table 7.2 *Number of copula and auxiliary tag questions per recording*

Subj.	Recording													
	1	2	3	4	5	6	7	8	9	10	11	12	13	14
Alex														
1	0	2	0	3	2	3	7	7	14	1	0	9	4	
2	1	4	0	0	0	5	1	7	19	7	3	4	3	
Betty														
1	0	0	0	0	0	0	0	0	0	1	8	0	0	4
2	0	0	0	0	0	0	0	0	0	1	10	6	7	10
Clare														
1	2	0	0	1	0	2	3	3	1	2	2	0		
2	2	5	5	0	0	4	1	3	2	8	3	6		
Daisy														
1	0	0	0	0	0	0	0	0	0	0	0	0		
2	0	0	0	0	0	0	0	0	0	0	0	0		
Eric														
1	0	0	0	0	0	0	2	2	1	4	1	0	2	
2	0	0	0	0	0	0	1	0	0	1	1	12	8	
Fleur														
1	0	0	0	0	0	0	0	0	0	0	0	0		
2	0	0	0	0	0	0	0	0	0	0	3	1		
Gemma														
1	0	0	0	0	0	0	0	0	0	0	0	0		
2	0	0	0	0	0	0	0	0	0	0	0	0		

Key: 1: Copula tag questions.
2: Auxiliary tag questions.

questions. When seen in conjunction with the frequency figures for auxiliary tags (Table 7.2) a correspondence can be observed for Betty, Eric and Fleur, between the greatest increases in frequency and the largest number of additions to the range of auxiliaries used in tags. This is based on a fairly restricted number of forms in the case of Fleur (Rec. 11), but is particularly marked for Betty and Eric. For Betty, Recording 11 shows the emergence of six new auxiliary subforms in ten tags, and for Eric, Recording 12 shows the inclusion of six new auxiliary forms in twelve tags. This is confirmation, then, that for these three children, increases in frequency do not mean stereotypical repetition, and suggests the rapid extension of a set of tag formation rules across the child's auxiliary class. For Alex and Clare, on the other hand, increments in the range of forms are more gradual. The peak of Alex's

Table 7.3 *MLUS and MLUL at: (1) emergence of tag questions; and (2) emergence of three auxiliary subforms in tags*

	1st emergence		3 subforms	
Subject	MLUS	MLUL	MLUS	MLUL
Alex	2.6	5.4	2.9	6.0
Betty	4.4	9.3	4.6	10.6
Clare	2.8	5.9	2.8	6.5
Daisy	[3.9]	[8.5]	[3.9]	[8.5]
Eric	3.6	7.0	4.0	7.8
Fleur	4.0	8.5	4.0	8.5
Gemma	[5.2]	[12.2]	[5.2]	[12.2]

Key: [ ]: Square brackets indicate highest recorded values for children who produced
no tags.

Table 7.4 *Cumulative range of auxiliary subforms used in tag questions*

	Recording													
Subj.	1	2	3	4	5	6	7	8	9	10	11	12	13	14
Alex	1	3	3	3	3	5	6	7	9	11	11	11	11	
Betty	0	0	0	0	0	0	0	0	0	1	7	10	11	14
Clare	2	4	5	5	5	7	8	9	9	11	11	13		
Daisy	0	0	0	0	0	0	0	0	0	0	0	0		
Eric	0	0	0	0	0	0	1	1	1	2	3	9	12	
Fleur	0	0	0	0	0	0	0	0	0	0	3	3		
Gemma	0	0	0	0	0	0	0	0	0	0	0	0		

tag usage (nineteen tokens in Recording 9) only adds two new auxiliaries
to the range. The transcript for Recording 9 shows that while some forms
such as 'don't' (ten tokens) are used repetitively, six auxiliary subforms are
distributed among the nineteen tags, so usage does vary. Nevertheless, the
pattern of development suggests early non- or partially analysed usage followed by later gradual extension of tag production rules to a wider range
of contexts.

7.4.2 Case studies
Preliminary analyses suggest contrasting styles of learning tags particularly for Alex and Clare on the one hand, and Betty and Eric on the other. This assumption will be tested by provisionally placing children in three groups and looking at each child in detail. Group 1 (Daisy and Gemma) show no evidence of tags. Group 2 (Betty, Eric, and Fleur) are expected to develop tags in an analytic sequence, while for Group 3 (Alex and Clare) a holistic, piecemeal style of learning is predicted.

Group 1: No recorded production of tag questions
DAISY. By Daisy's last recording (2;11.21) negation is well established and ellipsis and Y/N inversions have been observed since Recording 4 (2;5.27). Each of these operations is distributed across eight auxiliary subforms, though the only verbs for which there are tokens of affirmative *and* negative subforms, as well as use in ellipsis and Y/N inversions, are 'do', 'can' and 'will'.

Daisy's maximum values for MLUS and MLUL (Table 7.3) suggest that her failure to produce tag questions is by no means unusual at this stage. Declarative tags however are beginning to emerge:

> we got one of these we have [looking at a book]
> she want to get dressed she do [playing with a doll] *(Daisy, Rec. 12, 2;11.21)*

GEMMA. Despite being the youngest child, Gemma has attained the highest values for MLUS and MLUL by the end of the study. Similarly, her range of auxiliary subforms is equal to, or in advance of children who do use tags (see Fig. 5.3). After the emergence of ellipsis and Y/N inversion in Recording 4 (2;0.18) Gemma uses a range of ten auxiliary subforms in ellipsis, and twelve in Y/N inversions. In both case affirmative and negative forms are included. The emergence of negative questions outside tags is interesting, because like tag questions, and unlike most affirmative Y/Ns, they are always conducive (Quirk et al., 1985). Gemma is therefore producing lengthy and complex utterances which contain the features of tags and sometimes combine them. Nevertheless, neither declarative nor interrogative tags emerge even though attempts to elicit tag questions during Recordings 7 (2;2.26) and 9 (2;4.9) resulted in accurate imitations of Matrix + Tag.

It was suggested above that variation in input frequency might accelerate or delay children's learning of tags within a given sequence of development. The absence of tags for Gemma could therefore be attributable to low frequencies in the speech addressed to her. Fortunately it was possible to estimate the frequency of tag questions addressed to Gemma by her mother, using a transcript from an intermediate stage of the study (Rec. 6, 2;2.2). Excluding periods of verbatim reading, 448 utterances were addressed to Gemma by her mother, of which 53 are Declarative + Tag (11.8%); 42 of these were the standard falling intonation, reversed polarity model. This exceeds the highest mean input frequency of 8% from the studies quoted above.

Since Gemma's failure to develop tags cannot be attributed to an input deficiency nor to lack of grammatical competence, it seems likely that her precocity in the development of syntax is not yet matched by the skills and knowledge required to fit expressions of varying commitment to the truth of propositions into the framework of discourse.

Group 2: Analytic tag development
FLEUR. Fleur produces only four tags in twelve recordings and the first occurs at 2;9.1 (Rec 11). Auxiliary ellipsis and negation had been sampled sporadically since the earliest recordings, but Recording 11 shows the extension of these functions to a wider range of auxiliaries (five new auxiliary subforms in ellipsis, and two in negation). Surprisingly, however, Fleur's output is marked by an almost total absence of Y/Ns. There are only two Y/N inversions containing auxiliaries ('does' and 'shall') in twelve transcripts and only one precedes the appearance of tags. Inverted Wh- questions are also rare; three are sampled before Recording 11 and the status of two of these is doubtful because the auxiliary is contracted: 'what's' (= what does) and 'what's' (= what has).

That tags should emerge in Recording 11 is of interest because they coincide with major advances in Fleur's language development. It has already been noted that Recording 11 shows an increase in the contexts of ellipsis. It is also the occasion of the greatest increases in frequency of auxiliary usage, range per 100 utterances, and cumulative range of auxiliary forms (see Figs. 5.1, 5.2, 5.3). The first declarative tag ('I can ride it I can') also occurs. These developments are accompanied by a sharp rise in MLUS (see Table 4.3) and MLUL.

All four of Fleur's tag questions contain an auxiliary, have falling intonation and reverse the polarity of the matrix. Negative and affirmative tags occur equally:

1. 'ooh I can't take this off . can I' [playing with Lego]
2. 'you didn't come in Grandpa's did you' [telling R. about a visit]
3. 'he won't stay on there . won'tn't he' [playing with toy horse and rider]

(Fleur, Rec. 11, 2;9.1)

4. 'she can go on can't she' [playing with Lego]   (*Fleur, Rec. 12, 2;9.22*)

There are no pronoun or auxiliary matching errors but from the apparent polarity error in 3 we can see that 'won't' is unanalysed. The obligatory polarity reversal is therefore achieved by adding the contracted negative particle to a form which is already negative. Presumably, since Fleur has never used 'will' except as a contracted form or in imitation, she has no appropriate affirmative form to supply in this context.

Fleur's tag development does not unequivocally follow the separate mastery of the required syntactic processes but it does correspond with a dramatic extension of auxiliary forms across a range of functions and her single error suggests a 'bottom-up' construction of this particular tag. Why she uses so few questions remains a puzzle, but it may simply reflect the relatively passive role she adopted during recording sessions. Another possibility, which will be investigated as part of the analysis of CAN (Chapter 9), is that Fleur has other means of realising the functions usually performed by Y/Ns.

ERIC. There is no record of Eric producing declarative tags, but the first tag questions appear at 2;6.11 (Rec.7). Their development can be divided into three distinct stages: emergence, subsequent development and acquisition.

In the first stage tags are all negative, reverse polarity and have falling intonation (Rec. 7, 2;6.11):

1. 'it's gone now /enɪt/'
2. 'bird's gone /enɪt/'
3. 'got a zoo haven't you'

The first two are assumed to be copula tags; Eric seems to use 'gone' to describe the state of absence rather than the culmination of a process of disappearance. However, the prosodic features of /enɪt/ suggest that it functions as a single morpheme. The same analysis is suggested for 3; 'haven't' has no affirmative form in the matrix and up to and including this recording, Eric has only once supplied 'have' or contracted ''ve' before 'got' in a total of thirty-two declarative obligatory contexts. Evidence of the syntactic operations required for producing tags is also limited. Although Eric has used a wide range of affirmative and negative auxiliary subforms (twenty types), only two of these in each case have appeared in Y/N inversions or ellipsis. There is a strong suspicion, therefore, that the first tags are supplied in suitable contexts as rote-learned wholes.

During *Stage II* (Recs. 8 to 11) there is a gradual extension to Eric's range of tags. Initially, these follow the previous pattern with regard to intonation and polarity, and still have prosodic features which suggest lack of analysis. However, a new pronoun is introduced in Recordings 8 and 9:

> he lovely /ɪni:/ (*Eric, Rec. 8, 2;7.4*)
> he's nice /ɪni:/ (*Eric, Rec. 9, 2;7.26*)

and Recording 10 shows the presence of copula /ɪnɪt/ in contexts previously occupied by /enɪt/:

> /sgɒn ɪnɪt/ (It's gone isn't it?)
> ⟨that's/it's⟩ the same one /ɪnɪt/ (*Eric: Rec. 10, 2;8.17*)

Auxiliary tags occur only rarely:

> he have to get some more squeak won't him [a squeaky toy with a missing squeaker] (*Eric, Rec. 10, 2;8.17*)

Recordings 10 and 11 mark the introduction of affirmative tags. Some have falling intonation and reversed polarity:

> not his tail is it [doing animal jigsaws] (*Eric, Rec. 10, 2;8.17*)

Others have rising intonation and match the polarity of the matrix:

> this is a goat is it? [doing animal jigsaws]
> that go on this does it? [doing animal jigsaws] (*Eric, Rec. 10, 2;8.17*)

The emergence of this type of tag, which is closer to a genuine question (see Section 7.2.2), coincides with advances in Y/Ns. It will be recalled that when tags emerged for Eric, Y/N usage was restricted to two subforms. The frequency of Y/Ns has since increased, and the range of auxiliaries used in Y/Ns has widened to nine by Recording 10. These developments continue through Recordings 11 and 12 by which time fourteen subforms have appeared in Y/Ns.

If any sample can be taken as evidence of the acquisition of auxiliary tags (*Stage III*) it is Recording 12 (2;9.29), nearly four months after emergence. Before Recording 12 tags had been fairly infrequent and contained copula BE (ten tokens) rather than an auxiliary (three tokens). In Recording 12, however, all twelve tags sampled contained an auxiliary, including six subforms not previously recorded in tags. This increase in frequency continues in Recording 13 (2;10.19) with eight auxiliary tags containing a further three subforms.

In Recordings 12 and 13, the majority of tags (eighteen out of twenty-two) still have falling intonation and reversed polarity. The difference is that affirmative tags now outnumber negative tags by fifteen instances to seven. In addition, 'isn't it' now coexists with /ɪnɪt/, and negative DO forms are supplied where the matrix contains no auxiliary or copula:

> this goes in the bath don't it and then it goes squirt warting [squeezy toy which will squirt water] (*Eric, Rec. 12, 2;9.29*)

The auxiliary in the tag is now always matched by a corresponding auxiliary in the matrix:

> I haven't got one of these have I (*Eric, Rec. 12, 2;9.29*)

One final type of tag emerges in Recording 13. This is the first person singular, matched polarity, rising intonation tag containing 'shall':

> I will get Teebo shall I? [Teebo is a Star Wars toy] (*Eric, Rec. 13, 2;10.19*)

These tags are offers to perform an action and have no clear place in Berninger and Garvey's (1982) function categories, though they come closest to Permission Request. Certainly, they place an obligation on the addressee to respond before the action is performed but unlike other affirmative Y/Ns which ask for permission, these questions (like other tag questions) are conducive.

The development of Eric's tags can be summarised as follows: a restricted range of mainly copula tags occurs at a stage when ellipsis and Y/Ns are hardly established. Secondly, alternative patterns of polarity and intonation develop as the range of auxiliary tags gradually increases. Finally, the development of the auxiliary in syntactic frames other than the declarative culminates in a rapid increase in the frequency and range of auxiliary tags.

Eric's tags are remarkably free of error. The correct operator is always supplied (in contrast with the other children), though the auxiliary may be missing from the matrix. Neither are there any polarity or pronoun errors. One anomaly remains, however:

> we didn't see ⟨that⟩ in London did we (*Eric, Rec. 13, 2;10.19*)

This utterance, which was made to the researcher in response to a dinosaur picture, referred to a family visit to the Natural History Museum. In context it sounded inappropriate, though a corresponding declarative tag (# 'we didn't') would not have done. The reason is that there was no shared information to enable the listener to respond felicitously. To put it differently, Eric's tag has broken the sincerity condition for a Y/N, namely that: 'The speaker believes that the hearer knows at least as well as he himself does whether the proposition is true or false' (Hudson, 1975, p. 12). The implication is that before one can speak of 'mastery' of tags, an understanding of their felicity conditions has to be assumed, as well as the ability to 'decentre' sufficiently to assess the extent of the hearer's knowledge of the topic.

BETTY. The development of Betty's tags can be seen as five distinct stages, each of which marks a significant advance in grammatical complexity and is associated with necessary progress in associated areas of syntax. Nevertheless, even by her last recording Betty still lacks a final rule which would enable her to produce acceptable tag questions appended to affirmative matrices.

Stage I occurs between Recordings 2 and 6 (2;4.15–2;7.3) and is typified by primitive declarative tags, referred to here as prototags:

> We got ⟨?⟩ book we got   *(Betty, Rec. 2, 2;4.15)*
> I got my animal house . upstairs I got   *(Betty, Rec. 3, 2;4.3)*
> I like that big fish I like
> Daddy call her Buster Daddy call her [Betty's sister]   *(Betty, Rec. 6, 2;7.3)*

Although these examples satisfy Quirk et al.'s (1985) criterion for ellipsis of 'verbatim recoverability', they have no sentence-final auxiliary or copula functioning as an operator. This is a development which characterises *Stage II* (Rec. 6, 2;7.3 – Rec. 10, 2;10.2):

> it's bubbles it does   *(Betty, Rec. 6, 2;7.3)*

Some declarative tags supply auxiliaries which are absent from an obligatory context in the matrix:

> and I got some those I have   *(Betty, Rec. 6, 2;7.3)*

Interestingly, prototags disappear after Recording 6 except for a single token in the following complex sentence:

> I 'spect [expect] she goes on the little lamb 'spect she does [playing with farm animals]   *(Betty, Rec. 13, 3;0.6)*

Here, Betty has derived the operator and its grammatical subject ('she does') from the embedded clause, and attaches it to the top clause ('I 'spect'). Since the top clause contains a mental state verb in the first person singular, any tag *question* would be derived from the second clause down (see Cattell, 1973; Lakoff, 1969) giving the following:

> # I expect she goes on the little lamb doesn't she?

A tag question derived from the top clause would result in an unacceptable sentence:

> * # I expect she goes on the little lamb don't I?

On the other hand the rules for appending *declarative* tags to complex sentences appear to be more flexible; the tag is derived according to the desired emphasis:

#I expect she goes on the little lamb I do (emphasising her own mental state)

#I expect she goes on the little lamb she does (emphasising the truth of the second clause)

What Betty's error demonstrates is an incomplete knowledge of the conventions of ellipsis which make it possible to differentiate between these two shades of meaning in a complex clause.

The frequency of Betty's declarative tags declines after Recording 10 (2;10.2) when the first *interrogative* tags appear. Initially these are affirmative and have matched polarity and rising intonation (*Stage III*):

that is Mr ⟨Naughty⟩ is it? [looking at Mr Men books]
I throw this fish in shall I? [magnetic fishing game]

Despite its similarity to Y/Ns, Betty is the only child for whom this type of tag question precedes apparently more complex forms. Its emergence does, however, follow considerable progress in negation, ellipsis, and Y/N inversion. Negative auxiliary forms have been present from Recording 3 (2;4.23), and ellipsis develops across ten forms between Recordings 3 and 10. Y/Ns, which first appear in Recording 6, use eleven subforms by this stage.

Stage IV begins with a considerable increase in the frequency of tag questions in Recording 11 (2;10.24). These contain a sufficient number of auxiliary types (cf. Tables 7.2 and 7.4) to suggest that they are productive. In this sample fifteen out of eighteen have falling intonation. What is notable, though, is that negative tags are limited to three copula tokens:

's all sticky now /ɪnɪt/
That's your ⟨bit⟩ /ɪnɪt/
this go on this horse /ɪni:/   (*Betty, Rec. 11, 2;10.24*)

Otherwise tags only reverse polarity if the matrix clause is negative:

he not made of fabric is he
and we're not naughty am I
and I wouldn't like that would I   (*Betty, Rec. 11, 2;10.24*)

This means that falling intonation affirmative tags also follow affirmative matrices, a combination which Figure 7.1 shows to be ungrammatical:

there's the lid on top is it
he's holding on is he
this bit goes up does it [doing jigsaws]
yes that's right is it   (*Betty, Rec. 11, 2;10.24*)

Errors like these are still present in Betty's last recording. The problem is not that she is unable to reverse polarity because she gives affirmative tags to negative matrices. Neither can they be regarded as intonation errors since rising intonation tags are used appropriately from Recording 10. Rather, she seems to have assumed that all tags are affirmative, the only exceptions being /ɪnɪt/ and /ɪniː/ which probably function as single units.

At this stage Betty also has difficulty matching the auxiliary in the matrix, as the following examples show:

> cos it – cos cars might knock me down – w- were they
> I might get things all over me will I
> cos there might be crocodiles in it will there
> you – you should pull it along do you (*Betty, Rec. 11, 2;10.24*)

Errors like these might suggest that Betty is as yet unaware of subtle distinctions between degrees of modality expressed by modal verbs such as WILL and MIGHT. On the other hand, the frequency of tags containing MIGHT and SHOULD may be sufficiently rare in the speech she hears for Betty to be unaware of their full distributional potential.

In two cases a copula tag is used in a context where dummy DO would be expected. Here Betty is placing the collar on a toy carthorse:

> this go on the horse /ɪniː/ [falling intonation]
> over his head is it? [rising intonation] (*Betty, Rec. 11, 2;10.24*)

The use of rising intonation 'is it?' as a general purpose tag is part of the dialect of South Wales and although we have assumed that Betty's tags are now productive, this does not preclude the additional use of general purpose tags which may be only partially analysed.

Recordings 12–14 (*Stage V*) continue to extend the range of auxiliaries in tags (see Table 7.4), culminating in the emergence of the tagged imperative ('can you?'). The high frequency of auxiliary tags which was attained in Recording 11 (see Table 7.2) is maintained, but is accompanied by a decline in copula tags. The polarity errors noted above continue and there is only a single case of a negated auxiliary ('didn't') in a falling intonation tag despite twenty-two contexts which require them. In other respects, however, Betty's tags now conform to those of a mature speaker. In twenty-seven tokens produced during this period there is only one pronoun error, and only one matching error in twenty-three tags which require auxiliaries.

The evolution of Betty's tags can be seen as a process of gradually increasing syntactic complexity:

1. Recordings 2 to 6: declarative tags without an operator.
2. From Recording 6: declarative tags contain the copula and an increasing range of auxiliary forms.

3. From Recording 10: following developments in ellipsis and Y/N inversion, a small number of affirmative, rising intonation, matched polarity tags occur.
4. Recording 11: sudden emergence of copula BE and auxiliary forms in falling intonation tags. Except for two copula tags, assumed to be unanalysed, all are affirmative, regardless of the polarity of the matrix. The auxiliary in the tag may not match the form in the matrix.
5. Recordings 12 to 14: the frequency of auxiliary tags is sustained, while that of the copula falls. Polarity errors continue but there are fewer wrong auxiliaries. The tagged imperative emerges.

The persistence of Betty's polarity errors is puzzling although identical errors have been reported elsewhere. Brown and Hanlon (1970) found them to be rare and a temporary phase but Mills' subject, Nicky, was still making them nearly six months after the first formal tag had emerged (Mills, 1981). But Nicky's errors differed from Betty's because they were specific to certain contexts and auxiliary forms, namely DO-insertion and forms which undergo a root change in the negative : am/aren't, will/won't, etc. Todd (1982) reports a case where the problem continued for as long as two years. The child, Audrey, first used formal tags at 3;2, but apart from a small number of stereotypical forms, did not produce negative tags until 4;2. By 4;10 they occurred in about 50% of cases involving 'is' and 'will', but never with other forms. By 5;3 negation had spread to the full range of auxiliaries used in tags but at the same time the negation rule was overgeneralised to contexts which had previously been correctly given an affirmative tag: 'You don't see very much butterflies, don't you' (Todd, 1982, p. 107). One explanation for this phenomenon might have been that negation, on top of producing the matrix and its inverted and ellipsed tag, was simply beyond the child's processing capacity. Todd is able to reject this possibility on two grounds. Firstly, Audrey was capable of producing utterances of greater length and complexity. Secondly, once negative tags began to emerge, knowing the auxiliary form was a better predictor of whether the tag would be negative than knowing the length of the utterance in morphemes. The source of Audrey's polarity errors is attributed to an inadequate mastery of negation when tags were emerging. As a result, she learnt to supply affirmative tags in all contexts.

How do we explain Betty's errors? We can also probably discount processing limitations. Betty attains higher MLUS and MLUL values than any other child except Gemma. Besides, even short and simple utterances contain the error:

yes that's right is it   (*Betty, Rec. 11, 2;10.24*)

Similarly, no explanation can be found in Betty's learning of negation which was well established for both copula B E and auxiliaries by the time tags emerged.

A tentative suggestion is that Betty has acquired a rule that all tags (both declarative and interrogative) are affirmative, and the origin of such a rule could be her own output of declarative tags during Stages I and II. Although somewhat speculative, the data are consistent with this account in four ways. Firstly, Betty is unusual in the extent to which she develops declarative tags before tag questions. Secondly, declarative tags and falling intonation tag questions perform a similar function for her, namely to emphasise the proposition in the matrix clause. The tag question is in fact the more complex form at the discourse level as well as at the level of syntax because, in order to satisfy felicity conditions, the addressee's knowledge of the topic has to be considered. It is no surprise therefore that it should follow the declarative tag. Thirdly, the emergence of falling intonation tag questions coincides with the almost total disappearance of the declarative tag. Finally, up to the emergence of the falling intonation interrogative tag, almost all declarative tags (eighteen out of nineteen) have been affirmative.

The evidence is at least consistent with the hypothesis that the development of tag questions has been influenced by the predominant form of declarative tags. The transition from the declarative type to the interrogative type to perform similar functions goes as far as inversion, but stops short of transforming affirmative to negative. From this point onwards the position is as described by Todd (1982): correct exemplars in the input are assimilated to Betty's existing rule system, and disconfirmatory evidence goes unheeded.

Group 3: Tags occur prematurely
To talk of the 'development' of tags for the premature tag users is misleading. Rather, there is the piecemeal emergence of a repertoire of tags seemingly unrelated to the use of auxiliaries in negation, inversion or ellipsis.

A L E X. For Alex, at least, one can justifiably discuss two stages. The first extends from 2;7.6 to 2;8.3 (Recs. 1–3) and is followed by two samples during which no auxiliary tags occur. Recording 6 (2;10.12) then marks the beginning of the second stage which continues to the end of the study (Rec. 13).

During *Stage I* seven formal tags, five of which contain auxiliaries, are present in Samples 1 and 2 (2;7.6 to 2;7.13), a time when ellipsis is rare and restricted to three auxiliary forms. It is only in Recording 5 (2;9.22) that there is a significant increase in frequency and range of forms. The development of auxiliary inversion in Y/Ns also lags behind the occurrence of auxiliaries in tags. Apart from three anomalous utterances (e.g. 'can you hearing me?') in Recording 2, non-copula Y/Ns contain no auxiliary until Recording 5 (see Table 7.5) and are typically performatives:

> we do it together? (=shall we?/can we?)
> you come over? (=will you?) (*Alex, Rec. 1, 2;7.6*)
> I draw it? (=can I?/shall I?) (*Alex, Rec. 2, 2;7.13*)

As can be seen from Table 7.5, these decline as the range and frequency of Y/N inversions increase.

Table 7.5 *The development of Alex's Y/N questions (excluding tags). Number of tokens and range of forms*

Y/N	Recording												
	1	2	3	4	5	6	7	8	9	10	11	12	13
No. aux.	8	5	1	1	5	3	2	1	0	0	3	0	0
Inverted aux.	0	3	0	0	3	4	3	4	3	4	4	11	29
Range of aux. forms	0	3	3	3	3	5	5	7	8	8	9	9	11

The following are typical of Alex's tags during Stage I:

> got a mellow (= car) /æntʃuː/ (haven't you) (*Alex, Rec. 1, 2;7.6*)
> boat /ɪnɪt/
> and it go out/ dʌnɪt/ (doesn't it)
> you going home after /ʌnjuː/ (aren't you)
> and they gonna park /enðeɪ/ (aren't they) (*Alex, Rec. 2, 7.13*)

These early tags have a number of features in common. All are interrogative, negative, and have falling intonation and reversed polarity. Other shared characteristics such as phonological reduction, the absence of the operator from the matrix clause, and the substitution of inappropriate tags in an imitation test (see Fig. 7.2) lend weight to the view that there is little awareness of their constituent structure.

Nevertheless, a closer analysis of tags produced spontaneously during Stage I shows that all are appropriate to their matrix in three ways. Firstly, as falling intonation negative tags they correctly follow affirmative matrices. Secondly, the small range of pronouns which they contain are always suited to the context. Thirdly, they contain the phonetic contours of operators which

MODEL	IMITATION
hasn't it	/ænɪt/
hasn't it	/ɪnɪt/
doesn't it	/enɪt/
don't I	/ɑ:naɪ/

Fig. 7.2 Alex's imitations of tags (*Recording 3, 2;8.3*)

would be appropriate in the matrix. Under these circumstances we clearly have to regard Alex's tags as at the very least marked for those features which enable them to be supplied in the right context.

The utterances below illustrate developments during *Stage II*:

> I didn't did I
> That's a seat is it? [rising intonation]
> I did haven't I
> he's been work he is
> I' ⟨m⟩ gonna get two I am (*Rec. 6, 2;10.12*)
> you naughty boy /enju:/
> I have two /enaɪ/
> it's got rubbish on /dəʊnɪt/ (*Rec. 9, 3;0.21*)

By now the first affirmative tags, with both falling and rising intonation, have appeared, as well as occasional declarative tags. Frequencies are now higher (see Table 7.2), and both auxiliary and copula tags are more likely to be preceded by an appropriate verb form in the matrix. The range of operators in tags gradually increases (Table 7.4) but this is accompanied by the presence of matching errors which were previously absent. The predominant pattern for tag questions, however, remains the same. Out of thirty tags produced in Recordings 6 to 8, twenty-six are negative, and have falling intonation and reversed polarity. The remaining four are affirmative, three with falling, and one with rising intonation.

The rise in frequency to thirty-three tag questions in Recording 9 from a previous maximum of fourteen raises the possibility that advances in Alex's syntax development have enabled him to extend rules for tag production to a wider range of contexts. It is true that two new affirmative subforms ('can' and 'could') occur, but the range is still fairly restricted. The nineteen auxiliary tags contain only six different subforms: eleven contain /dəʊn/ ('don't') and nine of these are /dəʊnɪt/ ('don't it'). A further five auxiliary and three copula tags contain the multipurpose form /en/. This single form substitutes for auxiliary and copula 'aren't', copula 'isn't', and auxiliary and main verb 'haven't' (see examples above). It seems therefore that Alex's rule system is still context restricted, with holistic strategies enabling him to extend tag usage to a wider range of utterances. The rise in frequency can be seen from Table 7.2 to have been a temporary phenomenon, and an analysis of the polarity and intonation of tag questions contained in Samples 9 to 13 (3;0.21 to 3;3.20) shows no change in the previous pattern: fifty-five of sixty-four are negative with falling intonation and reversed polarity. The only significant development during this period is the appearance in Recordings 12 and 13 of the affirmative, matched polarity, rising intonation tag 'is it?':

> make windows is it again? (*Alex, Rec. 12, 3;2.25*)
> play here is it? (*Alex, Rec. 13, 3;3.20*)

This is another multipurpose form and functions as a suggestion or request for permission. In context they have the force of the 'let's ... shall we?' pattern, but they are the closest Alex comes to tagged imperatives.

In summary, tag questions emerge for Alex at a stage when their syntactic requirements are beyond his competence. However, although it is assumed that his knowledge of their internal structure is limited, early tags are marked in such a way that they always occur in appropriate contexts. After Recording 6, the frequency of tags increases but the limited range of auxiliary forms they contain and the strategy of using multipurpose forms in a variety of different, sometimes inappropriate, contexts suggests only a partial awareness of the role of auxiliaries in tags.

CLARE. The majority of auxiliary subforms which occurred in Clare's tag questions did so before they were recorded elsewhere. Some of these forms were present during the first three speech samples and a comparison with the development of Y/Ns and ellipsis supports the interpretation that her early tags are not productive. During Recordings 1 to 6 (2;4.3 to 2;7.26) there are twelve instances of auxiliaries in what appears to be ellipsis. However, these are restricted to four auxiliary subforms, the status of which is also in doubt; performative usage of 'don't!' and 'won't' account for seven tokens.

If ellipsis is rare or indeterminate before Recording 7 (2;8.17), auxiliaries in Y/N inversion (excluding tags) are even rarer. The first occurrence is not until Recording 5 (2;7.2) where 'can' is used twice, and the only other token before Recording 7 is a single example of 'have'. Recording 7 marks an increase in range and frequency of auxiliaries in both ellipsis and Y/N inversions, but, as Table 7.6 shows, the development of the range of auxiliaries used in Y/Ns is slow and gradual and parallels Clare's expansion of the range of auxiliaries used in tags (Table 7.4).

Table 7.6 *Clare's Y/N questions (excluding tags). Number of tokens and cumulative range of forms*

Y/N	Recording											
	1	2	3	4	5	6	7	8	9	10	11	12
No. aux.	0	0	0	0	0	1	0	1	2	0	1	3
Inversion	0	0	0	0	2	1	5	2	11	2	6	14
Range of aux. forms	0	0	0	0	1	2	4	4	5	6	7	9

While the majority (thirty-six out of fifty-four) of the tag questions produced spontaneously were of the negative, falling intonation, reversed polarity type, variations were present from the beginning and were sustained through all samples. Development cannot be analysed in terms of stages and Clare's tags will therefore be considered according to subcategories.

Declarative tags: Clare produces five declarative tags, four of which contain an auxiliary. The first, which is similar to Betty's prototags, appears in Recording 5, over four and a half months *after* the first recorded tag question:

> I want to do a butterfly . I want to [crayoning] (*Clare, Rec. 5, 2;7.2*)

The first declarative tag containing an auxiliary occurs two samples later:

> I getting that I am
> (*Clare, Rec. 7, 2;8.17*)

Intonation: Clare's tag questions always have falling intonation, except for a single case of a Permission Request in the first recording:

> ⟨let him⟩ go and mend it shall we? [playing with Lego]
> (*Clare, Rec. 1, 2;4.3*)

The only tagged imperative uses falling intonation, which in its context is the only option available since the polarity of the imperative matrix is negative:

> don't do it to me will you again [she had been bumped by a Lego car]
> (*Clare, Rec. 2, 2;4.25*)

Polarity: Clare is the only child apart from Betty to make polarity errors. Unlike Betty, however, these are rare (four cases), and co-exist with correct reversals. While Betty only failed to supply the negative forms, Clare makes both types of error:

> that's on top is it [falling intonation]   (*Clare, Rec. 7, 2;8.17*)
> not an elephant at all aren't you [falling intonation]   (*Clare, Rec. 8, 2;9.6*)

After Recording 8 no further errors are recorded.

Using the correct auxiliary: tags supplying DO after a matrix containing no auxiliary or copula occur from the second sample:

> this goed in my mouth . didn't it   (*Clare, Rec. 5, 2;7.2*)

The first time an appropriate auxiliary in a tag question follows the corresponding auxiliary in the matrix is in Recording 7:

> Panda can't draw can he   (*Clare, Rec. 7, 2;8.17*)

While tags of this type subsequently become more frequent, tags containing an auxiliary which is absent from the matrix persist:

> I got a Christmas tree home /hæntaɪ/ (haven't I)   (*Clare, Rec. 3, 2;5.22*)
> that broken haven't it   (*Clare, Rec. 10, 2;10.18*)

Similarly, matching errors occur at all stages:

> not wee-wee had he [taking the pants off a doll]   (*Clare, Rec. 2, 2;4.25*)

> no it can't fit you does it   (*Clare, Rec. 8, 2;9.6*)
> that—that's the one with the ⟨hole/home⟩ wouldn't it   (*Clare, Rec. 10, 2;10.18*)

Additional examples of attempts to tag matrices containing more complex modal meanings are provided by Clare's responses to the imitation test. Attempts to elicit tags always failed, but occasionally Clare spontaneously tagged her repetitions of the models presented. These responses, which are *not* included in the spontaneous speech data, are shown below. In each case the model sentence is placed in brackets beneath Clare's response:

> pig should really go home /ɪntɪt/
> [the pig should really be at home]   (*Clare, Rec. 6, 2;7.26*)
> really be at home wouldn't it
> [the pig should really be at home]   (*Clare, Rec. 10, 2;10.18*)
> her gets – give us a lot of wool can't it
> [she could give us lots of wool]
> those are really be at home won't they
> [the pig should really be at home]   (*Clare, Rec. 11, 2;11.8*)
> ⟨the other one⟩ lot /ə/ wool can't it
> [she could give us lots of wool]
> ⟨?⟩⟨?⟩⟨?⟩ the boy very careful don't you

[the boy has to be very careful] (*Clare, Rec. 12, 3;0.1*)

In summary, Clare's approach to learning and using tags is characterised by the high frequency of errors. In the early stages in particular, these result from applying a limited repertoire of tags to a wide range of contexts. Typical is the use of the general purpose /ɪntɪt/ in contexts which require both copula and auxiliary verb tags:

> they swimming /ɪntɪt/
> you found a horsie /ɪntɪt/ (*Clare, Rec. 6, 2;7.26*)

Like Alex, the place of Clare's early tags in her overall syntactic development is premature both from the point of view of the syntactic processes which are yet to be mastered, as well as such rule-of-thumb measures as MLUS and MLUL. Unlike Alex, however, Clare frequently supplies tags containing inappropriate auxiliaries during the earliest phase of usage and as a result of her /ɪntɪt/ strategy makes a small number of pronoun errors, something which never occurs for Alex despite his use of similar multipurpose forms.

It is impossible to identify a point at which Clare's tags become productive; development of both tags and the related syntactic processes is too haphazard. Interestingly, however, pronoun errors cease after Recording 6, matching auxiliaries first occur in tagged matrices in Recording 7, and polarity errors are absent after Recording 8. This suggests that it is during the period from 2;7.26 (Rec. 6) to 2;9.6 (Recording 8) that the most significant progress is made.

7.5 Summary and discussion

The implications of the results described will be discussed under two headings. Firstly, five general aspects of the analysis will be outlined and secondly, the evidence for style differences in the development of tags will be evaluated.

7.5.1 General findings
1. There is no evidence that copula tags appear before auxiliary tags. It is true, on the other hand, that copula forms such as /ɪnɪt/ are often among the first tags to emerge, and that these may function as general-purpose pro-forms which can also appear in contexts for auxiliary tags.
2. Most tags follow the 'standard' pattern of falling intonation and reversed polarity, and the majority are also negative. For three children, negative falling intonation tags are also the first to emerge. The exceptions are Betty, who begins with affirmative, matched polarity tags, and Clare, who produces

both types in her first recording. No conclusions can therefore be drawn about sequence of development, especially as the higher frequency of the negative form of the 'standard' model increases the probability of its being sampled first.

Theoretically there are arguments both for and against the prior emergence of the falling intonation tag. There is a good case for expecting the rising intonation tag to occur first, since rising intonation is associated with Y/N inversion. Polarity matching might also be expected early because it omits one of the transformations of the more complex tags. On the other hand, from the point of view of epistemic modality, it is the falling intonation, reversed polarity tag which expresses greatest commitment to the proposition, and just as the use of modal verbs to express *constraints* on the truth is a later development (Stephany, 1986), so one might also expect tag questions which express less commitment, or uncertainty, to appear at a later stage.

3. Only the data from Betty would be consistent with the idea that declarative tags are a precursor of tag questions. The development of prototags and declarative tags is clearly an area of individual variation.

4. Pronoun errors are rare – supplying the correct auxiliary is a much greater problem. It is common for children to go through a sometimes lengthy period during which some tags supply a correct auxiliary which is absent from its obligatory context in the matrix clause.

5. There is more to learning tag questions than bringing together a set of rules for negation, ellipsis, inversion and pronoun substitution. The child has to learn the role of tags in the dynamics of conversation, be aware of circumstances in which they can be uttered felicitously and understand the relationships between intonation and syntax, and varying expectations with regard to the truth of propositions to be communicated. By the end of this investigation even the most advanced producers of tag questions have only demonstrated any degree of competence in a single syntactic type, and even these usually follow single clause sentences. Deriving the tag from the correct clause in complex sentences is an ability which has yet to be demonstrated.

7.5.2 Differences in style of tag development

Evidence of early usage of tag questions and of the occurrence of previously unsampled auxiliaries in tags for two children had suggested contrasting styles of development for Alex and Clare on the one hand, and Betty, Eric, and Fleur on the other. It was thought that these styles would be characterised by either the use of partially analysed forms and piecemeal learning (Alex and Clare) or an analytic approach where the rules for producing tags are quickly generalised to a broad range of linguistic contexts. While the detailed analysis of the development of tags generally confirms the hypothesis, it is important to emphasise that these two styles are by no means mutually exclusive.

It is indeed the case that both Alex and Clare show a slow and gradual increase in their repertoire of tags after an early phase during which they appear to have little knowledge of the syntactic requirements for their production. Early phonologically reduced forms, assumed to be no more than partially analysed, are gradually replaced by prosodic contours which suggest a greater degree of segmentation. Adding a small range of rote-learned tags to appropriate contexts, or inappropriately appending a single rote-learned tag to sentences for which they have no tag readily available, is a strategy which enables Alex and Clare to function conversationally at a level above their syntactic competence. It must be remembered, however, that even if we regard early forms as syntactically unanalysed chunks, Alex demonstrates sufficient knowledge of their collocational restrictions to ensure that in most cases they are used appropriately.

It is also true that Betty, Fleur, and Eric delay the production of tags until there has been progress in MLUS and MLUL, in the use of the auxiliary, and in the syntactic operations which are needed to produce tags. It is possible to identify points at which there are significant developments consistent with the application of rules to a wider range of contexts. Betty, in particular, develops tags in a sequence which corresponds to a hierarchy of syntactic difficulty. Nevertheless, the development of this group of children is not unequivocally analytic; even Betty uses the reduced /ɪnɪt/ and /ɪni:/ at a time when all other tags are affirmative. Fleur never demonstrates competence in the production of Y/N inversions, though of course this doesn't mean that she has no such competence. In the case of Eric, tags emerge at a much higher MLUS than the corresponding figure for Alex and Clare, and at this stage negation is well-established. Ellipsis and inversion, however, are only just developing, and his early tags are restricted to a small number of forms which are reduced phonologically. Development is piecemeal for a period of nearly four months, after which there are rapid increases in frequency, range of auxiliaries and range of linguistic contexts. Eric, therefore, combines the style and strategies of both groups.

7.6 Conclusion

These results throw further light on questions arising from the attempt in Chapter 6 to identify areas of holistic learning in the development of the auxiliary. These questions concerned the problem of sampling error and whether Alex and Clare's tags were genuinely premature, and the fact that there were no recorded tags for Gemma.

Examination of Gemma's transcripts confirmed that neither deficient input, linguistic competence, nor processing capacity could explain the non-emergence of tags. A discussion of the meaning, function, and discourse role of tags, however, drew attention to areas of potential difficulty other than syntax. It was suggested therefore that although Gemma had sufficient knowledge to cope with the syntax of tags, she was not sufficiently mature (as the youngest child in the sample) to understand how tags function in conversation.

Finally, there was at least partial confirmation of two contrasting styles of development. The extreme cases, Betty on the one hand, and Alex and Clare on the other, certainly showed different developmental patterns, and a viable explanation for the persistence of Betty's polarity errors can be found in the analytical sequence of her tag development. However, while some children can be seen to be more analytical in their approach to learning tag questions than others, this is a matter of degree and does not preclude holistic strategies.

8 The development of auxiliary DO

8.1 Introduction

A dimension on which children might be expected to differ is the extent to which auxiliaries remain context restricted, or are applied to a variety of available contexts fairly quickly. In certain cases context-restricted usage would also indicate unanalysed usage. This is amenable to investigation by examining the set of main verbs with which specified auxiliary forms, or subforms co-occur. The forms chosen must, however, occur with sufficient regularity to allow comparisons both between children, and within children over time. For this reason, Chapters 8 and 9 concentrate on DO and CAN as the forms which occur most frequently.

8.2 DO as an operator

In standard English, forming the negative and in most cases the interrogative of main verbs requires DO-insertion (see Section 1.5). Auxiliary DO, therefore, plays a central role in the development of negation and questions. Like other auxiliaries, it is also available for emphasis and ellipsis. It can be supplied as a means of stressing the propositional truth of the predicate of a clause containing no auxiliary (# 'He went out' → # 'He 'did go out') and functions as an operator (with or without emphasis) where there is ellipsis of the main verb (# 'He did').

8.3 Unstressed forms

As a consequence of the limitation of auxiliary DO to the NICE operations and its lack of independent propositional content, its paradigm is deficient in comparison with that of other auxiliaries; there is no place for DO forms which are unstressed, declarative and affirmative (UDAs). Palmer (1965) suggests that such forms occur in 'code' (ellipsis) but their existence is difficult to substantiate. According to Quirk et al. (1985, p. 1595) 'a noncontrastive primary stress falls . . . on the operator in an elliptical verb phrase'.

The absence from standard English of what in other auxiliaries would be regarded as the base form has interesting consequences for the study of the development of DO. However, as Palmer also points out, UDAs can be found in certain dialects of British English, for example in the West, particularly Bristol and South Wales. This observation was borne out by both the Bristol and the Welsh children.

8.3.1 Unstressed DO in the Welsh data

While it was known that UDAs were a feature of the dialect of some of the children's parents, it was not known whether they would be present in the speech of children so young. The fact that the forms apparently performed no useful syntactic function and were semantically empty suggested that they might not. Kuczaj and Maratsos had far less success in eliciting imitations of 'semi-grammatical' unstressed DO forms than declarative CAN and WILL (Kuczaj and Maratsos, 1975, pp. 90–100). On the other hand, Fletcher (1979) reports unstressed 'did' in one child's speech for a six-month period after his third birthday. The presence of such forms would not of necessity be attributable to features of the linguistic environment. It is also possible that UDAs could be a temporary overregularisation of auxiliary verb usage, a temporary strategy, or a 'hypothetical intermediate' (Brown, Cazden and Bellugi, 1969). In all three cases, however, they would be unlikely to occur before other auxiliaries.

In fact, a small number of tokens of declarative unstressed 'do', 'does', or 'did' were found in the speech of all children except Eric. Typical examples are:

they eat the food when they get — when they /dʊ/ go home
[story of the three little rabbits] (*Betty, 2;10.24*)

it /dəz/ fit [playing with Lego] (*Betty, 2;10.24*)

Suzanne did come to my house yesterday (*Clare, 3;0.2*)

Nevertheless, Table 8.1 shows UDAs to be relatively rare, and Alex, Gemma and Fleur produce tokens involving only one subform.

All children, except Eric (for whom there are no recorded UDAs) and Gemma, had access to these dialect forms at home. Gemma's parents used standard English and by 2;0.17 when she first produced UDAs she had experienced little contact with other children. For her, then, the forms must derive from an idiosyncratic rule. Generally UDAs occurred most frequently after the age of 2;9, but Gemma is a clear exception. Of the six produced, two were present at 2;0.8, a further two at 2;1.15, and one each at 2;3.19 and 2;4.9. No further examples were found in recordings at 2;5.28 and 2;6.26,

Table 8.1 *Frequency of unstressed declarative DO forms (pooled for all occasions)*

| Subject | DO forms | | | Total |
	do	does	did	
Alex	4	0	0	4
Betty	2	2	5	9
Clare	3	0	11	14
Daisy	1	0	2	3
Eric	0	0	0	0
Fleur	0	1	0	1
Gemma	0	0	6	6

nor in subsequent follow-up visits. This, and the fact that all six involved 'did', suggests that their use might be a temporary strategy during a period when past time reference was emerging.

Data were examined from the three children whose use of UDAs was most frequent. The first question was whether Gemma, as an exceptionally fast developer, was producing unstressed 'do' forms at an early *stage*. The second question asks more specifically whether unstressed 'did' occurs before, during or after learning the past tense. If it occurs before, then this would suggest a strategy to compensate for difficulties in producing past tense forms of main verbs.

The first of these questions is partially answered by reference to Table 8.2. MLUS values for Betty, Clare and Gemma fail to confirm that Gemma was producing unstressed forms at an earlier stage. Gemma's forms all occur at an MLUS of between 3.6 and 5.0 (her ceiling was 5.2 at 2;4.9). For Betty and Clare most occurrences are between an MLUS of 4.4 and 4.9, and 3.7 and 4.8 respectively. However, both have produced isolated tokens at 2.8–3.7 morphemes (Betty) and at 2.8–3.3 morphemes (Clare).

A comparison between the production of unstressed DO and other aspects of auxiliary verb learning shows that for Gemma the emergence of UDAs at 2;0.18 (Rec. 4) corresponds with the first growth spurts in range of auxiliary forms per 100 structured utterances, in her cumulative range of forms, and in the frequency of auxiliaries per 100 structured utterances. Up to this point, Gemma's only recorded auxiliary forms had been 'can' and 'can't', restricted to non-ellipsed declarative frames expressing ability, and to performative utterances. Now, however, unstressed 'did' co-emerges with 'didn't', ellipti-

Table 8.2 *Age and MLUS of three children in recordings containing UDAs*

	Betty						
MLUS	3.3	2.8	3.7	4.4	4.6	4.9	4.4
Age	2;4.8	2;4.15	2;7.3	2;10.2	2;10.24	2;11.17	3;1.2
Tokens	1	1	1	1	2	1	2
	Clare						
MLUS	2.8	3.2	3.3	3.7	4.0	4.8	
Age	2;4.3	2;7.2	2;7.26	2;9.28	2;11.8	3;0.1	
Tokens	1	1	1	3	4	4	
	Gemma						
MLUS	3.6	5.0	4.9	5.0			
Age	2;0.18	2;1.15	2;3.19	2;5.7			
Tokens	2	2	1	1			

cal usage of 'did', 'has' + 'got', and five subforms of auxiliary 'be' (three contracted and two noncontracted). For the first time auxiliaries are used in both Y/N and Wh- questions – with no evidence of a 'hypothetical intermediate' stage of non-inversion (see Brown, Cazden and Bellugi, 1969; Bellugi, 1971; Menyuk, 1969).

While for Gemma the emergence of UDAs coincides with the onset of competence in using the auxiliary verb system, the position is very different for Clare and Betty.

Clare's first token was produced during her first recording session:

I /dɪ/ goggle /mɪm/ (I did cuddle him) [a Lego man].

Clare uses five other subforms in this sample, but all are represented by single tokens. Two of these occur in tag questions (see Chapter 7) and the remainder are negative forms used for emphatic interpersonal meanings ('don't!', 'won't!'), also assumed to function as single morphemes. The emergence of unstressed declarative 'did' is therefore not an integral part of a developing system of auxiliary verbs although by her period of maximum usage after 2;9.28 (Rec. 9) Clare is showing much greater competence with the auxiliary.

The pattern for Betty is very similar. Again, the first recorded UDA was in the first speech sample (2;4.8) and it results in an overmarking error: 'I did got my ⟨road roller⟩'. This is followed by a more 'correct' usage in the second sample at 2;4.15: '/dɪ/ buy ⟨?⟩ pape' [pretending a toy had bought some paper]. Between this and 2;10.2, after which there are a further six, there is only a single token at 2;7.3.

It is unlikely that these forms are fully productive; there is no evidence from Betty's first two speech samples that there has been anything more than piecemeal learning of a small number of declarative forms, and no other DO forms are present. By contrast, after 2;10.2 (Rec.10) Betty uses all three types of UDA, by which time there has been a dramatic increase in the frequency of auxiliaries to 34.7 per 100 structured utterances. Range of subforms per 100 structured utterances has also undergone a rapid rise by the previous sample (2;9.8), reaching a figure of 9.9, and in the imitation test Betty now includes the auxiliary in 17 out of 19 items. All DO forms now occur regularly, and ellipsis and inversion in questions are well established.

In summary, Clare and Gemma's UDAs emerge well before any evidence that auxiliaries in general, or DO forms in particular, are functioning as a system. Frequency of occurrence, however, is greatest at a later stage following a period of rapid auxiliary verb learning. Gemma, by contrast, only uses UDAs during a period of initial rapid growth in her repertoire of auxiliaries. Since UDAs are not part of Gemma's linguistic environment, their production is considered to be rule based, compared with a restricted, only partially analysed initial usage, probably derived more directly from input for Betty and Clare.

8.3.2 An explanation for Gemma's unstressed forms

Gemma's only unstressed form is 'did', and it was suggested above that its use may be a strategy for referring to past events where past tense forms of main verbs are in doubt.

The order of appearance of past tense forms is well documented (see Brown, 1973; De Villiers and De Villiers, 1973; Ervin, 1964; Kuczaj, 1977). Children first learn irregular forms as syntactically unanalysed units; the child is not yet aware of the relationship between, say, 'eat' and 'ate' (Kuczaj, 1981a). Some time later, the -ed suffix on regular verbs is acquired and a period of overregularisation follows, during which the -ed suffix is applied to verbs with irregular past tense forms which were formerly produced correctly. This phenomenon which often extends into school age is frequently taken as evidence of the acquisition of a rule for past tense production (though see Fletcher, 1985, for a note of caution) and for Slobin it exemplifies the operating principle: avoid exceptions (Slobin, 1979, p. 108).

Clare shows overregularisation of the -ed suffix from the very first speech sample. Early recordings contain 'broked', 'hurted' (Rec.1), 'comed', 'goed' (Rec. 2), and 'boughted' (Rec. 3). It is unlikely therefore that Clare's eleven tokens of unstressed 'did' are part of a strategy for past reference at any period.

Betty uses both regular and irregular past forms correctly from Recording 1, but it is only in the sixth sample (2;7.3) that overgeneralisation errors appear ('bited', 'comed'). They are rare and subsequently only occur in Sample 10 at 2;10.2 ('fallededed') and in Sample 11 at 2;10.24 ('bringed'). The frequency of overgeneralisation errors may itself be an area of individual differences, and their absence during the early stages is not evidence that no productive past tense rule exists, since overgeneralisation necessarily *follows* the induction of a rule. Nevertheless, most of Betty's unstressed 'did' forms precede her first overregularisation, and their use as a strategy cannot be ruled out.

Clare and Gemma are well matched on MLUS for the first four samples, after which Gemma enters a period of accelerated development. In learning the past tense, however, she was less advanced. As shown above, Clare appeared to have a past tense rule from the outset. Gemma, by contrast, uses few past tense forms until her fourth recording (2;0.18). This coincides with the emergence of UDAs and, as Table 8.3 shows, is followed in Sample 5 (2;1.15) by an impressive increase in the range of past tense forms.

Table 8.3 *Gemma – range of past tense forms per recording (Recordings 1–10, 1;10.6–2;5.7)*

	Recording									
Past forms	1	2	3	4	5	6	7	8	9	10
Irregular	2	2	0	4	13	4	2	4	7	5
Regular	0	1	0	0	5	2	0	1	5	2
Overregularisation	0	0	0	0	1	0	0	0	2	1

Gemma's first UDAs occur in Samples 4 and 5, after she has started to use past tense forms, but at a time when they are restricted almost exclusively to irregular verbs. Figures for Sample 5, however, indicate a period of growth which may suggest the development of a productive rule for the past tense.

Possibly, there are two facets to Gemma's use of UDAs. Firstly, she has developed a functional need for past time reference by Sample 4, which is also the first sample to contain unfilled obligatory contexts for the past tense morpheme. Unstressed 'did' provides a means of marking a wider range of verbs for past tense than those she has thus far succeeded in learning by rote. It is interesting that all Gemma's UDAs co-occur with irregular verbs, though this may result from nothing more than a statistical tendency for irregular forms to occur more frequently (see Fletcher, 1985, for an analysis of regular and irregular forms for one child).

Secondly, as part of the process of learning a past tense rule, Gemma has begun to pay attention to a potentially bewildering aspect of her input: the same function is achieved in different ways for different populations of verbs. Unstressed 'did' provides a means of creating order in an area of confusion; a single rule avoids the problem of choosing between competing options. Again, we might invoke Slobin's (1979) operating principle: avoid exceptions. Unfortunately, this is a strategy which leads to overmarking errors at a later stage:

> and I did took it off *(Rec. 8, 2;3.19)*
> and I did did it like this *(Rec. 10, 2;5.7)*

Despite the paucity of the data, the case for unstressed 'did' as a strategy for past time reference is a fairly strong one. What remains a matter of speculation is how Gemma acquired a rule for supplying dummy DO for this function in the absence of exemplars in the input.

Five possibilities present themselves and these will be evaluated in turn:

1. Unstressed 'did' is a hypothetical intermediate.
2. Declarative usage of other auxiliaries has been overgeneralised.
3. Usage of negative declarative DO has been overgeneralised.
4. Usage of auxiliary DO in contexts with contrastive stress has been overgeneralised to unstressed contexts.
5. Usage of main verb 'did' in declaratives has been overgeneralised.

Some forms which are peculiar to early language learners are termed 'hypothetical intermediates' (Brown et al., 1969). These are structures which, because of limitations on a child's processing capacity, differ from the correct form by one transformation or more. The term has been applied to non-inverted Wh- questions (Brown et al., 1969), and non-negated falling intonation tag questions (Todd, 1982). For UDAs to be a hypothetical intermediate would require a theoretical framework in which all finite declarative sentences contain an auxiliary in deep structure (e.g. Akmajian, Steele and Wasow, 1979; Pullum and Wilson, 1977). Failure to carry out a deletion transformation would result in sentences containing an unstressed declarative DO form to which

Tense is attached. However, if such an interpretation were correct, we would also expect to hear unstressed present tense DO forms from Gemma, and these are never in evidence.

For Gemma to overgeneralise the privileges of occurrence of other auxiliaries (Possibility 2) there are two preconditions: firstly, she would already have to be aware of a range of declarative usage where the auxiliary precedes the infinitive of a main verb. Knowledge of BE + ING or HAVE + EN would therefore not assist induction of the UDA rule. Secondly, she would have to know that DO belongs to the same class of verbs as other auxiliaries. However, apart from CAN Gemma shows no productive knowledge of the modal auxiliaries in spontaneous speech when UDAs emerge, though two more modals are supplied in the imitation test, and a combination of imitation test and spontaneous speech yields a further four on the following occasion (Rec. 5, 2;1.15). It is possible that this is sufficient to fulfil Condition 1, particularly if her knowledge is greater than is revealed in production. But does she have sufficient knowledge of other aspects of DO-support to identify DO as a member of the same class of verbs? The only DO form present in the data up to, and including, the emergence of 'did' is the corresponding negative form 'didn't', but this could be sufficient to identify common privileges of occurrence with other auxiliaries and to infer that they extend to all DO forms.

Possibility 3 is a simpler version of 2. It omits data from other modal verbs, requiring the declarative function of 'did' to be inferred from the behaviour of 'didn't'.

Possibility 4 posits a derivation of UDAs from the use of the auxiliary in contexts of emphatic affirmation. These have not yet emerged in Gemma's speech for any auxiliary, and will not do so until Sample 6 (2;2.2.). Frequencies of these are low, however, and they may simply not have been sampled. It is also possible that in input they are already available, attended to, and understood.

Possibility 5 suggests that UDAs are derived from usage of unstressed main verb 'did' in declarative contexts. This is not incompatible with stress patterns of sentences containing DO as a lexical verb or pro-verb, but the class of word which follows DO is clearly different when it functions as a main verb. In fact, Gemma's first recorded use of main verb 'did' is in Sample 5 (2;1.15), shortly after the emergence of the unstressed auxiliary. There is therefore no evidence to support this explanation.

Of the possible sources of Gemma's rule, Possibility 1 seems the least likely, and of the other four only 2 and 3 are supported by evidence from her own speech output. Of these, 3 has the merit of simplicity, but otherwise it is impossible to assess their relative probability on the evidence available.

Finally, it is interesting to note that English is not the only language in which auxiliary DO before a main verb infinitive exists, but is considered to be nonstandard. As a language which marks mood by other means, German has little need to use the verb 'tun' (= DO) as an operator. Nevertheless, in the speech of children and many adults, weakly stressed declarative forms of 'tun' frequently precede an infinitive, as in 'Sie tut gerade schreiben': She's writing (Literally: She does just write) (Berger, Drosdowski, Grebe and Müller, 1972, p. 648). Such usage is regarded as nonstandard, the High German equivalent being # 'Sie schreibt gerade.' The only acceptable usage of 'tun' as an operator occurs where topicalisation of the main verb is achieved by a change of word order (Grebe, 1966): # 'Schreiben tut sie gerade.'

While many German children obviously hear this function of 'tun', it is not known whether such structures ever result entirely from the development of idiosyncratic rules in the way that appears to have happened with Gemma.

8.4 The range of contexts of 'don't'

As the most frequent subform of DO, 'don't' was chosen for the analysis of the linguistic contexts in which DO forms occur. The aim was to identify sudden increases in the range of contexts which might be indicative of analytic processes, or highly restricted or stereotyped usage indicative of a piecemeal approach. The analysis concentrates on the range of main verbs which co-occur with 'don't', but it also considers the relationship between the nouns and pronouns in subject position and the function of early utterances.

Table 8.4 shows the development of types and tokens of lexical verbs which co-occur with 'don't'. Figures include imperatives, but omit elliptical utterances, including tags. As might be expected, usage is context restricted in the early stages, but there are no dramatic increases in the range of contexts. Instead there is a slow and steady rise in the number of types. While there appears to be a certain amount of stereotyped usage for all children except Gemma, for whom there are very little data, Fleur's production is particularly repetitive. During the nine recordings since the first emergence of 'don't' + Main Verb (Rec.4), Fleur produces thirty-four tokens but only three types. Of these, twenty appear in one recording (Rec.10, 2;8.10).

A closer look at the verbs themselves (Table 8.5) helps to explain how 'don't' is functioning. Between them, the children use twenty-seven different main verbs with 'don't', but 69% of all tokens during the period of the

Table 8.4 *Cumulative types and tokens of main verbs which co-occur with* '*don't*'

| | Recording | | | | | | | | | | | | | |
Child	1	2	3	4	5	6	7	8	9	10	11	12	13	14
Eric	1/1	2/3	2/3	2/3	2/6	3/8	4/15	6/18	7/21	10/31	12/33	13/39	16/45	
Betty		1/4	2/7	4/10	4/10	4/11	4/11	5/13		5/16	5/23	6/24	7/26	7/30
Clare			2/2	3/3	3/3	4/4	4/4	4/5	6/7	6/13	7/14	7/14	9/18	
Daisy		1/4	2/7	3/10	4/11	4/12	5/14	5/15	6/17	10/24	12/30			
Eric								1/2	1/4	3/6	3/6	4/7	5/11	5/11
Fleur				2/2	2/3	3/6	3/6	3/6	3/26	3/26	3/32	3/34		
Gemma					1/1	2/3	4/6	4/6	4/6	4/6	4/6	4/6		

study are accounted for by just three verbs ('know', 'like', and 'won't'). These are also the only verbs to co-occur with 'don't' for Fleur, and are the first to be used by Betty and Alex. For the other children, one or two of these are always among the first to emerge and, except for Gemma who produced the smallest number of tokens, each child has one verb which occurs with a relatively high frequency. In the case of Alex, Betty, and Fleur this is 'know'. For Clare, and to a lesser extent Eric, it is 'like', and for Daisy it is 'want'. Invariable early pronunciation of 'don't know' as /dənəʊ/ (Alex and Fleur) or /dəʊnəʊ/ (Betty) suggests that these are acquired as unanalysed wholes.

It is no coincidence that the four verbs which occur most frequently express cognitive or affective states. In spite of the use of 'don't' for the third person singular in the dialect of most of the parents, its use has a first person singular orientation for all children and is used in this way in 79.8% of occurrences. The combination of reference to self with the negation of main verbs which express cognitive or affective states frequently corresponds with a performative function enabling the child to reject objects and activities, and to regulate the behaviour of the addressee so that more acceptable alternatives are provided.

Fleur, for example, developed a strategy of using '(I) don't know' to brush aside display questions asked by her mother. In Recording 9 (2;7.17) she had been asked a series of Wh- questions about some wedding photographs. Her mother's style of conducting this interrogation was non-supportive. Sequences followed two main patterns. In the first, Fleur would give the wrong response and the identical Wh- question would be repeated. Again Fleur would give the wrong response, and again the question would be

Table 8.5 *Frequencies of verbs which co-occur with 'don't'*

	Subjects								
Verb	Alex	Betty	Clare	Daisy	Eric	Fleur	Gemma	Total	%
know	15	20		2		27	2	66	37.9
like	8	3	9	3	5	1		29	16.7
want	3	2	2	12		6		25	14.4
want to	4	2		1	1		2	10	5.7
break	2				3			5	2.9
go	2			1	1			4	2.3
live		1	1	1				3	1.7
put		1		2				3	1.7
suit				3				3	1.7
do			1		1			2	1.1
have	1	1						2	1.1
look	1		1					2	1.1
pinch	1						1	2	1.1
play				2				2	1.1
say	2							2	1.1
think	1			1				2	1.1
turn	1			1				2	1.1
care	1							1	0.6
catch							1	1	0.6
cheat	1							1	0.6
come	1							1	0.6
drop			1					1	0.6
feel			1					1	0.6
lift			1					1	0.6
make				1				1	0.6
talk	1							1	0.6
work			1					1	0.6
Total	45	30	18	30	11	34	6	174	99.8

repeated. This could happen from two to five times when the sequence would be terminated by a negative evaluation (e.g. 'You daft bat!'). The second pattern involved no response from Fleur and was followed by an immediate negative evaluation. Only rarely was the null response or wrong response followed up with a Yes/No question, a common way of facilitating conversation when children fail to answer Wh-s (Gleason, 1977). By the following session (2;8.10) Fleur had learnt how to deal with the situation, and all twenty of her 'don't know' utterances in Recording 10 were part of display question sequences.

Elsewhere, 'don't know' was used as a refusal to continue with an activity such as the imitation test. This is a function for which 'don't want' and 'don't like' were also used. Eric had a more subtle approach. When he was tired of 'telling the story to Teddy' he would say, for example, ''e [= Teddy] don't like this story'.

Utterances containing 'don't' also frequently function as requests for action at this stage. Daisy's 'don't go' (2;10.30) referring to a Lego train was in fact a request to make it work. Similarly, Gemma's 'you don't want to pinch mine' (2;2.26) was an instruction not to touch her fish during a magnetic fishing game.

8.5 DO forms: summary and conclusion

Six children developed early unstressed DO forms in declarative frames (UDAs). Because such forms were also a feature of the dialect of the area, the processes by which they were acquired are difficult to specify. Basically, there are three possible mechanisms, and various combinations of these. The first is rote-learning from input. The second is the induction of a DO + Main Verb rule derived from exemplars in declarative sentences. The third is the acquisition of a rule either directly from the observed syntactic behaviour of DO or from a distributional analysis of other members of the auxiliary class.

For one child (Gemma), however, there is no evidence of UDAs in the speech addressed to her. Only the last, the most indirect, and hence arguably the most analytical of the three mechanisms proposed above, could account for these structures in the speech of Gemma. Since the only form used by her is 'did' and since it emerges at a transitional stage in the development of the past tense, its use is interpreted as a strategy for regularising past time reference.

Except for Fleur, whose use of 'don't' is frequent but highly stereotyped, there are no clear indications of individual differences in style of development across contexts. During the period of the study, contexts, as defined by the lexical verbs with which 'don't' co-occurs, were fairly limited, though they do vary from a final cumulative figure of sixteen for Alex to three for Fleur. Developments were slow and steady for all children with no evidence of simultaneous acquisition. At this stage, usage is overwhelmingly performative, a fact which is reflected in the first person subject orientation of 'don't', and the predominance of a small number of cognitive and affective state verbs with which it combines.

9   The development of CAN

9.1 Introduction

It was shown in Chapter 4 that the order of emergence of CAN forms in spontaneous speech was:

can't (D) → can (D) → can (Q) → can't (Q)

This sequence contravenes the general trend found in Section 6.1 for affirmative forms to precede corresponding negative forms. However, given reports of negatives such as 'can't' and 'don't' as early rote-learned items (Bloom, 1970; Ervin, 1964; Fletcher, 1979; McNeill, 1966), and considering that we are talking of emergence rather than acquisition, it is hardly surprising.

What was less predictable was that in the imitation test 'can' (D) emerged later than both 'can't' (D) and 'can' (Y/N) for all children (see Section 4.4.3). The explanation suggested was a tendency to attribute an exclusively interpersonal, in particular a regulatory, meaning to utterances (in this case the model sentence) whose semantics are not fully understood. No such meaning could be attributed to the 'can' (D) item, hence its late appearance. This interpretation is consistent with the view that early modals are 'without exception interpersonal and action-oriented' (Fletcher, 1979, p. 282; see also Stephany, 1986).

On the other hand, it will be shown that there is a deep-seated inconsistency in the literature on this subject. If comprehension and production are based on interpersonal function, why does Wells (1979a) find meanings of permission and ability to emerge *before* the performative meanings? One possibility is that this is an area of individual differences in functional orientation, similar to Nelson's (1973) Referential/Expressive distinction but at a later stage. Another explanation lies in a possible mismatch between the development of the child's interpersonal aims and the researcher's reading of the underlying modality of utterances.

These possibilities will be considered below, as part of an analysis of function and meaning. Initially, however, the sequence described above will be illuminated by examining trends for the frequency of CAN in the various syntactic frames, and an indication of the degree of restriction in usage will again be obtained by examining the linguistic contexts in which it occurs.

9.2 Frequencies of CAN

Previous research attests the high frequency and early emergence of CAN in comparison with other modals. In Shields' (1974) cross-sectional study of modality in 107 children between 2;6 and 4;11 CAN was the most frequent form until after 4;6 when it was overtaken by WILL/SHALL. Perkins (1983a) found that for ninety-six children aged 6 to 12, CAN accounted for over a quarter of modal expressions, while for the sixty younger Bristol children (Wells, 1979a) it had the highest frequency and, together with WILL, was the first form to emerge for 50% of the children.

Findings from the subjects in the current study are consistent with those outlined above. Forms of CAN were present in the first recording of all children except Clare, who was also the only child for whom CAN did not precede the other modals. For all seven children the frequency of this form overwhelmingly exceeds that of any other modal.

9.2.1 'Can' versus 'can't'

Table 9.1 *Frequencies of 'can' and 'can't' (pooled for all samples)*

Subject	can	can't
Alex	35	65
Betty	64	88
Clare	44	48
Daisy	19	43
Eric	45	64
Fleur	32	159
Gemma	79	21
Totals	318	488

Although it has been shown that the reverse is true of slightly older children (Shields, 1974) and of 5-year-olds (Raban, 1988), it can be seen from Table 9.1 that for six out of seven subjects, 'can't' exceeds 'can', and that in extreme cases the imbalance is in a ratio of approximately two to one (Alex and Daisy), and even five to one (Fleur). Gemma, surprisingly, presents exactly the opposite picture. She produces nearly four times as many tokens of 'can' as 'can't'.

Table 9.2 *Development of frequencies of 'can' (+) and 'can't' (−)*

Child		1	2	3	4	5	6	7	8	9	10	11	12	13	14
								Recording							
+	Alex	0	0	0	0	1	4	3	7	4	8	1	5	2	
−		5	2	2	2	3	4	4	3	5	12	6	12	5	
+	Betty	1	0	2	0	2	5	4	7	9	14	2	3	6	9
−		3	1	2	16	5	6	6	2	6	16	11	6	5	3
+	Clare	0	0	0	0	2	1	11	2	2	2	2	22		
−		0	0	5	4	1	3	5	5	3	11	4	7		
+	Daisy	0	2	1	3	0	1	0	1	0	2	3	6		
−		3	1	0	1	2	5	5	11	4	3	4	4		
+	Eric	1	0	0	1	0	3	1	4	4	8	7	8	8	
−		0	6	1	0	5	5	3	4	6	0	4	20	10	
+	Fleur	0	0	1	0	0	3	1	1	0	1	24	1		
−		7	26	24	8	12	17	9	19	11	8	13	5		
+	Gemma	1	1	0	1	0	0	15	3	35	9	8	5		
−		0	1	0	2	0	1	2	7	5	2	0	1		

Key: +affirmative; −negative.

Since it cannot be assumed that over a lengthy period these asymmetries are consistent, the figures above have been broken down to show trends over time (Table 9.2). These confirm that for six children 'can't' consistently exceeds 'can', at least until the latter form becomes established as a regular feature, when there may be a temporary reversal (Fleur, Rec. 11; Clare, Rec. 12). The earlier consistent usage of 'can't' is also confirmed for six children but for Gemma a different order of development is suggested, with 'can' and 'can't' occurring with equal rarity until Recording 7 (2;2.26), when there is a sudden increase in the affirmative form. This is then followed in Recordings 8 and 9 (2;3.19 and 2;4.9) by an increase in the occurrence of 'can't'. The significance of this idiosyncratic approach will be discussed later in this chapter.

9.3 CAN and the development of questions

An examination of declarative and interrogative frames for 'can' and 'can't' (Table 9.3) shows that while 'can' occupies a variety of syntactic frames for most children, the use of 'can't' is much more restricted. In part, this most probably results from the additional syntactic complexity of using the negative in questions, but it is undoubtedly also related to meaning and function. Analysis of the affirmative form shows that while declaratives and Y/Ns are most frequent, declaratives substantially exceed Y/Ns for five of the children. The total absence of Y/Ns for Fleur will be considered below.

Table 9.4 gives a longitudinal perspective to the relationship between 'can'

Table 9.3 *Percentage of 'can' (N = 318) and 'can't' (N = 484) in declaratives and interrogatives (combined for all samples)*

Child	can				can't			
	D (%)	Y (%)	W (%)	T (%)	D (%)	Y (%)	W (%)	T (%)
Alex	17	15	0	3	65	0	0	0
Betty	28	11	1	1	58	0	0	0
Clare	37	11	0	0	49	0	0	3
Daisy	21	10	0	0	69	0	0	0
Eric	17	19	3	2	59	0	0	0
Fleur	16	0	0	1	83	0	0	1
Gemma	61	18	0	0	21	0	0	0
Total	27	11	0.5	1	60	0	0	0.5

Key: D = Declarative.   Y = Y/N.
W = Wh- Question.   T = Tag Question.

Table 9.4 *Frequencies of 'can' per recording: declaratives (D) and Y/Ns (Y)*

Child		1	2	3	4	5	6	7	8	9	10	11	12	13	14
								Recording							
D	Alex	0	0	0	0	1	2	1	5	3	3	0	2	0	
Y		0	0	0	0	0	2	2	2	1	2	1	3	2	
D	Betty	1	0	2	0	2	2	3	4	9	7	2	2	4	5
Y		0	0	0	0	0	2	1	2	0	7	0	1	2	2
D	Clare	0	0	0	0	2	1	8	2	0	1	1	19		
Y		0	0	0	0	0	0	3	0	2	1	1	3		
D	Daisy	0	2	1	1	0	1	0	1	0	1	2	4		
Y		0	0	0	2	0	0	0	0	0	1	1	2		
D	Eric	1	0	0	1	0	1	1	2	2	3	1	3	4	
Y		0	0	0	0	0	2	0	2	2	3	6	3	3	
D	Fleur	0	0	1	0	0	3	0	1	0	1	24	1		
Y		0	0	0	0	0	0	0	0	0	0	0	0		
D	Gemma	1	2	0	1	0	0	15	3	25	7	4	3		
Y		0	0	0	0	0	0	0	0	10	2	4	2		

in declaratives and Y/N inversions. Two features are of particular interest. Firstly, the pattern for all Y/N users other than Daisy is of emergence followed soon after by regular and consistent usage. Secondly, although the affirmative declarative clearly *emerges* before the affirmative Y/N, the further *development* of declarative 'can' in terms of frequency of use takes place concurrently with the development of the interrogative. Again, Gemma is an exception; an increase in the frequency of declarative 'can' in Gemma's Sample 7 is not accompanied by the emergence of Y/Ns, and this is consistent with other evidence from Gemma which shows her as a child for whom syntactic complexity and order of emergence are more closely matched than for most other children, and two samples later (Rec. 9) a second increase in the frequency of declarative 'can' coincides with the first ten Y/Ns (Sample 9, 2;4.9).

For five children, then, and especially for Alex, the order of development of declarative and polar interrogative uses of 'can' is not as clear-cut as would be predicted by syntactic complexity. This has implications when one considers the possible role of Y/Ns in the speech addressed to the child. In Chapter 11 evidence will be presented of a statistical relationship between the frequency of Y/Ns in input and the rate of auxiliary verb learning in children. One problem in explaining such a result has been in discovering a possible route from the question forms the child hears to the declarative forms which are used first (Fletcher, 1983; 1985). If, however, there are some verbs in the auxiliary system for which declarative and interrogative development is concurrent (and perhaps even complementary) rather than consecutive (and additive), such a relationship might be easier to explain. The question of input will be considered in detail in Chapters 10 and 11.

9.3.1 Absence of CAN (Y) for Fleur – a functional explanation

It will have been observed that for Fleur there is no record of Y/N inversions containing 'can'. Taken together with her almost excessive use of 'can't' this feature is of sufficient interest to warrant a closer examination of both spontaneous and elicited data. If Fleur has developed an understanding of the syntax for producing Y/Ns with 'can' or other auxiliaries in initial position, but does not do so spontaneously, this could point to a functional explanation.

For Fleur the development of modal meanings in Y/Ns begins in Sample 3 (2;3.11) with three 'semantically modalized utterances' (Stephany, 1986). These utterances contain no modal verb, but their modal meaning is suggested by the linguistic and extralinguistic context (see also Klima and Bellugi, 1966, pp. 347 and 349). They will be referred to here as *Contextually Modalised*. As in the two examples quoted below, Fleur's Y/Ns, both in elicited imitation and in spontaneous speech, are syntactically complete but for the verb 'can':

> F: you see baa lamb?
> R: ask Humpty if he can hear you
> F: ⟨you⟩ hear me? (*Fleur, Rec. 3, 2;3.11*)

It is interesting that 'can' has already co-occurred with 'see' in declaratives in Recording 2 (2;2.14) and will shortly do so with 'hear' in Recording 5 (2;4.22), but it is only in Recording 6 (2;5.15) that Fleur includes 'can' in a Y/N in the imitation test, even though the item also contained the main verb 'see'. It then disappears for the next three samples, but re-emerges for Recordings 10, 11 and 12, albeit in a non-inverted form in Sample 10 (2;8.10). Therefore, while spontaneous speech shows no sign of 'can' in Y/Ns (except for a single non-inverted case in Sample 7), there is evidence from elicited imitation that Fleur has some understanding of its use in this function. Interestingly, this development in elicited speech coincides with the emergence of isolated single tokens of 'does' and 'shall' in spontaneous Y/N inversions, as well as four auxiliary forms in tag questions in the final two recordings. However, such instances are rare and despite attempts on eight different occasions, Fleur never imitates 'does' (Y/N).

The most that can be said, therefore, is that by the end of the study Fleur was developing an understanding of the syntax of auxiliaries in Y/Ns, having demonstrated knowledge of the function of Y/Ns at a much earlier stage. One factor may have been limitations on her processing capacity, which could have precluded the retention of the auxiliary in polar interrogatives. It will be recalled that Fleur's MLUS development was slower than for the other children, despite the fact that it had been relatively high during Samples 1 and 2. In addition, she was the only subject who failed to imitate sentences of over five morphemes. On the other hand, instances of the contextually modalised Y/N function are also rare, only occurring in Samples 3 and 7. This raises the question of whether Fleur has a different functional orientation, or whether she has a different means of realising the functions for which Y/Ns containing modals are used by the other children. This, and the related question of Gemma's preference for the affirmative form of CAN, will be illuminated firstly by examining the contexts of use, and secondly by a detailed coding of the meaning and function of CAN.

9.4 Range of linguistic contexts of 'can' and 'can't'

Tables 9.5 and 9.7 show cumulative types and tokens of the verbs which co-occur with 'can' and 'can't'. These are presented cumulatively across occasions. Tables 9.6 and 9.8 then indicate which verbs these figures refer to for each child.

Results indicate a slow and steady extension to the range of contexts in which 'can't' appears (Table 9.5); rapid increases in range do not occur, even where there is an increase in frequency and an examination of the utterances themselves in conjunction with the figures above shows that in several cases there is an early period dominated by a single verb. This is true of Alex, Betty, Eric, and especially Fleur whose range of types in Table 9.5 is consistently low in comparison with the number of tokens produced. For

Table 9.5 *Cumulative types and tokens of verbs which co-occur with 'can't'*

Child							Recording							
	1	2	3	4	5	6	7	8	9	10	11	12	13	14
Alex	1/3	1/3	3/5	3/5	5/8	6/11	6/11	6/12	8/17	11/24	11/24	12/35	13/37	
Betty	1/3	1/4	3/6	6/15	7/20	8/25	8/30	9/31	9/37	12/52	12/59	12/63	12/68	13/71
Clare			2/5	3/9	3/10	4/13	5/17	7/22	9/25	11/32	12/34	13/37		
Daisy		1/1	1/1	1/1	2/2	3/5	4/7	9/12	11/16	12/19	12/23	15/28		
Eric		1/6	1/6	1/6	1/6	3/11	3/13	4/16	6/20	6/20	7/24	8/40	11/48	
Fleur	1/7	4/31	4/55	4/63	6/75	7/91	9/100	9/119	11/130	12/138	15/150	15/153		
Gemma		1/1	1/1	2/3	2/3	2/4	2/6	4/12	4/15	5/16	5/16	5/16		

Table 9.6 *Frequencies of verbs co-occurring with 'can't'*

	Subjects								
Verb	Alex	Betty	Clare	Daisy	Eric	Fleur	Gemma	Total	%
do	14	24	9	2	21	105	7	182	46.7
put	2	6	2	5	6	26		47	12.1
get		12	11	6	4	1	5	39	10.0
catch	3	6	4	1	2	1	1	18	4.6
go	2	3	1	1	3	3		13	3.3
see	2		1	1	1	6	2	13	3.3
find	1	4	3	1		1	1	11	2.8
remember		6			1			7	1.8
squeak					7			7	1.8
hear		3		1		2		6	1.5
take				3		2		5	1.3
draw		2	1	1				4	1.0
move	4							4	1.0
know		2				1		3	0.8
read				2		1		3	0.8
say	3							3	0.8
fit			1	1				2	0.5
open	1					1		2	0.5
play	1				1			2	0.5
pull	2							2	0.5
sit			1	1				2	0.5
climb			1					1	0.3
come	1							1	0.3

	37	71	37	28	48	153	16	390	98.6
cut		1						1	0.3
eat		1						1	0.3
have					1			1	0.3
make			1					1	0.3
miss			1					1	0.3
pick					1			1	0.3
press						1		1	0.3
reach				1				1	0.3
stand				1				1	0.3
stick						1		1	0.3
tell	1							1	0.3
wind						1		1	0.3
write		1						1	0.3
Total	37	71	37	28	48	153	16	390	98.6

three of these children the main verb in question is 'do'. In fact early co-occurrences of 'can't' are restricted to a small set of main verbs. If the first three main verbs to co-occur with 'can't' is taken for each child, the total range for the seven children is only nine verbs, the most common being 'do' (six children), 'get' (five children), and 'find', 'see' and 'put' (two children each). In addition, Table 9.6 indicates the extent to which usage of 'can't' is dominated by a small number of main verbs over the period of the study. Although there are thirty-six main verb types and 390 tokens, three verbs ('do', 'put', and 'get') account for 68.8% of co-occurrences, figures which are almost identical to those obtained for verbs co-occurring with 'don't' (see Table 8.5, p. 123).

The analysis of contexts for 'can' presents a very different picture (Table 9.7). There is no evidence here of stereotyped usage and the set of main verbs first used by the children is more heterogeneous than those first used with 'can't'. The first recorded main verb is different for each child, though taking the first three yields only a slightly wider range (twelve verbs). Again, main verb 'do' is among the first three to be used by most children (five out of seven). This picture is complemented by Table 9.8 where it can be seen that although there are fewer main verb tokens than for 'can't', the number of types is greater. Here, the three most frequent verbs ('do', 'have', and 'put') account for only 45.5% of co-occurrences.

For 'can' there are also identifiable points for three children (Gemma, Fleur, and Clare) at which the range of contexts for 'can' increases. For Gemma and Clare these correspond with the emergence of Y/Ns (see Table 9.4). It seems therefore that for these two children the extension of 'can' to a new syntactic frame is accompanied by or follows a wider understanding of its privileges of occurrence.

The only other frequency surge of the affirmative declarative (Clare, Rec. 12, 3;0.1) suggests more repetitive usage. There are only four types to nineteen tokens on this occasion, and an inspection of transcripts shows why. As was usual, Clare chose to play with the 'funny faces', a set of interchangeable hats, chins, pairs of eyes, mouths and noses which combine like a jigsaw. This time, Clare decided that each face she designed was to represent a member of her family. 'Can', in combination with 'have' was used to allocate parts of the face to the chosen family member. The result was a paradigm similar to a 'sentence switchboard' for foreign language learners:

Table 9.7 *Cumulative types and tokens of verbs which co-occur with 'can'*

Child	Recording													
	1	2	3	4	5	6	7	8	9	10	11	12	13	14
Alex	1/1				1/1	3/4	4/6	5/12	5/15	6/16	7/17	10/22	11/24	
Betty		1/1	1/1	1/1	2/3	4/7	4/10	7/16	7/24	11/35	12/36	12/38	14/44	15/48
Clare					1/2	2/3	7/10	7/10	7/12	7/13	7/15	10/34		
Daisy		1/2	1/3	2/4	2/4	2/4	2/4	2/4	2/4	4/6	5/7	8/13		
Eric	1/1	1/1	1/1	2/2	2/2	3/5	3/6	5/10	6/14	6/21	8/27	10/34	11/41	
Fleur			1/1	1/1	1/1	4/4	4/5	4/6	4/6	5/7	10/24	10/25		
Gemma	1/1	2/3	2/3	3/4	3/4	3/4	10/18	10/21	21/51	23/58	25/65	26/68		

Table 9.8 *Frequencies of verbs co-occurring with 'can'*

Verb				Subjects				Total	%
	Alex	Betty	Clare	Daisy	Eric	Fleur	Gemma		
do	5	13	4	1	13	2	12	50	19.8
have	7	6	16		7	1	4	41	16.2
put	1	5	4	4	3	7	1	24	9.5
go	1			1	7	2	5	16	6.3
see	1	6		3	2	1	3	16	6.3
catch		2	3				5	10	4.0
read	3	2	1		1		3	10	4.0
pick							7	7	2.8
ride						7		7	2.8
get		3			3			6	2.4
find							5	5	2.0
play	2	1			2			5	2.0
sit	1			1	1		2	5	2.0
draw		3		1				4	1.6
take						1	3	4	1.6
eat		1				2		3	1.2
swim			2				1	3	1.2
be		1					1	2	0.8
count							2	2	0.8
dig		2						2	0.8
hear		1					1	2	0.8
join							2	2	0.8
push							2	2	0.8

	24	48	34	13	41	25	68	253	100.5
bend							1	1	0.4
boing[a]							1	1	0.4
build							1	1	0.4
carry			1					1	0.4
come	1							1	0.4
cuddle					1			1	0.4
cut				1				1	0.4
drive						1		1	0.4
hang		1						1	0.4
help	1							1	0.4
keep	1							1	0.4
let			1					1	0.4
listen							1	1	0.4
look					1			1	0.4
mix				1				1	0.4
move	1							1	0.4
open	1							1	0.4
rest			1					1	0.4
ring						1		1	0.4
sing		1						1	0.4
squeeze							1	1	0.4
squirt							1	1	0.4
tie							1	1	0.4
turn							1	1	0.4
work			1					1	0.4
Total	24	48	34	13	41	25	68	253	100.5

[a] bounce.

[Subject NP] + 'can' + have + [Object NP]

Mummy	a funny mouth
Daddy	a funny chin
Neil	those eyes
Linda	a head
that	a neck
	that ⟨hair/head⟩
	that mouth

With regard to the distinctive styles of using CAN which have been seen in Fleur and Gemma, it can be seen from Tables 9.5 and 9.6 just how context restricted Fleur's use of 'can't' is, given her clear preference for this form. Gemma, on the other hand, whose preferred form is 'can', uses the latter in combination with twenty-seven different main verbs by her last recording.

Once again the figures showing developments over time fail to discriminate clearly between the children, and the general trend seems to be one of piece-meal development apart from more rapid extension of the usage of 'can' at one point for Gemma, Clare, and Fleur. The analysis discriminates more effectively between the development of 'can' and 'can't'. Even when Fleur's contribution is removed, the latter is more context restricted than the former.

In order to throw further light on the distinctive features of Gemma's and Fleur's usage of CAN, particularly Gemma's preference for the affirmative form and the possibility of a connection between Fleur's lack of Y/Ns and her stereotypical usage of 'can't', an analysis of modal meanings will now be undertaken.

9.5 The meaning and function of CAN

The problem with any analysis of modality in child language is the complexity of the system which is developing. The interaction of mood, tense, illocution-ary force, and degrees and types of modal meaning, not to mention prosodic features, gives rise to an enormous range of subtlety of expression in which such factors as extralinguistic context, including situation, relative status of speaker and addressee, and the knowledge and beliefs they share, may deter-mine the form and subsequent interpretation of an utterance (Lakoff, 1972). As Leech has pointed out, modal notions such as Permission and Necessity 'become remoulded by the psychological pressures which influence everyday communication between human beings: factors such as condescension, polite-ness and irony' (Leech, 1971, pp. 66–7).

Such complexity is reflected in the multiplicity, and sometimes incompati-bility of approaches to modality in the literature. Several of these 'semantic proposals' are summarised in Palmer (1979, pp. 10–16). They range from the speech act analysis of Boyd and Thorne (1969), to Leech's (1969) componential analysis. Elsewhere, attempts are made to take up an intermediate position between semantics and pragmatics, and relate meaning and conversational context to modal logic (e.g. Groenendijk and Stokhof, 1975). A basic meaning approach has been taken by Ehrman (1966), Haegeman (1983), and Perkins (1983a,b). Others (Twadell, 1960; Joos, 1964) have based their analysis on the diversity of meaning expressed by various modals, assigning these to two-, or even three-dimensional matrices. A fundamental question, therefore, is whether to treat each modal as having a basic, or core meaning (monosemy), or whether a single modal form can be regarded as having several meanings (polysemy) though Coates (1983) goes some way towards reconciling this apparent incompatibility (see Perkins, 1984). Related to this is the extent to which modal meanings are identifiable as discrete categories (Leech and Coates, 1980). These two problems have fundamental relevance for the study of child language, as will be seen below.

The following serves as an illustration of the problem. Halliday (1985) analyses the Probability and Obligational meanings of the modal system in relation to polarity, and 'value' (referred to elsewhere as 'degree' of modality). Even Halliday's 'thumbnail sketch', as he calls it (p. 339), produces a three-dimensional matrix capable of containing forty-eight categories. He continues, 'These are, of course, only the broad outlines; the actual number of distinctions that can be recognised as systematic within the modality system runs well into the thousands' (Halliday, 1985, p. 335). Other dimensions include Modality/Modulation (Halliday, 1970) and Potential (Halliday, 1985), Subjectivity/Objectivity (Lyons, 1977), and Formal Explicitness (Perkins, 1983a,b).

The child language researcher is faced therefore with the dilemma of determining which of the many possible semantic contrasts are relevant, or have psychological reality for the stage of linguistic and cognitive development of the subjects under investigation. Not surprisingly, there has been much variation in approach, to some extent determined by the age of subjects. Although a great deal of work on modal verbs has concentrated almost exclusively on syntax (e.g. Major, 1974), several studies, some with children older than those being considered here, have looked at meaning and function. Kuczaj, for example, tests the Form-Function Hypothesis by looking at the relationship between the development of modal forms and modal meanings in fifteen children between 2;6 and 5;6. His coding follows the traditional classification of modality (Permission, Ability, Possibility, Obligation/Necessity) with the addition of Hypothetical, and three categories of futurity (Kuczaj, 1982b). Hirst and Weil (1982) studied comprehension of degrees (strength) of epistemic and deontic modality in fifty-four children between the ages of 3;0 and 6;6, while Wells combines these two approaches in a two-dimensional matrix consisting of degrees (Possible, Predictable, Necessary, Neutral) and types of modality (Inference, Likelihood, Constraint, Potential, Performative) (Wells, 1979a, p. 254). Excluding the Neutral type, which by its very nature is nonmodalised, this gives a total of fifteen cells. An earlier scheme (Wells, 1975) was based on Halliday's original (1970) distinction between Modality and Modulation, Modality being the equivalent of Epistemic Modality (expression of the speaker's commitment to the truth of the proposition), and coded according to categories which are in practice a mixture of degree and type (Certain, Possible/Probable, Inference). Modulation includes Palmer's (1979) Deontic and Dynamic modalities which express meanings of Obligation/ Necessity and Potential.

Shields (1974) studied the development of modal auxiliaries in 107 children aged 2;6–4;11. Just as Wells (1979a) has separate categories for performatives and other types of modal meaning (i.e. either performative function or modal meaning is coded, but not both) so Shields allocates to each modal verb a set of mutually exclusive categories of which some are semantic, others pragmatic. 'Can', for example, could be allocated to the semantic categories of Possibility and Ability, or to the pragmatic categories of Role (the use of 'can' to allocate roles in imaginary play contexts) and Permission/Refusal, a category which combines Wells' Performative (Permission) and Constraint (Permission) categories.

Finally, Perkins (1983a) relates modal verbs in 6- to 12-year-olds to age, sex and social class variables. Modal meanings are related to number and person of the verb subject, and are analysed according to the theoretical framework developed in his previous ten chapters. Basically, Perkins attempts to explain how the modal system expresses the constraints on, and the potential of the truth of propositions and the occurrence of events. He does so by reference to rational, social, and natural laws, and to the situation or circumstances in which these laws operate. These situational characteristics can be of three types; they can be evidence, a deontic source, or they can be empirical circumstances. The core meaning of MUST, by Perkins' analysis, is that by dint of the authority of the speaker (deontic source), social laws (or conventions) entail the occurrence of an event (Perkins, 1983a,b).

Of course, it does not necessarily follow that a theoretical framework derived from an adult speech corpus, or from the judgements of mature speakers, fulfils criteria of relevance and psychological reality, even if the utterances under scrutiny do fall relatively easily into the categories devised. The appeal of Perkins' framework, however, lies in the ease with which it can accommodate performatives which are predicted on different underlying modal meanings. The sentence # 'You can do it!', for example, can function as an indirect request (performative) by appealing to the inherent characteristics of the addressee (ability meaning), to the authority of the speaker (permission meaning), or to external conditions (circumstantial possibility). Neither does Perkins' analysis preclude an approach which would allow the child a developing understanding of the sources of constraint and potential, and the laws which operate on them to allow and restrict freedom of action and expression.

For these reasons the analysis below has been strongly influenced by Perkins' work. However, Leech and Coates (1980) and Coates (1983) draw attention to problems of the indeterminacy of modal meanings, which also have a bearing on the interpretation of children's utterances. Three types of indeterminacy are identified:

1. Gradience: the tendency of a modal meaning to fall at some point on a cline linking poles of meaning, for example a continuum from Ability to Root (as opposed to Epistemic) Possibility, or from Permission to Possibility. 'Every believer can be a faithful distributor of the gospel' (Coates, 1983, p. 14), for example, lies somewhere between Ability and Root Possibility.
2. Ambiguity: the utterance 'He must understand that we mean business' (Coates, 1983, p. 16) can be understood as either Epistemic (= 'I strongly believe that he understands . . . '), or Root Possibility (= 'Circumstances make it vital for him to understand . . .'), or even Deontically (= 'Somebody go and make sure that he does understand . . .').
3. Merger: a type of ambiguity where meanings merge, but where understanding is not hindered. In the sentence 'Rutherford suggested to Marsden that he should follow this up' (Coates, 1983, p. 17), the meaning of 'weak obligation' merges with the 'quasi-subjunctive' meaning, but there is no danger of this leading to a misunderstanding.

Leech and Coates (1980) suggest that it will be the non-fuzzy poles of their clines of modal meaning which will be established first in the language of children and support this view with evidence from Anderson (1975) that children's concept boundaries may become more fuzzy with age. In the case of CAN therefore one would expect the clear-cut Ability, Permission and Root Possibility meanings to emerge first as prototypes, followed only at a later stage by indeterminate tokens.

On the other hand, it might be the case that the first meanings to emerge are primitive core meanings such as a notion of Possibility founded on nothing more than an awareness (in the case of CAN) of constraint or potential. The development of modal meanings would consist of gradually understanding and differentiating between the combinations of laws and circumstances under which truths of propositions, or the occurrence of events are, or are not precluded. Indeterminacy would therefore occur from the earliest stages.

9.5.1 Coding categories for CAN in previous research

Since Wells (1979a) provides the most fine-grained analysis, his definitions will be used as a base-line for interpreting the categories of other researchers. Two of Wells' degrees of modality (Possible and Predictable) and all five types of modality (Potential, Constraint, Likelihood, Inference, Performative) encompass CAN, yielding eleven meanings. Examples are taken from Wells (1979a, p.255):

1. Potential × Possible (Ability): 'I can write my own name now.'
2. Potential × Possible (Intrinsic Potential): 'My bike can go very fast.'
3. Constraint × Possible (Lack of Constraint: Permitted): 'I can play outside till tea-time.'
4. Constraint × Possible (Circumstantial Possibility): 'There's nothing coming. We can cross now.'
5. Likelihood × Possible: No example given.
6. Inference × Possible: No example given.
7. Performative × Possible (Request Permission): 'Can I go out to play?'
8. Performative × Possible (Grant/Refuse Permission): 'You can't have that.'
9. Performative × Possible (Request Action): No example given.
10. Performative × Possible (Offer Action): No example given.
11. Performative × Predictable (Command): No example given.

Kuczaj (1982b) identifies six meanings for 'can/can't'. Where appropriate, Wells' approximate equivalent is given in brackets:

1. Ability (Potential × Possible)
2. Willingness (Offer Action)
3. Permission (Performative or Constraint)
4. Possibility (Possible × Constraint/Likelihood/Inference)
5. Hypothetical (Likelihood × Possible)
6. Future of Prediction

Perkins (1983a) uses four categories, three semantic and one performative:

1. Ability (Potential × Possible)
2. Permission (Performative or Constraint)
3. Circumstantial Possibility (Constraint × Possible)
4. Suggestion (Perkins' example is: 'That can be a bus station' (p. 144) – this can be interpreted as Intrinsic Potential, but it is also Performative × Predictable – see discussion below.)

Shields (1974) makes a five-way distinction of which two are based on function:

1. Ability/Inability (Potential × Possible)
2. Permission/Refusal (Performative or Constraint)
3. Possibility/Impossibility (Possible × Constraint/Likelihood/Inference)
4. Rule (as Shields acknowledges, this is a subcategory of Possibility/Impossi-

bility. She lists it separately because it involves generalisations from experience, in which case it would be coded under Inference in Wells' scheme.)
5. Role (the equivalent of Perkins' Suggestion).

Anomalies in the above schemes arise where a single token has to be assigned to either a functional category (Performative, Suggestion, Role) or a semantic category. Conceptually it would be neater to think in terms of a three-dimensional matrix: Type of Modality × Degree of Modality × Illocutionary Force. Wells' scheme has the advantage that Performatives can be coded according to degrees of modality. It does not, however, recognise that Performative utterances can be predicated on different *types* of modality. Take for example Perkins' category of Suggestion: 'That can be a bus station.' If stating the utterance allocates a new role to the referent then it is performative. In Austin's classification this would be exercitive: the child is exercising 'powers, rights, or influence' (Austin, 1962, p. 151). The problem is that Perkins describes this example as one where natural laws act on empirical circumstances. If this is the case, how does it differ from Ability (or Wells' Intrinsic Potential), which is also derived from 'empirical circumstances originating within the subject of the sentence' (Perkins, 1983a, p. 144)? The answer is that there is a difference in function rather than modality. In discussions relating to Austin's (1962) Constative/Performative distinction, attention is often drawn to the fact that performative utterances are not concerned with truth values (e.g. Robinson, 1972), but what is happening here is that performing the act of role allocation is dependent on the truth value of the underlying proposition that the inherent characteristics of the referent do not preclude its functioning as a bus station. Having established this, the effective transfer of role will depend on social factors such as the relative status of other participants in the interaction, and the rules which have been negotiated to regulate their fantasy play. In cases like this the modal meaning is a statement of the felicity condition which allows the speech act to achieve its purpose, and an adequate analysis of CAN in performatives has to take this into account.

9.5.2 Coding scheme for CAN
In the light of all that has been said above, it is with some hesitation that one attempts to code modal meanings for young children at all. Firstly, there is the potential problem of indeterminacy and its possible effects on reliability. Secondly, as was observed above, early usage of modals is generally assumed to be action oriented with little or no access to the full range of adult meanings (e.g. Fletcher, 1979). On the other hand, according to Wells (1979a) meanings of permission and ability precede performative meanings.

Unfortunately there is no way to judge the psychological reality of modal meanings in spontaneous speech samples. Nevertheless if we assume that the child begins with a primitive core meaning which is progressively differentiated, it is only through the linguistic and extralinguistic contexts of use that this process can occur and the same information can inform research into the course of development and any individual differences which may arise. The coding scheme outlined below attempts therefore to attribute a small number of semantic distinctions on the basis of factors in the linguistic and extralinguistic context which indicate Perkins' (1983a) laws and circumstances: social laws and a deontic source give a Permission meaning; natural laws and inherent characteristics give Ability; natural laws and external circumstances give Circumstantial Possibility, and the pairing of rational laws and evidence gives Epistemic Possibility. Performatives are dealt with in two ways. Any performative utterance is given an additional semantic tag from one of the above categories if performative usage appeared to be predicated on a modal meaning. Otherwise it is possible to code for Performative meaning only, as in Wells' scheme:

1. ABILITY: 'Can't catch anything' [Fishing game] (*Eric: 2;10.19*)
   'What can it do?' [Squeezy toy] (*Eric: 2;8.17*)
2. PERMISSION (Nonperformative): 'She can't' (= The girl next door is not allowed to play with Alex's toys) (*Alex: 3;2.4*)
3. CIRCUMSTANTIAL POSSIBILITY: 'He can't go to sleep' [The doll can't sleep because of the noise] (*Alex: 3;2.4*)
4. EPISTEMIC POSSIBILITY: # 'That can't be mine'
5. PERFORMATIVE (ABILITY): 'Can you do it?' [Mr Men puzzle] (= Will you. . .?) (*Eric: 2;5.21*)
6. PERFORMATIVE (PERMISSION): 'Can I go (= have a go) with the money now?' [Wants to put researcher's money into a toy telephone] (*Eric: 2;8.21*)
7. PERFORMATIVE (CIRCUMSTANTIAL POSSIBILITY): 'Now you can read it' (= Now that I've read the book, you must read it to me) (*Gemma: 2;5.7*)

9.5.3 Evaluation of the coding

A total of 807 tokens of CAN were coded. Because of the difficulties of coding for modal meaning, all instances were coded twice and overall agreement was 95%. Reliability, however, is only a necessary condition for validity, not a sufficient one, and this relatively high figure conceals what were some very real problems. It was certainly not the case (as suggested in Leech and Coates, 1980) that indeterminacy is less of a feature of modality in child language, and in one way this is reassuring since indeterminacy seems to be part of the very nature of the modal system. It also suggests that children do not begin with one or more stereotypical, clear-cut meanings but with a basic meaning for each modal verb which will continue to be the foundation of a more finely-grained understanding. Some of the coding problems are illustrated below.

Firstly, in child language, as in adult language, many uses of CAN lie somewhere on a gradient between Circumstantial Possibility and Ability (e.g. 'I can't do this 'cos they're too hard', Betty: 2;9.8). A smaller number lie on a gradient between Circumstantial Possibility and Permission ('Can't draw on this', Betty: 3;1.2), and an even smaller number of cases were ambiguous between Permission and Ability ('I can put this one on' [a cassette in the cassette player], Daisy: 2;11.21). To enlarge on the examples given above, when Betty says 'I can't do this 'cos they're too hard', two factors conspire to restrict potential action: her own inherent skills, and external circumstances consisting of the characteristics of the funny face jigsaws she was trying to do. We have no way of knowing which, *if any*, of these sources of restriction were most salient for her. Similarly, Betty's 'Can't draw on this' referred to one of the researcher's flashcards. Was the statement motivated by the knowledge that social laws preclude scribbling on objects belonging to others, or was she referring to the fact that the flashcard already had pictures on, and was therefore unsuitable for drawing? It is possible that she was doing neither. For the gradients Ability–Possibility and Permission–Possibility these problems were dealt with during coding by allocating tokens to the category which seemed most salient, but giving them an additional coding to show which other area of meaning appeared to be present in the context. Ambiguous cases were treated as unanalysable.

A second problem was that CAN frequently co-occurred with 'private verbs' of perception (see Quirk et al., 1985) such as 'see', 'hear', and 'feel', in sentences such as: 'I still can't see it' (Eric: 2;9.8). Although this might look like an ability meaning, private verbs express states which lack the subject-as-agent orientation, associated with ability. One analysis is to treat CAN as redundant in these contexts. As Palmer points out, there is little difference between 'I see the moon' and 'I can see the moon' (Palmer, 1979, p. 74). On the other hand, Perkins' (1983a) position is that CAN relates the verb of perception to external circumstances and the same view is taken here. Usually this usage was coded as Circumstantial Possibility. Occasionally, however, the context was such that the vision of the grammatical subject was salient. This occurred because one of the toys provided was a one-eyed doll. In this context, 'Want to see 〈only〉 he can't . can he?' (Clare: 2;10.18) was coded as Ability.

Thirdly, as could be predicted from Austin (1962), the dividing line between performative and nonperformative utterances is not always clear. A large number of tokens have been coded as Ability, Permission, or Circumstantial Possibility when the child's intention was not overtly performative. Nevertheless, many of these clearly have 'further implications for action' (Wells, 1982b), at least in as far as the effect on the addressee is concerned. A common example is the utterance: '(I) can't do it'. Depending on the context, it can be interpreted as a statement of inability, a refusal to do something, or a request to the addressee to do something for you. In Fleur's case, this sentence was nearly always used to initiate exchanges, and was accompanied by passing objects to the addressee. For example, if she couldn't put two Lego pieces together and these were handed to her mother or to the researcher while the sentence was spoken, a Performative was indicated. Whether this was predicated on a meaning of ability is doubtful, but it was coded as such to denote that the context was one where the child's limitations would have prevented a certain course of action. At other times the same utterance could be much more difficult to interpret. 'Can't do it' or 'Can't' often function as a refusal and were used, for example, by Alex if he didn't feel like starting, or continuing the imitation test, or as a way of verbalising non-cooperation with his parents' wishes. As in Wells' scheme these were coded as performative when the intention was clear. The intention was not always sufficiently clear, however, and utterances of this form may occasionally have been wrongly treated as nonperformative if the intention was to transfer turns during games, change the activity, or request the addressee to perform the action.

It is with such reservations in mind that the results of the coding are presented.

9.5.4 Results

Totals and percentages of meanings of each CAN form are given in Table 9.9 below. There were no tokens of Epistemic Possibility and this category has been omitted from the tables.

It is evident from these figures that usage of CAN arises predominantly from contexts where actions and events appear to be constrained or made possible by Ability. This tendency is even more pronounced if Performative utterances are allocated to the modal meaning on which they are predicated, though, as might be expected, interrogative Performatives are usually predicated on a Permission meaning. This can be seen from Table 9.10. Here, tags are excluded because in most cases the modal form in the tag is the same modal as in the matrix clause, but with opposite polarity. The verb

Table 9.9 *Percentages of meanings of CAN forms pooled for all children and all recordings*

Meaning	CAN forms and syntactic frames						
	can't (D)	can (D)	can (Y)	can (T)	can't (T)	can (Wh)	Total
Ability	39.9	13.1	0.4	0.1	0.1	0.4	54.0
Permission	0.9	1.7	0.0	0.2	0.1	0.1	3.1
Circ. Poss.	4.8	5.0	0.9	0.0	0.2	0.1	11.0
Perform.	14.1	6.7	9.5	0.6	0.0	0.0	31.0
Unanalysable	0.4	0.2	0.1	0.0	0.0	0.2	0.9
							100.0

Key: D = Declarative.   Y = Y/N question.
T = Tag question.   Wh = Wh- question.

in the tag therefore has the same modal meaning as the verb in the matrix clause. Y/N questions have been combined with the very small number of Wh- questions to form an overall question category.

Table 9.10 *Percentages of meanings of* CAN *forms (Performatives only)*

	CAN forms			
Meaning	can't (D)	can (D)	can (Q)	Total
Ability	53.6	14.6	1.9	70.1
Permission	2.4	5.1	8.3	15.8
Circ. Poss.	5.3	7.3	1.5	14.1
				100.0

Key: D = Declarative.
        Q = Wh- and Y/N questions (tags excluded).

One study which relates meanings of C A N to mood and polarity is Shields (1974). Shields' subjects were in playgroups and nurseries and therefore older than the Welsh children, and a context where children are interacting with each other may allow the child greater flexibility in the use of areas of modality which depend on the authority or status of the speaker. Nevertheless it is interesting to compare Shields' results with those above.

The most striking feature of Shields' figures is that 'can' tends to be used when the meaning is Permission, and also tends to be interrogative. 'Can't' tends to be declarative and used for Ability. Permission meanings are the most frequent (43%), followed by Ability (35%) and Possibility (13%). The remainder is accounted for by the Role and Rule categories (see above). The results reported here differ in several respects. Though the negative form is also mainly used for Ability, affirmative C A N is used mainly in declarative mood, also for Ability. In fact, Ability is considerably more frequent than for Shields, and Permission much less frequent. This variation probably reflects the differences in age and context discussed above, and the fact that during most of the study the Welsh children were relatively limited in their use of Y/Ns. At the same time, they had other means, such as the performative use of affirmative and negative declaratives, of expressing their needs and wishes, and of influencing the behaviour of others.

The main purpose of the coding for meaning and function was to throw light on individual differences in the frequency of polarity and mood types. Particularly striking were an apparent emphasis on 'can' rather than 'can't' by Gemma, and a lack of Y/N forms but an inordinate number of instances of 'can't' in declarative mood for Fleur. Table 9.11 shows the percentage of CAN meanings for each child.

The proportion of Performatives is notably higher for Fleur and Alex. An inspection of the data shows that for Alex, this is partly the result of using 'can't' or 'can't do it' as a refusal to act (23.3% of his Performatives), but mainly it is due to an underlying sense of giving, refusing or asking for permission (55.8%). In Fleur's case the reason is different. 'Can't' predicated on Ability accounts for 98.8% of her Performatives. These utterances, which occur regularly from her first speech sample, take the form of either 'can't', or '(I) can't do it' and initiate exchanges as requests for action (see Section 9.5.3). This is a highly effective strategy for Fleur which enables her to influence the behaviour of others without having to learn Performative functions of Y/Ns, and may account for the delay in the development of Y/Ns. It also explains Fleur's stereotypical usage of 'can't' which was identified in Section 9.4.

In the development of CAN, Gemma has been shown to differ from the other children in two important respects. Firstly, in the frequency of forms, Gemma uniquely shows a strong overall emphasis on 'can' rather than 'can't'. Secondly, CAN emerges and develops in various syntactic frames in an order which corresponds more closely with their syntactic complexity than is the case for the remaining children. Table 9.11 suggests that Gemma does not differ substantially from most of the other children in the meanings expressed by CAN. Although the proportion of tokens which appear to express Circumstantial Possibility (17%) is comparatively high, Performatives account for a similar proportion to all other children except Alex and Fleur.

One explanation for these features could be that while other children initially use 'can't' as a Performative to influence the behaviour of others, Gemma achieves similar functions with the affirmative form. At first sight, the evidence seems to be consistent with this hypothesis. Gemma certainly uses the affirmative form as a Performative in declarative sentences.

> you can read it [= I want you to read me the book]
>
> [*Gemma, Rec. 2, 1;10.30*)

She also uses the affirmative form in Y/Ns in Performatives. At 2;4.9 (Rec. 9) 'can' first emerges in polar interrogatives (see Table 9.4), and the ten tokens

Table 9.11 *Percentages of meanings of CAN forms for each child*

Meaning	Subjects						
	Alex	Betty	Clare	Daisy	Eric	Fleur	Gemma
Ability	43.0	56.6	60.9	61.3	60.6	46.6	58.0
Permission	2.0	5.3	2.2	4.8	5.5	1.6	1.0
Circ. Poss.	12.0	13.2	8.7	9.7	8.3	8.9	17.0
Perform.	43.0	22.4	28.3	22.6	25.7	42.9	23.0
Unanalysable	0.0	2.6	0.0	1.6	0.0	0.0	1.0
Totals	100.0	100.1	100.1	100.0	100.1	100.0	100.0

sampled during this recording all appear to be predicated on a deontic source:

> 'can I. . .?' (1 token) to ask permission.
> 'can we. . .?' (6 tokens) to request action *and* ask permission (dual function).
> 'can you. . .?' (3 tokens) to request action.

The six 'can we. . .?' utterances fall into an intermediate category. While on the one hand they request permission to engage in some activity, they also require the interlocutor to perform certain actions which make that activity possible. Hence, 'can we find er fish game?' (Gemma, Rec. 9, 2;4.9) asks the researcher's permission to change the current activity, but also requires him to find and set up the magnetic fishing game.

Gemma clearly does use performative 'can' in both declarative and Y/N interrogative frames. Nevertheless, if the explanation for Gemma's unique 'can'-orientation were to lie in the performative category, we would expect Gemma to be using a lower proportion of performative 'can't' than the other children, and a higher proportion of performative 'can'. It can be seen from Table 9.12 that, while there are some substantial individual differences in these two categories, Gemma does not differ sufficiently from the majority of children to account for the predominance of 'can' in her speech samples. What does emerge from Table 9.12, however, is that the largest category, Ability, is an area where Gemma, in contrast with the other children, tends to use 'can' rather than 'can't' as the vehicle of expression,. While most children use CAN forms to express inability, or lack of potential, Gemma has the reverse tendency. Why this should be the case is a question which an examination of the transcripts does little to illuminate. Nevertheless, it is worth noting that this tendency is already present in Recording 7 (2;2.26) when CAN forms are first produced in quantity. As Table 9.2 showed, Recording 7 contained fifteen tokens of 'can', all of which were in declarative mood. Of these, fourteen were coded as Ability and one as Circumstantial Possibility. This ratio of Ability to other meanings of 'can' is not sustained, however. From Recording 9 (2;4.9) when 'can' emerges in performative Y/Ns and the frequency of Circumstantial Possibility increases, there is a fall in both the absolute and proportional frequency of the ability meaning. As an illustration, if the tokens are pooled for Recordings 7, 8, and 9 and compared with the pooled tokens for Recordings 10, 11, and 12 we find that the absolute frequency of Ability falls from twenty-six to six, and the proportional frequency falls from 49.1% to 27.3%. In the majority (54.4%) of cases of Ability, the referent is Gemma herself, either in the first person singular ('I can pick yours up' (magnetic fish): Rec. 7, 2;2.26), or the third person

Table 9.12 *Meanings of 'can' and 'can't' as a percentage of all tokens of CAN for each child*

Meaning	Subjects						
	Alex	Betty	Clare	Daisy	Eric	Fleur	Gemma
'can'							
Ability	5.0	10.5	15.2	8.1	7.4	12.0	42.0
Permission	1.0	3.3	1.1	4.8	3.7	1.0	1.0
Circ. Poss.	5.0	6.0	3.3	4.8	6.5	3.1	15.0
Perform.	24.0	19.7	28.3	12.9	23.9	0.5	21.0
'can't'							
Ability	38.0	46.1	45.7	53.2	53.2	34.6	16.0
Permission	1.0	2.0	1.1	0.0	1.8	0.5	0.0
Circ. Poss.	7.0	7.2	5.4	4.8	1.8	5.8	2.0
Perform.	19.0	2.6	0.0	9.7	1.8	42.4	2.0
'can' and 'can't'							
Unanalysable	0.0	2.6	0.0	1.6	0.0	0.0	1.0
Totals	100.0	100.0	100.1	99.9	100.1	99.9	100.0

singular ('Boo [= Gemma] can build it' [Lego]: Rec. 4, 2;0.18), but it is also interesting that from the earliest recording Gemma is also using 'can' with animate second and third person singular subjects.

The basis for differences between Gemma and the other children in sequence of emergence and distribution of C A N forms appears, therefore, to lie in a motivation during the early development of C A N to express the potential of herself and others to carry out various actions and intentions. While the other children in the study draw attention to constraints on behaviour through the negative C A N form, it is the lack of such constraints which is more salient for Gemma.

9.6 Summary and discussion

1. C A N was the earliest modal verb to occur for six children, and the most frequent to occur for all seven. This is in keeping with other accounts of the development of the modals.

2. An examination of the distribution of C A N showed that for six children 'can't' outnumbers 'can', in one case by a ratio of 5:1. The exception is Gemma who uses 'can' four times more frequently than 'can't'. Sequence of emergence and subsequent development also differ for Gemma. For the group as a whole, *emergence* tends to follow the pattern:

can't (D) → can (D) → can (Y/N) → can't (Y/N)

Further *development*, that is to say the production of more than isolated, sporadic tokens, follows a slightly different sequence. Declarative 'can't' again precedes Declarative 'can', but the affirmative form tends to develop concurrently in declaratives and Y/Ns. This order of development is different for Gemma in several respects. Firstly, in both emergence and development 'can' (D) precedes 'can't' (D). Secondly, 'can' in Y/Ns, which suddenly emerges with a relatively high frequency in a variety of performative linguistic contexts, follows the development of both 'can' (D) and 'can't' (D). In their analytic sequence these features of C A N parallel other aspects of Gemma's auxiliary verb learning. At the same time it can also be seen that the imbalance between 'can' and 'can't' continues even after 'can't' has become more frequent. It was shown that Performative usage cannot account for this phenomenon. Instead, it was found that Gemma was oriented towards the expression of affirmative Ability meanings, particularly during the early stages of the development of C A N.

3. Differences between 'can' and 'can't' were noted in their development across a range of linguistic contexts. Whereas usage of 'can't' was highly stereotyped during the early stages, and subsequently developed piecemeal,

'can' was more heterogeneous in the range of lexical verbs with which it co-occurred, and for three children (Gemma, Clare, and Fleur) relatively rapid increases in range could be identified. This is consistent with the view that children's understanding of 'can't' in particular is initially restricted in respect of syntax, function, and semantics.

4. In the development of Y/Ns, contextually modalised utterances frequently preceded Y/Ns which contained 'can' but non-inverted Y/Ns containing 'can' were almost completely absent.

5. It was pointed out that the literature on the development of modality contains a fundamental contradiction. On the one hand, it has been argued that only a performative meaning can be attributed to the modal verbs produced by the 2-year-old. On the other hand, Wells' coding of auxiliary meanings expressed by the sixty younger Bristol children shows Permission and Ability meanings to precede performative usage of CAN. Two possible explanations were advanced for this discrepancy: misinterpretation of the function of the child's utterance and individual differences in the extent to which interpersonal functions are effected by modal verbs, particularly CAN. These two possibilities will be examined in turn.

The analysis of meanings of CAN shows that for this coding scheme, there was an overall majority of tokens which expressed a nonperformative meaning, most frequently Ability. However, there were serious difficulties in coding modal meanings and since most performatives and nonperformatives were predicated on an Ability meaning, it was frequently difficult to decide whether a token was primarily interpersonal or a statement relating to the presence or absence of constraints on an action or event. Even if the token could satisfactorily be allocated to the performative or nonperformative category, the indeterminacy of modal meanings could still make coding problematic. It was suggested above that the development of modality might begin with a nonspecific awareness of potential and constraint – the expression of a 'core' Possibility meaning in which the sources of limitations on various behaviours are not yet differentiated. In order to 'acquire' the Permission meaning, the child would have to appreciate the context of social laws and sources of power and authority which give rise to such meanings, and distinguish them from the laws and circumstances which separate them from other types of Possibility. This presupposes a fairly sophisticated knowledge of cause and effect and suggests that the allocation of tokens of CAN to modal categories was, at least partly, unjustified. What the coding scheme has tapped is the linguistic and situational context in which the modal verb is embedded. It is this context which forms the basis of the researcher's coding decisions, and which is also the child's primary source of information during the gradual and perhaps lengthy process of differentiation of the 'core' meaning. It may therefore be the contexts of the child's own output which allow the process of learning modal meanings to take place.

From the outline above it seems possible that discrepancies in the literature with regard to the relative order of emergence of performative and nonperformative usage could result from the unwarranted attribution of complex modal meanings to utterances whose meaning is purely interpersonal, or at most based on a primitive concept of possibility, or constraint. The discussion so far has centred on the pooled data for all occasions, but even if we take a longitudinal perspective and examine the first two recordings for each child during which CAN forms occurred, we still find that in six out of seven cases Performatives are in a minority.

The second suggestion to account for the discrepancy was that the emphasis may vary from child to child. There is certainly evidence that two children (Alex and Fleur) produce a much higher proportion of Performatives, but they develop concurrently with the Ability meaning, and do not clearly precede it. The only child for whom Performatives clearly emerge before the development of modal meanings is Gemma. These consist of a very small number of forms (four) during Recordings 2 and 4.

The issue of the function of early CAN forms, and the place of Performatives in the sequence of development is still to be resolved, but it is fair to say that all the 2-year-olds in this study produced verbs which conveyed at least a primitive modal meaning without being overtly performative.

6. The frequency of Performatives was considerably higher for Alex and Fleur than for the other children. As a proportion of all tokens of CAN, Performatives accounted for 43.0% and 42.9% respectively. The other children fall within a range of 22.4%–28.3%. What is interesting about the figures for Alex and Fleur is not just the similarity of their magnitude in comparison with frequencies for other children, but the fact that such similar frequencies are produced from Performatives which function quite differently. For Alex, Performatives are mainly to do with refusing, asking for, and giving permission and they contain declarative 'can't' and declarative and Y/N 'can'. In addition, Performatives which are apparently predicated on inability serve as a means of refusing to comply with regulatory requests. Fleur's Performatives, on the other hand, contain declarative 'can't' in eighty-one cases out of eighty-two. These utterances are nearly always a request for action predicated on her own inability and this is probably linked with another feature of Fleur's development – the total absence of Y/Ns containing CAN. Once

the syntax of Y/Ns has developed, other children use these as part of their repertoire of means of influencing the behaviour of their interlocutors. By the end of the investigation Fleur is able to imitate Y/Ns containing 'can', and occasionally produce contextually modalised Y/Ns and Y/Ns containing auxiliaries other than CAN. However, she may have found the use of sentences containing 'can't' to be so effective in the contexts sampled that developing 'can' in Y/Ns was unnecessary.

These findings will be related to other aspects of the children's auxiliary verb development in Chapter 12, but first in Chapters 10 and 11 the role of the language addressed to children in the development of the auxiliary verb class will be considered.

PART III

Environmental influences and individual differences in auxiliary verb learning

10 *Previous research*[1]

10.1 Introduction

Since 1977 a number of correlational studies have appeared which examine relationships between linguistic input and subsequent rate of language development. These studies, which have produced conflicting results, have evoked considerable theoretical and methodological controversy. Nearly all have included a measure of the child's auxiliary verb development, and it is this aspect which appears to have given rise to one of the most consistent findings to date, namely an association between Y/Ns in input and rate of auxiliary verb learning.

It will be argued, however, that this finding is not as clear-cut as is often assumed, and it will be shown that the usual explanation for this relationship is unable to account for most of the results published. While the investigation to be described finally produces evidence consistent with current hypotheses relating to the mechanisms involved in extracting the auxiliary from input, it will be stressed that these mechanisms are far from being fully understood.

10.2 Naturalistic studies

Nine naturalistic investigations into relationships between input and subsequent rate of language development use an index of auxiliary verb development. Eight proceed from a common research paradigm and will be treated together. The ninth by Keith Nelson and his colleagues is rather different and will be considered separately. The eight are:

1. Newport, Gleitman and Gleitman, 1977 (NGG)
2. Gleitman, Newport and Gleitman, 1984 (GNG): a reanalysis of NGG.
3. Furrow, Nelson and Benedict, 1979 (FNB).
4. Barnes, Gutfreund, Satterly and Wells, 1983 (BGSW).
5. Hoff-Ginsberg, 1985 (HG1): the influence of discourse features and sentence type.

6. Hoff-Ginsberg, 1986 (HG2): structural and functional influences in the same data.
7. Scarborough and Wyckoff, 1986 (SW).
8. Yoder and Kaiser, 1989 (YK).

All eight investigate the effect of the frequency of selected linguistic variables heard by the child, on selected measures of rate of language development. The procedure is as follows:

1. At a suitable point in time (T1) a spontaneous speech sample of children interacting with caretakers or other adults is recorded.
2. At a later time (T2), usually six or nine months later, a second sample of spontaneous speech is collected.
3. The speech addressed to the child at T1 is coded according to the independent variables selected and proportional frequencies are calculated. The variables are typically derived from features of the 'motherese' register (see, for example, Snow and Ferguson, 1977) or test hypotheses relating to the relative simplicity or complexity of features of input.
4. The child's stage of development at T1, and later at T2, is assessed on the measures chosen as dependent variables.
5. The child's progress between T1 and T2 is measured by calculating a gain score for each dependent variable.
6. It is assumed that neither the child's gains nor the input received are independent of the child's initial status. If the sample of children was inadequately matched at T1, statistical adjustments are made to control for differences in age and stage of development at T1 (see GNG for discussion).
7. Correlations between input frequencies at T1 and children's gain scores by T2 are computed.

Since results have been inconsistent, and since attitudes to the role of input are often the products of polarised theoretical positions, it is hardly surprising that these procedures and the interpretation of results have caused controversy. This has perhaps been most evident in exchanges between GNG and FNB (Furrow and Nelson, 1986; Furrow, Nelson and Benedict, 1979; Gleitman et al., 1984). The objective here is to concentrate on those aspects which relate to the auxiliary, so this is not the place for a full-scale critique. Points of methodology specific to the study of the auxiliary will be considered below. Other statistical and methodological issues have been dealt with by Schwartz and Camarata (1985) and the NGG study has been evaluated by Cromer (1981) and Lieven (1982). Naturalistic and experimental research into effects of input is also reviewed in detail in Wells and Robinson (1982) where the results of three of the correlational studies (NGG, FNB, and preliminary analyses of the BGSW data by Wells, 1980a) are compared. K. E. Nelson (1980) discusses the effects of the most commonly used input variables on syntax development while the theoretical implications of the findings of these studies are addressed in Hoff-Ginsberg and Shatz (1982) and in Gleitman and Wanner (1982).

One investigation which has received less attention is K. E. Nelson, Denninger, Bonvillian, Kaplan and Baker (NDBKB, 1984), the ninth study referred to above. The work dates back to 1972 and the 'Fiffin Project', an experimental study of the conceptual development of twenty-five children between 2;0 and 4;6 (K. E. Nelson and Bonvillian, 1978). NDBKB collected naturalistic child language and maternal input data from the same children at 22 months (T1) and 27 months (T2) and carried out simple correlations between input variables at T1 and child language score at T2. This study lacks the controls of the other eight; no adjustments were made for variation between the children at T1 and some correlations are with language level at T2, not always with gains. Since the children's vocabulary size varied from 18 to 300 words at T1 (K. E. Nelson and Bonvillian, 1978), it is unlikely that the children were well matched initially on the five language variables which were used in the correlations. Nevertheless, the research is introduced here because of its relevance to the auxiliary, and because the finding of a relationship between simple recasts and auxiliary growth (Table 10.1 below) is consistent with other evidence (see Section 10.3).

10.2.1 Predictors of auxiliary verb development

Table 10.1 lists variables which have been found to be associated with rate of auxiliary learning. In some cases the variables are only roughly comparable between studies. Nevertheless, the table gives an indication of findings across the nine studies referred to. In the GNG study significant effects are for the six younger children (18–21 months) except for the correlation with Y/Ns which was only significant for the older group (24–27 months at T1). Results for subcategories of Y/Ns will be reviewed separately.

These results are highly disparate and in one case contradictory. However, Y/N questions enter into significant correlations with auxiliary growth more frequently than any other variable. This relationship figures in the results of five out of the nine studies, the strongest correlations being in NGG and GNG.

With a sample of fifteen children, NGG obtained a double partial correlation as high as .88 between Y/Ns and auxiliaries per verb phrase, the most powerful of the fifty correlations they computed, and this increased to .91 in a reanalysis for the six older children (GNG, 1984).

Table 10.1 *Input variables found to be correlated with auxiliary gains*

Input variables	NGG	GNG	FNB	BGSW	HG1	HG2	SW	NDBKB	YK
					Correlational studies				
Y/N questions	+	+	+	+	+	ns	ns	0	0
Wh-questions	ns	*−	ns	0	+	+	ns	0	0
Real questions	0	0	0	0	0	+	0	0	ns
Display questions	0	0	0	0	0	ns	0	0	−
Verbal reflective questions	0	0	0	0	0	+	0	0	0
Imperatives	−	ns	ns	ns	ns	ns	ns	0	ns
MLU	ns	+	ns	ns	0	ns	ns	0	0
S-nodes/utterance	ns	+	ns	0	0	0	ns	0	0
Repetitions (of child)	−	−	0	0	ns	ns	0	ns	0
Expansions	+	+	0	0	ns	0	ns	+@	ns
Acknowledgements of declaratives	0	0	0	0	0	0	0	0	0
Deixis	ns	*+	ns	0	ns	ns	ns	0	0
Interjections	+	+	0	0	ns	0	0	0	0
Unintelligible	0	*−	0	0	0	0	0	0	0
Aux./Verb phrase	ns	0	0	0	0	ns	0	+	0

Key: + Significant positive correlation.
− Significant negative correlation.
ns Nonsignificant.
* Significant but lacking consistency on GNGs split half reliability procedure.
Real questions: the opposite of display questions (Hoff-Ginsberg, 1986).
Verbal reflective questions: questions as partial repetitions (Hoff-Ginsberg, 1986).
@ These were simple recasts, altering only one constituent of the child's utterance.
0 Not included.

10.3 Experimental studies

The work of Keith Nelson and his colleagues has shown that 'recasting' can be effective in developing areas of syntax in which the auxiliary plays a central part. Recasts, like grammatical expansions, semantic extensions, repetitions or various combinations of these, such as 'embedded extensions' (Howe, 1980) or 'synergistic sequences' (Cross, 1977), are responses by the child's interlocutor which incorporate various, particularly semantic, features of the child's previous utterance: 'Recasts pick up the child's basic meaning but redisplay or recast this meaning into a sentence structure that is in some way different from the child's original utterance' (K. E. Nelson, 1983, p. 53). K. E. Nelson, Carskaddon and Bonvillian (1973) have shown that for children of 32–40 months, a programme of recasting spontaneous utterances over a period of thirteen weeks (two 20-minute sessions per week) can bring about overall gains in language development significantly greater than for a control group. Results show higher scores on elicited imitation and in spontaneous production on the number of verb elements/verb construction and the number of auxiliaries/verb construction. Effects can also be highly specific; K. E. Nelson (1977) recast the utterances of two groups of children aged between 28 and 29 months. One group heard recasts containing complex questions (negative Y/N and Wh- questions, and tag questions). The other group heard complex verb groups (sentences containing two verbs, or containing the future tense or conditionals). Each group subsequently began using the targeted structures, but not the nontargeted structures. Finally, Baker and K. E. Nelson (1984) successfully used recasts to introduce passives, relative clauses and previously unused auxiliary verb forms to the speech of 2- and 3-year-olds.

While Nelson's experimental research has not usually been directly concerned with the auxiliary, the work shows that auxiliaries and the structures which contain them are sensitive to this type of intervention. One experiment which was designed to examine the relationship between input and auxiliary verb learning is Shatz, Hoff-Ginsberg and McIver (1989). Shatz et al. compare the effects on auxiliary growth of pairs of utterances which place the modal 'could' in contrasting positions. In the experimental groups the Y/N-initial position was found to be the most facilitative condition, but there was no clear advantage over their control group.

10.4 Yes/No questions and auxiliary verb learning

It is clear from the nine naturalistic studies in Section 10.2 and experimental work by Shatz et al. (1989) that the Y/N auxiliary relationship is a recurrent theme. It is also of interest that in the studies by Keith Nelson, recasts frequently redisplay the child's meaning as a Y/N, particularly as a tag question (see K. E. Nelson, 1977; K. E. Nelson et al., 1973).

More recently, evidence from blind children has shown a link with Y/Ns. Landau and Gleitman (1985) found the auxiliary to be the only language measure on which three blind children were delayed in comparison with sighted children. Maternal speech to two of the blind children and to sighted children matched for age and MLU were compared. The frequency of Y/Ns addressed to the blind children was found to be lower, and the authors conclude that there is a causal relationship between the relative paucity of Y/N input to blind children and their delay in learning the auxiliary.

10.4.1 Function and form of Y/Ns

Y/Ns function as questions to which a felicitous answer could be as minimal as 'yes', 'no' or 'I don't know' but which do not preclude more complex responses, nor responses which omit these three minimal options. However, Y/Ns may also have a directive function: # 'Can you pass the salt?' is usually intended and interpreted as a request for action rather than an enquiry about the addressee's abilities. Despite such discrepancies between form and function the term 'Y/N' is used here to describe utterances which are marked for interrogative mood either by inversion of subject and verbal operator or by intonation, and which, unlike Wh-questions, request no further propositional content.

The well-formed Y/N requires the inversion of an auxiliary or copula verb and its subject:

> # Is that your book? (copula inversion)
> # Did you see that? (auxiliary inversion)

These will be referred to as 'Y/N inversions'.

Colloquially, in the speech addressed to young children, and in the early stages of language learning by 2- and 3-year-olds (Bellugi, 1971; Menyuk, 1971), the auxiliary or copula is frequently omitted, the mood being marked by rising intonation:

> # That your book?
> # See that?

This type will be referred to as 'intonation only Y/Ns'.

Occasionally, a third type occurs:

I'm going out!
You're going out?
Yes

Here, the auxiliary is retained but there is no inversion. Again, interrogative mood is marked by intonation only. These will be referred to as 'non-inverted Y/Ns'.

10.4.2 Y/Ns as a feature of 'motherese'

A high frequency of questions in general, and of Y/Ns in particular, is well established as a characteristic of speech adjustments made to children varying in age from 1;0 to 3;0 and beyond. Drach (1969) observed that the number of questions (and especially Y/Ns) one mother addressed to her child was many times greater than those she addressed to two female adults. Broen (1972) found questions to account for approximately 40% of utterances addressed to children, of which 36% were Y/N inversions and 35% intonation only Y/Ns. For NGG 21% of mothers' utterances to their children were Y/Ns, compared with only 8% addressed to the experimenter. Similarly, Cross (1977) found that for sixteen fast developers, 33.4% of mothers' utterances were questions, and 18.2% were Y/Ns. Inversions accounted for 7.7%, 5% were intonation only questions, and 5.6% were tags. While there is a suggestion that a high proportion of interrogatives may be an artifact of the settings in which speech data are collected (D'Odorico and Franco, 1985), high proportions are also reported for fathers (Gleason and Weintraub, 1978; Kavanaugh and Jen, 1981), and for some cross-cultural research (Blount, 1972), although in cultures where the child is not given equal status as a conversational partner, interrogatives are likely to function very differently.

There is now a general consensus that speech adjustments to young language learners are motivated by the desire to communicate rather than to teach (Lieven, 1982; Newport, 1977; Shatz and Gelman, 1977; Wells, 1980b). This is not the place to outline the features of motherese. These have been extensively discussed and summarised elsewhere (Cromer, 1981; De Villiers and De Villiers, 1978; Lieven, 1982; Wells, 1980b) but it has been pointed out (Brown, 1977; Colmar and Wheldall, 1985) that these features have two main functions, the facilitation of understanding, and directing and sustaining attention. The view is taken here that Y/Ns perform both these functions as well as serving to regulate children's behaviour (see also Newport, 1977). In furthering the interlocutor's comprehension of the child, Y/Ns occur in conversational exchanges as utterances which can either initiate or respond. They are a means of requesting information which places less of a burden on the child than, say, a Wh- question, and the child can be presented with a series of binary alternatives which gradually narrow down the available range of meanings until the required information is obtained. This accounts for the observation that mothers often immediately follow a Wh- question with a Y/N (Gleason, 1977). Y/Ns can therefore be regarded as a means of facilitating the child's participation in conversation with a more mature speaker. As responses, they occur both in motherese and in adult conversation as communication checks: what Quirk et al. call 'recapitulatory echo questions'. This type of question is defined as one which 'repeats part or all of a message, as a way of having its content confirmed' (Quirk et al., 1985, p. 835). As such, they belong to the much investigated category of contingent responses and may additionally be expansions, extensions or repetitions. However, several analyses (see Wells, Montgomery and Maclure, 1979, pp. 348–9), and this author's own observations of parental interaction with the Welsh children, suggest that the motivation behind many ostensibly 'clarification' sequences may be more subtle and complex than is often assumed. Wells et al. (1979) discuss the way in which less obvious intentions such as 'invitation to self-correct', 'stalling for time', or 'showing surprise or disbelief', are realised through their discourse function categories of 'requesting reiteration' and 'requesting confirmation'. The view here is that Y/Ns in these categories can also realise the procedural function of sustaining the interaction and maintaining joint attention on the theme of the child's previous utterance. The motivation for this may be purely affective, the enjoyment of non-essential interaction, or it may be indirectly regulatory, perhaps to prevent restlessness during caretaking activities. This would help to explain exchanges such as the following where Harriet (2;3, Occ.5) and her mother are looking at a picture of a doll:

> M: what's that?
> H: dolly
> M: dolly is it?
> H: yeh

The discourse role of Y/Ns addressed to thirty-two of the Bristol children will be analysed in Chapter 11. Here it has been suggested that like other characteristics of the motherese register they perform three broad functions: regulation of the child's actions, facilitating comprehension of the child, and promoting the joint focus of attention.

10.5 The Auxiliary Clarification Hypothesis

When NGG (1977) first reported the association between Y/Ns and auxiliary growth, their discussion emphasised the sensitivity of the auxiliary as a language-specific component to environmental influences (pp. 133–5), and the child's processing biases (p. 138). Subject–auxiliary inversion in Y/Ns displays auxiliaries at the front of the sentence where their position is congruent with children's tendencies to pay attention to the beginnings of utterances. In GNG (1984) the emphasis changes slightly. Processing bias is seen in terms of a memory factor, presumably a primacy effect, and two further aspects are highlighted: the role of complex input data (interrogatives rather than declaratives) in giving the child information about syntactic structure, and the special characteristics of the auxiliary as a member of the closed class. These features, which have been discussed in Section 1.3, include their contractibility[2] and occurrence in unstressed positions. The auxiliary in medial position, it is argued, tends to be contracted and unstressed, while the auxiliary in inverted Y/N position is stressed and uncontracted and therefore salient. Compare, for example: # 'You've got a new car' and # 'What /əv/ you got?' with # 'Have you got a new car?' The stress/contraction dimension seems to be a strong candidate to account for the fact that, for NGG, Y/Ns and not declaratives or even Wh-questions predict auxiliary gains.

This explanation will be referred to as the Auxiliary Clarification Hypothesis, borrowing the term 'clarification' from Fletcher's (1983, 1985) treatment of the same issue.

10.5.1 Problems with the Auxiliary Clarification Hypothesis

The fact that NGG's result has apparently been replicated by three other groups of researchers and confirmed by their own reanalysis (GNG, 1984) hardly serves to weaken the Auxiliary Clarification Hypothesis. Nevertheless, there are at least five factors which make the issue much less straightforward.

Firstly, Malan (1983) analysed stress and contraction (i.e. reduction) in Y/N-initial auxiliaries addressed to one child aged 2;4–2;5. Of these, 82% were found to be unstressed. Using the same data, Fletcher (1985) shows that there is considerable variation in sentence-initial auxiliary forms, including degree of reduction, and strength of vowel sound.

Secondly, children appear to be learning about these verbs from the beginning of sentences, but first use them in medial position in simple declaratives (this volume, Chapter 6). GNG (1984) seek explanations in learnability theory (e.g. Wexler and Culicover, 1980), and the child's processing biases. Children pay attention to the stressed elements in the input (auxiliaries in Y/Ns) while they also need data of moderate complexity (questions as opposed to declaratives) to be able to construct the relationship between different sentence types which contain auxiliaries. The resulting output (declarative sentences) shows an additional bias towards the reconstruction of canonical form. However, neither NGG nor GNG produce any evidence to show that the children have made any generalisation linking the same auxiliaries in initial position with those in medial position (Fletcher, 1985). Neither has it been demonstrated that the auxiliaries learned by the child by T2 are the same as the ones heard in Y/Ns at T1. In addition, since the measure used by NGG was auxiliaries per verb phrase, we don't know whether gains reflect developing knowledge of the auxiliary system, or frequent use of a limited range of forms.

Thirdly, as already indicated, there is no universally accepted set of auxiliaries included in child language research. The status of some of the marginal modals and semi-auxiliaries is particularly controversial. It is also often assumed, especially in American studies, that at least in the early stages of language development concatenatives (WANNA, HAFTA, GONNA, TRYNTA, LIKETA, GOTTA) are analysed as auxiliaries. Of these it is WANNA which is likely to contribute most significantly to auxiliary measures because of its high frequency. However, since none of the concatenatives and few of the marginal modals or semi-auxiliaries can be inverted at the beginning of a Y/N question, they must be irrelevant to the Auxiliary Clarification Hypothesis. On the other hand it may be possible for them to contribute to correlations if they occur in initial position in intonation only Y/Ns (# 'Wanna have some tea?').[3] Unfortunately, of the published studies referred to, only BGSW make information available about the classification of auxiliaries. However, communications from some of the researchers involved have at least partially clarified the issue. SW, for example, state that though the question of including concatenatives was taken seriously, it made no difference because no significant correlations were found (Scarborough, p.c.). NGG (Newport, p.c.) include auxiliary HAVE and BE, the modals CAN, MAY, and WILL (and related forms), and the 'semi-auxiliaries': GONNA, WANNA and HAFTA. Hoff-Ginsberg (p.c.) widens the range to include DO, SHALL and MUST, and GOTTA. However, HAVE TO and the negative forms CAN'T and DON'T are specifically excluded. The decision to omit what Hoff-Ginsberg's coding manual refers to as early 'unanalyzed negative markers' (Hoff-Ginsberg, n.d., p.19) is an interesting one. Whatever the degree of analysis of these forms, their occurrence in the data is not incompatible with the Clarification Hypothesis if they are addressed to the child in Y/N initial position.

The widest definition of the auxiliary appears to be used by BGSW (1983), but WANNA is excluded, and other concatenatives such as GONNA are coded as the corresponding semi-auxiliary (e.g. GOING TO). The auxiliaries used are those in Wells (1979a) (see Section 2.2.2).

Fourthly, Y/N inversions do not only place auxiliaries in initial position. Copula 'be' and, occasionally, main verb 'have' also allow subject/verb inversion. As far as is known, no research has separated out nonauxiliary inversions. NGG and GNG included copula inversions unless they were deictic: 'Is that a dog?' (Newport, p.c.).

Fifthly, and lastly, a closer look at the results of studies other than NGG and GNG shows that none actually supports the Clarification Hypothesis, the crucial difference being that while NGG treated Y/Ns as a single category, other studies used at least two subcategories. These subdivisions and their correlation with the auxiliary are as follows:

BGSW: 1. Y/N inversions (including tags) ($r = .16$; ns; $N = 32$)
        2. Intonation only Y/Ns ($r = .42$; $p < .05$; $N = 32$)

FNB: 1. Total Y/Ns ($r = .85$; $p < .025$; $N = 7$)
     2. Y/N inversions ($r = .48$; ns; $N = 7$)
     3. Other Y/Ns ($r = .72$; $p < .05$; $N = 7$)

HG1: 1. Total Y/Ns (ns)
     2. Y/N inversions (ns)
     3. Y/N not inverted ('Doggie wants a cookie?') ($r = .46$; $p < .01$; $N = 22$)
     4. Y/N tags (ns)
     5. Y/N elliptical ('Wanna cookie?') (ns)

SW: 1. Total Y/Ns ($r = -.42$; ns; $N = 9$)
    2. Y/N inversions ($r = -.54$; ns; $N = 9$)
    3. Other Y/Ns ($r = -.16$; ns; $N = 9$)

What is interesting about these results is that it is never the *inversion* category which produces the significant correlation. For BGSW and FNB it is the Intonation Only type which predicts auxiliary gains, the very type which omits the auxiliary or copula. Hoff-Ginsberg's correlation is with non-inverted Y/Ns, but she regards this to be spurious, the true effect being brought about by Wh-questions. There is nothing here, then, to support NGG's explanation of their result. NGG and GNG give no precise description of their Y/N variable. Newport (p.c.) confirms that it included inversions as well as intonation only and non-inverted Y/Ns, but excluded all tags. Newport also reports that when correlations between different types of Y/N and auxiliary gains are calculated separately, the only effect is for Y/N inversions. Unfortunately, no details of significance levels or reliability tests are given, nor whether the effect was common to the NGG analysis of all fifteen children and to the GNG reanalysis of separate age groups.

10.6 Summary

One group of researchers has found a relationship between Y/Ns addressed to children and rate of auxiliary development which is of a magnitude not normally found in psychological research. Even though there is a coherent and highly plausible explanation for this finding, it is not supported by other studies using a similar research design. It is possible, given the variation in magnitude and even direction of correlations in these investigations, and the scarcity of significant effects considering the large number computed, that such results have occurred by chance (Schwartz and Camarata, 1985). Neither do the results of Shatz et al.'s (1989) experimental study unequivocally support the Auxiliary Clarification Hypothesis. Of the three experimental conditions, pairs of Y/Ns were more beneficial than pairs of declaratives containing auxiliaries or pairs of utterances which contrasted the auxiliary in sentence initial and medial positions. However, children exposed to the paired Y/N condition failed to develop the auxiliary at a significantly faster rate than a control group.

In order to clarify the picture it was decided to undertake a reanalysis of the BGSW data to address the following areas in particular:

1. Why should two of the correlational studies find a relationship between learning auxiliaries and intonation Y/Ns which omit auxiliaries?
2. Unless the auxiliary really does receive greater prominence in Y/Ns, the GNG explanation must be rejected. What are the patterns of stress and reduction in Y/N-initial auxiliaries?

11 *Yes/No questions and rate of auxiliary learning for thirty-two children*

11.1 The Barnes, Gutfreund, Satterly and Wells study

Of the research outlined in Chapter 10, BGSW's use of the Bristol child language corpus (Wells, 1985) gives them the strongest claim to a representative sample of the population, and naturalistic and spontaneous speech undistorted by the presence of an observer (see Section 2.1). BGSW selected sixteen boys and sixteen girls with a broad range of family background and coded the speech addressed to them by adults in the recording when the child's MLUS was closest to 1.5 morphemes (T1). Because intervals between speech sampling were three months in the Bristol Study, exact matching for MLU was not possible and actual values for MLUS ranged from 1.0 to 2.21 (mean = 1.68). The mean age at this point was 2;0 (range 1;6–2;9). To assess the children's progress, transcripts from a point nine months later (T2) were used. Children's gains were indicated by residual gain scores, the difference between predicted scores at T2 and actual scores at T2 (see Barnes et al., 1983; O'Connor, 1972). For the auxiliary there were three measures: range of auxiliary meanings, auxiliary frequency,[1] and range of auxiliary forms. Meanings and forms are as defined in Wells (1979a), forms being major forms rather than subforms (see Section 2.2.2). Only the correlations with range of auxiliary meanings are reported.

11.1.1 Strengths and limitations of BGSW

1. Size of population sample: BGSW's sample of thirty-two children is the largest of the published studies and only HG1 and HG2 approach this figure ($N = 22$). NGG's original sample of fifteen is reduced to two groups of six in the reanalysis (GNG). For FNB, SW, and YK, sample sizes are seven, nine and ten respectively.
2. Make-up of population sample: the BGSW sample was constructed to ensure balance for sex and range of family background. Other studies used middle-class children, except YK, whose subjects were working class.
3. Speech sampling: data for all studies were collected in the home. Only BGSW increase representativeness by a time-sampling procedure for which the presence of a stranger was not required.

4. Input: except in BGSW, only the interaction between child and mother was sampled. BGSW included input from all adults, aiming for a more representative sample from the child's interlocutors.

5. Input variables: BGSW reduced the number of input variables and ensured their independence by means of factor analysis. This also reduced the possibility of significant correlations occurring by chance. Intercorrelations between T1 input variables and correlations between input and child language variables at T1 are reported by BGSW. Otherwise only HG1 describes procedures for checking independence of relationships and eliminating spurious effects, and only YK systematically address the issue of indirect relationships between T1 input variables and child outcomes.

6. Size of input corpus: the studies give few details of the size of corpus on which input frequencies are based, and there are no details of ranges or standard deviations. This is also true of BGSW. However, FNB used 100, and NGG 'approximately' 100 maternal utterances. An inspection of BGSW's data shows that the number of utterances addressed to the children by adults in eighteen 90-second samples varies from 22 to 279 (mean = 105.3; $SD = 69.4$). For some subjects the size of input sample must be regarded as unacceptably small; seven children (out of thirty-two) have fewer than 50 utterances addressed to them.

7. Stability of relationships over time: for BGSW and FNB the interval between T1 and T2 is nine months. This is a relatively long time in children's language development, and the GNG reanalysis and results from HG1 and HG2 suggest that some effects of input are specific to certain ages or stages. It is possible therefore that effects which are real in the short term become obscured over the longer period. Other studies (NGG, GNG, SW) use a span of six months, and YK bring this down to five months. HG1 and HG2 are the only studies which address this question systematically, by sampling at four points separated by three two-monthly intervals.

8. Matching of children at T1: FNB and SW assume that subjects are sufficiently well matched for age and stage at T1 that no adjustment is required to partial out the effect of children on their adult interlocutors, nor to compensate for the effect of different starting points on subsequent growth scores. FNB's children were perfectly matched for age (1;6) but as GNG have pointed out, one of the children may have been well in advance of the others. In addition, the remaining six subjects are attributed an MLU of 1.0, a value which can encompass a wide variety of significant linguistic developments (BGSW). SW's attempt at matching is more successful. All children at T1 are 2;0 and the MLU range is small (1.30–1.42). However, since there are many ways of arriving at any given MLU (Wells, 1985) this is no guarantee that children were well matched on the other dependent variables chosen.

Another approach is to assume that children are sufficiently well matched for age and linguistic ability to discount effects of the child on the quality of input, but to attempt to remove the negative effect of the child's initial status on subsequent growth. This is the approach taken by BGSW with their use of the residual gain score.

NGG make no assumptions as to adequacy of matching and have found it necessary to partial out the effect of both age and stage. In their reanalysis, GNG match children for age, and partial out initial stage only. HG1 and HG2 combine several approaches – growth scores are computed which remove the influence of initial status, and effects of the child on the mother are adjusted for where necessary.

While BGSW have dealt with the problem of the nonlinearity of crude gain scores, the attempt to match children on an MLUS of 1.5 was less successful. The result is that there is considerable variation at T1 in both MLUS (1.0–2.21) and age (1;6–2;9).

11.1.2 BGSW child auxiliary measures

It was observed in section 10.5.1 that if the dependent variable is the frequency of auxiliaries, as in all studies except BGSW, there is no guarantee that children are learning an integrated system of auxiliaries rather than stereotyped usage of a restricted range of forms. FNB, in particular, found auxiliaries per verb phrase to be unsatisfactory in discriminating between children, though this was partly because their subjects were at such an early stage of development.

BGSW report correlations with range of auxiliary meanings, which clearly avoids this problem. Nevertheless, as Wells' (1979a) analysis indicates, it is possible for a single form to express more than one meaning, just as it is possible for different forms to convey a similar meaning. Ideally, therefore, a profile of auxiliary development would include information about range of forms and meanings as well as frequency. This information was available to BGSW, but as their aim was to look at several different areas of language growth, it was necessary to reduce the number of variables. Because the current investigation is concerned solely with the auxiliary all three variables will be used in the reanalysis which follows.

First of all, however, so that the BGSW results may be better interpreted, full details of the relevant auxiliary and input variables will be given, as well as correlations between T1 input variables and residual gain scores for the three auxiliary measures. These have all been recalculated, partly because BGSW had no record of correlations with two of the auxiliary measures, and partly to confirm that all the published values could be reproduced. Since the SPSS file created by BGSW contained 161 variables, it was also a check that they had all been identified correctly.

Table 11.1 shows details of the three auxiliary measures at T1 and T2. Two things become clear. Firstly, and this is also true of the other studies, auxiliaries are extremely rare at T1, most children using none at all and, secondly, usage is restricted to a small number of forms and meanings. Intercorrelations reported in Table 11.2 show that these correspond perfectly at this stage.

Table 11.1 *Child auxiliary measures at T1 and T2*

Child aux. measures	Mean	SD	Range
T1 Range aux. meanings	0.47	0.88	0–4
T1 Range aux. forms	0.47	0.88	0–4
T1 Aux. frequency	0.43	1.01	0–4.4
T2 Range aux. meanings	9.20	4.50	0–17
T2 Range aux. forms	5.50	2.30	0–9
T2 Aux. frequency	2.10	1.48	0–5.6

Table 11.2 *Intercorrelations between auxiliary measures at T1*

	2	3
1 Range aux. meanings	1.0	.58
2 Range aux. forms		.58
3 Aux. frequency		

Residual gain scores show a similar pattern of intercorrelations (Table 11.3). Forms and meanings correspond closely, while correlations with frequency are only of moderate strength. This supports the claim that frequency alone is an inadequate index of progress.

11.1.3 Interrogative input measures available from BGSW
At 12% the mean number of Y/Ns in the Bristol corpus (Table 11.4) is low in comparison with, for example, Cross (1977) (18.2%), FNB (16.9%), HG2 (17%), and especially NGG (21%), despite the fact that NGG code deictic copula Y/Ns separately (Newport, 1977). It can be seen from the range in Table 11.4 that even the child who hears the most Y/Ns fails to

Table 11.3 *Intercorrelations between auxiliary residual gain scores*

	2	3
1 Range aux. meanings	.92	.50
2 Range aux. forms		.37
3 Aux. frequency		

reach the average for NGG's subjects. D'Odorico and Franco (1985) have suggested that high frequencies of questions may be a product of the contexts in which data are collected. The relatively artificial setting of free play or 'focused play between mother and children with a large toy' (HG1, 1985, p. 371) compared with the Bristol recording procedures might therefore account for this difference.

Table 11.4 *Interrogative input measures from the BGSW data: proportional frequencies*

Input measures	Mean	*SD*	Range
Y/N inversions	0.05	0.04	0–0.15
Decl. + tag	0.03	0.02	0–0.08
Intonation only Y/Ns	0.03	0.03	0–0.09
All Y/Ns	0.12	0.05	0–0.19
Wh- questions	0.09	0.06	0–0.24

Table 11.5 shows intercorrelations between types of question coded by BGSW. Not surprisingly, the strongest relationships are found between subcategories of Y/N and the global category. Between subcategories, tag questions are significantly correlated with other Y/N inversion. No relationships are found with Wh- questions.

11.1.4 Correlations between BGSW's interrogative variables and auxiliary measures

Apart from the correlation between intonation only Y/Ns and auxiliary meanings reported by BGSW, the only additional effect found in their data was between all Y/Ns and auxiliary frequency (Table 11.6). These results do little to make sense of the relationship between intonation only Y/Ns and

Table 11.5 *Intercorrelations between BGSW's interrogative input measures*

	2	3	4	5
1 Inversions	.39*	.02	.82‡	−.26
2 Decl. + tag		−.15	.52†	−.29
3 Intonation			.40*	−.10
4 All Y/Ns				−.20
5 Wh- questions				

*$p < .05$; †$p < .01$; ‡$p < .001$; $df = 30$; two tailed.

auxiliary learning. The association is only significant with one of the three auxiliary measures. Relationships with inversions which would be consistent with the Auxiliary Clarification Hypothesis only approach significance for auxiliary frequency.

Table 11.6 *Correlations between interrogative input variables and child auxiliary gains*

	Aux. gain scores		
Input variables	Meanings	Frequency	Forms
Y/N inversions	.16@	.33	.19
Declarative + tag	−.16	.26	−.05
Intonation only Y/Ns	.42@†	.26	.26
All Y/Ns	.31	.49‡	.28
Wh- questions	−.15	.07	−.20

@ As published in BGSW.
*$p < .05$; †$p < .01$; ‡$p < .001$; $df = 30$; two-tailed.

11.2 First attempts to account for the relationship between intonation only Y/Ns and auxiliary growth

Initially, four explanations for the effect of Y/Ns which apparently omit the auxiliary will be considered. These will be followed by a description of the effects of recoding the input in BGSW's transcripts.

A first possibility, which would be consistent with the Auxiliary Clarification Hypothesis, is that the association is spurious because inverted and intonation Y/Ns are themselves correlated at T1. But an inspection of inter-correlations between the interrogative input measures (Table 11.5 above) shows no relationship ($r = .02$). Nevertheless, the very independence of these variables, despite their apparent functional similarity, suggests further hypotheses relating to form/function relationships within the overall category of Y/N. This theme will be taken up on Hypothesis 4.

A second hypothesis might be that the intonation only category contains a high proportion of non-inverted Y/Ns (# 'You're going out?') which retain the auxiliary. Similar utterances had been observed as contingent responses addressed to the Welsh children. However, a preliminary check of the Bristol transcripts found almost no tokens at T1, and detailed coding of Y/Ns (see 11.3) for all thirty-two children produced a total of only six.

The third hypothesis considers direction of causality. BGSW themselves argue for an interpretation of their results based on 'reciprocal, rather than one-way facilitation' (p. 65). As they point out, children were matched for MLU only. It is possible therefore that intonation only Y/Ns are a response to children's use of auxiliaries at T1. However, as there are no significant relationships between interrogative input variables and any of the auxiliary measures at T1, this explanation also receives no support.

On the other hand, this is not the only way in which adults might respond to different levels of auxiliary development. BGSW intended that the range of auxiliary meanings should include cases, such as obligatory contexts, where despite the absence of an auxiliary, the context indicated a latent auxiliary meaning (Wells, p.c.). But again, an inspection of transcripts shows that no such instances could possibly have been coded at T1 and for each child BGSW obtained a perfect correspondence between auxiliary forms and meanings. At the same time, it is clear that there are latent auxiliary meanings at T1, even though one might hesitate to define them as obligatory contexts. It is also true that these sometimes evoke Y/N responses which may expand or extend these utterances in one way or another. Nevertheless, these also proved to be rare, and recoding Y/Ns for the thirty-two subjects produced only seventeen Y/N responses to latent auxiliary meanings.

The final hypothesis is derived from the statistical independence of inverted and intonation Y/Ns, and an awareness of the extent to which the Welsh mothers had used the latter in particular as contingent responses.

Contingent responses are reported to be associated with various child measures either as a general category (Hardy-Brown, Plomin and DeFries, 1981), as repetitions (Smolak and Weinraub, 1983), acknowledgements (Ellis and Wells, 1980), expansions (BGSW, 1983; Cross, 1978; GNG, 1984; HG1, 1985; K. E. Nelson et al., 1973; K. E. Nelson et al., 1984; NGG, 1977) or extensions (BGSW, 1983; Cross, 1978). Of course, these results also vary from study to study (repetition, for example, is negatively correlated with several measures for NGG and GNG) and are subject to similar reservations to those already discussed. Nevertheless, it is possible that any effects of questions on auxiliary verb learning are less direct than has often been suggested. If intonation only Y/Ns were a feature of a responsive style of interaction which is generally facilitative, then the auxiliary measure could be functioning as an index of overall language development. This interpretation would, of course, presuppose that the period T1 to T2 is one in which the development of the auxiliary plays a central role. This assumption is examined below.

11.2.1 Auxiliary proficiency between T1 and T2

Statistical descriptions of child language, based on measures of frequency, complexity or diversity, are difficult to translate into any meaningful concept of the type of utterances that children are actually producing. This is even more so with a feature such as the auxiliary which can enter into so many different semantic, syntactic and pragmatic roles. Neither does knowing the rate of occurrence of auxiliaries in verb phrases, or diversity of meanings or forms, give us much indication of whether the auxiliary is analysed as a class of words which exhibit a common set of syntactic behaviours.

In the present analysis this problem was addressed in two ways. Firstly, an assessment of the children's general language development between T1 and T2 was made by reference to their level on the Bristol Language Development Scales (BLADES) (Gutfreund, Harrison and Wells, 1989) on each of these occasions. The BLADES levels which were encompassed were then inspected to discover which features were most indicative of linguistic progress during this period. The median level of children at T1 was Level 3 (range 0–4), and at T2 it was Level 5 (range 3–7). An inspection of the items which appear at these levels suggests that, while it would be rash to attribute an integrated system of auxiliaries to the children by T2, this is a period during which the emergence of meanings and functions associated with the auxiliary is a particular feature. This includes progressive and perfective meanings, the first intonation Y/N questions, future time reference, meanings of permission and ability, and the first Subject + Aux + Verb constructions. By T2, some of the most advanced children have also produced subject–auxiliary inversion in Y/N and Wh- questions, meanings of obligation and necessity, and indirect requests.

The second approach was a more detailed analysis of auxiliary tokens produced in recordings made before T1 and in the two recordings made between T1 and T2.

Table 11.1 indicated the rarity of the auxiliary at T1. Closer inspection shows that for twenty children there was no record of any auxiliary up to and including T1, while for a further seven, T1 was the first occasion of emergence. No child had attained Wells' criterion of five major forms (see Chapter 2), though twenty-one of the children had done so by T2. If the number of subforms (as defined in Section 2.2.3) at T1 is examined, we find that only two children are on record as having produced more than two, and the pooled range of subforms to have emerged for all children is only eleven. All are used in declaratives although a few also occur in Wh- questions (two forms), Y/Ns (one form), and imperatives (1 form). Of the twelve children recorded as using an auxiliary by T1, eight had done so in declarative frames, five in imperatives, two in Wh- questions, and one in an inverted Y/N.

Nine months later at T2 the picture has changed considerably. All children now use auxiliaries in declarative sentences. Auxiliaries in Y/N inversions have emerged for three-quarters of the children, in tags for nearly a quarter, and in Wh- questions for one third. Three-quarters of the sample use auxiliaries in ellipsis, and half the children produce at least one stressed auxiliary for emphatic affirmation. Of the meanings expressed by the auxiliary system thirty-one children have used auxiliaries to express a modal meaning, twenty-three for the perfective, and twenty-five for continuous aspect. Dummy DO has been sampled for twenty-seven children, and three have included BE in truncated passives. On the other hand, when we examine the number of subforms to have emerged in the various syntactic frames since T1, it is only in non-ellipsed declaratives that there is a substantial increase: mean number of new subforms per child $= 8.6$ ($SD = 6.0$; range: 0–23). The next highest category is non-ellipsed Y/N questions where the mean increase is only 1.5 ($SD = 1.7$; range: 0–6). Even in declaratives some children are still using a restricted range of forms; seven children are on record as using three subforms or less. While all children may have used declaratives, of the other syntactic features of the auxiliary, less than half (fourteen) have produced a token of all four of the NICE properties.

In conclusion, it can be said that for the majority of children, auxiliaries are well established in declarative utterances by T2. However, there is less evidence that they are part of a wider syntactic system.

11.2.2 Summary

Four possibilities have been examined which might have accounted for a statistical relationship between Y/Ns which omit the auxiliary and rate of auxiliary learning. Three of these were easily rejected. The fourth hypothesis is that during a period of development which is particularly dependent on emerging auxiliaries, any measure of growth which relies on the auxiliary will be sensitive to general linguistic developments facilitated by intonation Y/Ns as contingent responses. This hypothesis, which will be referred to as the Responsive Style Hypothesis, will be tested in two stages following recoding of BGSW's Y/N input. There are two predictions: firstly that intonation Y/Ns will tend to have a responding function, and secondly that auxiliary gains will be correlated with Y/Ns which are responses to child utterances rather than those which initiate exchanges.

11.3 Coding scheme for Y/Ns

A coding frame was devised which allowed syntactic features such as inversion to be related to exchange-initiating and response function. The scheme also allowed the role of tags to be investigated separately, since in their various forms these can reveal much of the syntactic behaviour unique to the auxiliary and copula and, by repeating the operator, assist with the identification of constituent boundaries in the matrix clause.

The scheme to be described uses BGSW's coding scheme (Wells, 1980c) as a basis, but its further evolution was influenced by two other schemes associated with the Bristol project (Wells, 1979b; Wells and Gutfreund, 1984), and in particular the theoretical framework developed by Wells, Montgomery and MacLure (1979). Basically their approach is derived from Halliday (1984) and sees conversation as a process of exchange of the discourse commodities: GOODS-&-SERVICES and INFORMATION.

Initially, the relevant categories from BGSW's coding (the four types of Y/N and the contingent response discourse functions) were tried out on a subsample of ten children chosen at random. Unfortunately there were immediate difficulties in reproducing BGSW's input frequencies in the four Y/N categories. There are a number of reasons why the recoding might produce such discrepancies. One is that there is some doubt at this stage about the number of 90-second samples which were used by BGSW for some of the children. In addition, BGSW defined input as utterances addressed to the child by adults. In the trial coding here 'adult' was taken literally, but it was discovered later that this included any person over the age of 12 who spoke to the target child (see Ellis and Wells, 1980). But even these two factors could not account for all the differences between the original and recoded frequencies. The figures for Stella (1;9) illustrate a typical pattern. The overall frequency of polar interrogatives was almost identical (about 19% in both cases), but there were differences in the incidence of intonation only Y/Ns (9% for BGSW as opposed to 11% here), Y/N inversions (9% versus 6%) and Declarative + Tag (1% versus 2.5%). It seems likely that one problem lies in the coding of Declarative + Tag. It was shown in Chapter 7 that tags and the matrices to which they are appended have many different forms. One factor which may help to explain coding discrepancies is that a tag can be transcribed as a separate utterance from its matrix if there is an intervening utterance by another speaker or a slight pause in between. In these cases, the BGSW approach, unlike the reanalysis, seems to have been to code the 'tag' as a separate Y/N inversion. The justification for treating them as tag questions in the recoding is the hypothesis that tags can facilitate the development of an integrated *system* of auxiliaries by presenting pairs of auxiliaries for comparison in declarative and interrogative frames, and can (depending on their form) also illustrate the same auxiliaries in affirmative/negative, and ellipsed/non-ellipsed contrasts. For the same reason, the final version of the coding frame includes information about presence of the auxiliary in the matrix, polarity reversal, and whether the operator was an auxiliary or copula verb.

Another possible source of discrepancy are matched polarity copula tags which follow a matrix with absent copula: # 'Book, is it?' These have been treated as tags in the reanalysis but may have been coded as Y/N inversions by BGSW.

Whatever the reasons for being unable to reproduce BGSW's frequency counts, it will be shown that recoding input had interesting and far-reaching consequences.

11.3.1 Coding Y/N function

Following Wells, MacLure and Montgomery (1980), the basic unit of conversational analysis is taken to be the EXCHANGE. An exchange consists of two moves, and each move consists of or contains an INITIATING and a RESPONDING utterance or nonverbal acknowledgement. This was the major distinction in coding the discourse role of Y/Ns (Fig. 11.1).

However, Y/Ns which answer a request for GOODS-&-SERVICES or

Fig. 11.1 Discourse role of Y/Ns

INFORMATION, or acknowledge the utterance of a previous speaker, both respond *and* re-initiate. Kaye and Charney (1981) have described this type of move as a 'turnabout'. They are therefore dual-role conversational acts which link exchanges in longer sequences of discourse (Wells et al., 1980). These moves, and the exchanges in which they are embedded, have been given various other names, including side sequences, contingent queries, procedural exchanges, clarification request sequences, text contingent exchanges, continues, and bound exchanges (see Wells et al., 1979, 1980; Wells, 1980c). Here, Wells and Gutfreund's (1984) term BOUND EXCHANGE is used. This is appropriate because in contrast with their role in NUCLEAR EXCHANGES, Y/Ns are inextricably part of the following exchange (Fig. 11.2).

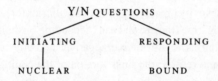

Fig. 11.2 Autonomy of exchanges introduced by Y/Ns

It is important to distinguish two types of bound exchange which are introduced by Y/Ns (Fig. 11.3). The first is opened by a RE-INITIATION as in the sequence below where a tagged response to Stella's question extends the conversation:

Stella: Zat?
Father: That's a carpet-sweeper isn't it like Mummy's?
Stella: Yes like Mummy's *(Stella, 2;0)* *(Wells, et al., 1980, p.3)*

In the second type, the Y/N is a device which ostensibly allows the conversation to proceed without communication breakdown. The resulting bound exchange adds nothing to the content of the conversation and could be removed from the sequence without affecting its validity. Unlike re-initiation, it does not extend to *topic*, though it may add syntactic or semantic units which were not contained in the sentence on which it is contingent:

Child: Hold it
Mother: Mummy hold it?
Child: Mm
Mother: All right then *(Adapted from Wells et al., 1979, p.347)*

Here the Y/N requests confirmation of the mother's interpretation of the child's intended meaning. Frequently this would be interpreted as a clarification request. However, as pointed out above, the psychological motivation behind these utterances is not always clear; clarification often seems unnecessary. For this reason Garvey's (1977) term CONTINGENT QUERY (CQ) will be used instead.

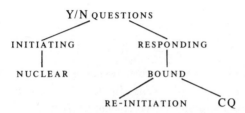

Fig. 11.3 Types of exchange introduced by Y/Ns

In their analysis of the development of conversation, Wells and Gutfreund (1984) omit all CQs from their Expansion category, even though they acknowledge that CQs frequently include morphemes omitted by the child. Since the focus of their attention was the sequence of emergence of conversational features, this was an appropriate decision. However, in this study where hypotheses relate to the facilitative possibilities of certain types of response, the opposite course was taken. It seemed clear that both CQs and re-initiations could be realised as repetitions, expansions or extensions (Fig. 11.4).

At first sight these three dependency categories seem easy to define. All three are frequently referred to in 'motherese' investigations. Expansion 'completes or expands the form of the child's utterance to make it a well-formed sentence' (Wells, 1980c, p.22), while extensions add relevant or contrasting information to the child's topic or request further information. Y/N repetitions include part or all of the previous utterance with no additions other than those required to recast the content in the form of a question. The problems arise in making these categories mutually exclusive. A repetition which adds a copula inversion (# 'Book.' 'Book, is it?') rather than just rising intonation (# 'Book.' 'Book?') is approaching an expansion. And expansions vary

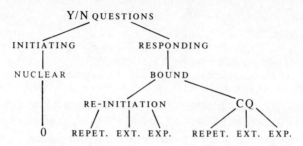

(REPET.: repetition; EXT.: extension; EXP.: expansion)

Fig. 11.4 Dependency of Y/Ns on previous utterances

on a continuum from partial expansions which do not result in a well-formed utterance to 'elaborated expansions' (Wells, 1979b) which not only supply missing functors but also add propositional content (# 'Book.' 'It's a lovely book isn't it?'). In turn, the dividing line between these and extensions is an extremely narrow one, and a check on coding reliability for the transcripts of five children produced a figure of 83% agreement, the expansion/extension distinction being the major source of error. In the BGSW study Wells (p.c.) had instructed coders to opt for the extension category if in doubt between extension and expansion. Of course, the problems are slightly different in the current analysis where only one mood category is coded for dependency, but attempting to apply Wells' criterion results in an almost empty expansion category and a large number of extensions. Consequently, these categories were merged (Fig. 11.5, Level 4).

One additional distinction was made, this time within Y/Ns which initiated nuclear exchanges: an additional identification was given to Y/Ns which were indirect requests. This resulted in a binary division of the initiating utterances into requests for goods-and-services and requests for information (Fig. 11.5).

It can now be seen from Fig. 11.5 that the coding scheme operates at five levels:

1. Discourse role.
2. Autonomy of the exchange.
3. Type of exchange.
4. Dependency of the Y/N on the previous utterance.
5. Discourse function.

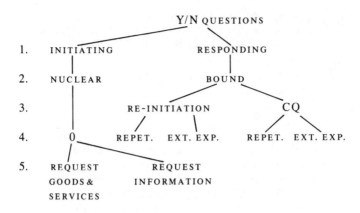

(REPET.: repetition; EXT.: extension; EXP.: expansion)

Fig. 11.5 Final scheme for Y/N coding

This outline does not claim to be a complete model of the operation of Y/Ns in conversations with children, but it is worth noting that the right-hand side of the scheme can easily be extended to include Level 5. This would entail the addition of responding functions such as CLARIFY, COMMENT, CORRECT, and AGREE. Although the process of coding gave insights into how this level might operate, they are not included here, because the separate discourse functions of Y/N responses had no immediate relevance to the hypotheses being tested.

The examples below summarise the coding categories for discourse features:

1. Initiating (Request information): 'Did you hurt yourself?' (*Benjamin, 1;9*)

2. Initiating (Request goods-and-services): 'Will you put this on the table for your dinner?' (*Jonathan, 1;9*)

3. Responding (Re-initiate: repetition):
   Child: ⟨Motor-bike⟩
   Mother: ⟨Um⟩
   Mother: Bike isn't it? (falling intonation) (*Debbie, 2;3*)

4. Responding (Re-initiate: expand/extend):
   Child: Meat
   Mother: Is it nice? (*Benjamin, 1;9*)

5. Responding (CQ: repetition):
   Child: Ice-cream
   Father: Ice-cream is it? (*Neville, 2;0*)

    6. Responding (CQ: expand/extend):
        Child: More
        Mother: Do you want another bic? (biscuit) *(Benjamin, 1;9)*

11.3.2 Coding the syntax of Y/Ns

Syntax was coded using the categories below:

    1. Operator: operators in Y/Ns (including tags) were coded as COPULA or
        AUXILIARY. Auxiliaries included only the primary forms DO, BE, HAVE
        and central modals (CAN, MAY, SHALL, WILL, MUST) and related forms.
        There were no tokens containing the marginal forms NEED and DARE.
    2. Y/N inversion (excluding tags): 'Did you hurt yourself?' *(Benjamin, 1;9)*
    3. Non-inverted Y/Ns: 'You don't want anything to eat?' *(Iris, 2;0)*
    4. Intonation only Y/Ns: 'You want to see the cats?' *(Jonathan, 1;9)*
    5. Informal tags: 'O.K.?' 'Right?' 'Eh?'
    6. Tags (reversed polarity): '⟨Making⟩ that silly noise won't help will it?'
                                                    (Benjamin, 1;9)
    7. Tags (matched polarity): 'You're going to knock it down are you?'
                                                      (Sean, 2;0)
    8. Tags (same operator in matrix and tag): 'You're going to knock it down
        are you?' *(Sean, 2;0)*
    9. Tags (different operator, or no operator in the matrix): 'You singing magic
        are you?' *(Tony, 2;0)*

11.3.3 Definition of 'input'

On one point there is a major departure from the methodology adopted by
BGSW. The original study defined 'input' as utterances addressed to the
child by any person over the age of 12. For the reanalysis it was believed
that there were sound theoretical and practical reasons for extending this
definition to include *all* utterances addressed to the subject. This seemed
necessary since adult–child interaction was not always representative of
the child's linguistic environment. Indeed, there were some children for whom
the majority of input at T1 was received from older siblings. Since one of
the strengths of the Bristol corpus is the degree to which it provides a typical
cross-section of language heard by the child, it is unnecessary to exclude
a portion of the data without strong reasons for doing so. The hypotheses
to be tested have to do with the syntactic and phonological properties of
certain utterances together with their conversational role. If an utterance fulfils
the required syntactic, phonological and functional criteria, it is not part of
the current theoretical framework to exclude it on grounds of the age of
the speaker.

11.4 Results

Tables 11.7 and 11.8 indicate proportional frequencies and intercorrelations at T1 for all fifteen input variables. Table 11.9 shows correlations between the same variables and the child auxiliary scores at T1. In each table and in the exposition of the results in 11.4.2, Y/N variables are grouped as follows: combined discourse categories (variables 1–7), responding categories (8–10), and initiating categories (11–15).

Table 11.7 *Distribution of Y/N input variables*

Y/N input variables	Mean	SD	Range
1 All Y/Ns (incl. tags)	.12	.05	.02–.22
2 Y/Ns (excl. tags)	.09	.05	.02–.20
3 Y/N inversions (excl. tags)	.05	.03	0 –.15
4 Aux. inversion only	.03	.03	0 –.10
5 All tag questions	.03	.02	0 –.10
6 Aux. tags only	.02	.01	0 –.04
7 All intonation only Y/Ns	.05	.03	0 –.11
8 All responding Y/Ns	.04	.03	0 –.10
9 Intonation only responses	.02	.02	0 –.08
10 All extensions/expansions	.02	.02	0 –.07
11 All initiating Y/Ns	.08	.05	.01–.22
12 Initiating Y/Ns (excl. tags)	.07	.05	.01–.20
13 Initiating inversions (excl. tags)	.04	.03	0 –.15
14 Initiating aux. inversion only (excl. tags)	.03	.03	0 –.07
15 Initiating intonation only	.02	.02	0 –.08

11.4.1 Relationships between form and discourse role of Y/Ns

The hypothesis relating syntactic features to discourse role was partially confirmed. It is true that Y/N inversions usually initiate exchanges, but the intonation only type is fairly evenly distributed between initiating and responding roles. It is clear, however, that Y/Ns which respond to the child usually omit the auxiliary or copula unless they also happen to be tag questions (Table 11.10). Even though nearly half the intonation only Y/Ns initiate exchanges, these figures are not inconsistent with a Responsive Style Hypothesis to explain correlations between intonation only Y/Ns and child auxiliary growth.

Table 11.8 *Intercorrelations between Y/N input variables at T1*

	1	2	3	4	5	6	7	8	9	10	11	12	13	14	15
1 All Y/Ns (incl. tags)	1														
2 Y/Ns (excl. tags)	‡.88	1													
3 Y/N inversions (excl. tags)	‡.68	‡.78	1												
4 Aux. inversion only	†.54	‡.60	‡.86	1											
5 All tag questions	*.45	−.03	−.03	.07	1										
6 Aux. tags only	.27	−.09	−.03	.00	‡.74	1									
7 All intonation only Y/Ns	‡.62	‡.70	.09	−.02	−.01	−.11	1								
8 All responding Y/Ns	†.46	.19	−.10	−.06	‡.62	*.44	*.42	1							
9 Intonation only responses	*.44	*.37	−.08	−.05	.23	.14	†.67	‡.82	1						
10 All extensions/expansions	.35	.12	−.03	.10	†.50	*.38	.23	‡.79	†.55	1					
11 All initiating Y/Ns	‡.79	‡.85	‡.83	‡.64	.07	.00	*.40	−.18	−.08	−.16	1				
12 Initiating Y/Ns (excl. tags)	‡.67	‡.83	‡.82	‡.62	−.12	−.13	*.39	−.21	−.15	−.10	‡.90	1			
13 Initiating inversions (excl. tags)	‡.64	‡.72	‡.94	‡.78	.00	.00	.07	−.10	−.13	.02	‡.78	‡.88	1		
14 Initiating aux. inversion only (excl. tags)	†.52	‡.60	‡.85	‡.98	−.04	−.04	−.02	−.15	−.09	−.04	‡.68	‡.62	‡.79	1	
15 Initiating intonation only	*.40	‡.58	.21	.05	−.24	−.26	‡.67	−.26	−.10	−.22	.62	‡.68	.23	.08	1

*p < .05; †p < .02; ‡p < .01; *df* = 30; two-tailed

Table 11.9 *Correlations between Y/N input variables and child auxiliary measures at T1*

| Y/N input variables | T1 aux. scores | | |
	Meanings	Frequency	Forms
1 All Y/Ns (incl. tags)	.05	−.18	.05
2 Y/Ns (excl. tags)	.01	−.20	.01
3 Y/N inversions (excl. tags)	.07	−.24	.07
4 Aux. inversion only	.08	−.20	.08
5 All tag questions	.08	.00	.08
6 Aux. tags only	−.04	−.02	−.04
7 All intonation only Y/Ns	−.06	−.05	−.06
8 All responding Y/Ns	.27	.24	.27
9 Intonation only responses	.19	.26	.19
10 All extensions/expansions	.29	.23	.29
11 All initiating Y/Ns	−.14	−.37*	−.14
12 Initiating Y/Ns (excl. tags)	−.10	−.36*	−.10
13 Initiating inversions (excl. tags)	.03	−.27	.03
14 Initiating aux. inversion only (excl. tags)	−.03	−.22	−.03
15 Initiating intonation only	−.25	−.31	−.25

*$p < .05$; $df = 30$; two-tailed.

Table 11.10 *Discourse role and syntactic feature of Y/Ns addressed to thirty-two children*

| Syntactic type | Discourse role | |
	Respond	Initiate
Y/N inversions	23	161
Intonation only	99	85
Tag questions	76	86

11.4.2 Relationships between Y/Ns and auxiliary gains

It should be pointed out that cross-tabulating the syntactic variables with the discourse categories gives a potential of ninety cells. If the frequencies in each cell were correlated against all three sets of residual gain scores, the result would be 270 correlation coefficients. In an analysis of this size one might expect approximately fourteen correlations to be statistically significant at the .05 level by chance alone. In practice, of course, such fine divisions result in some empty cells and many with low frequencies. Even so, the possible number of correlations is still very large. Here, correlations have only been computed which have direct relevance to the hypotheses being tested: the Auxiliary Clarification Hypothesis, the role of tag questions in displaying the behaviour of the auxiliary, and the Responsive Style Hypothesis.

Testing these hypotheses and obtaining results which are interpretable in relation to other published studies entails using both global categories as well as separate analyses for tags, auxiliary operators (excluding the copula), and initiating and responding utterances. Correlations were therefore computed between fifteen Y/N input variables and BGSW's residual gain scores for the three auxiliary measures. These will be reported in three sections beginning with the combined discourse categories (variables 1–7).

Results confirm the existence of a relationship between Y/Ns and subsequent rate of auxiliary verb learning (Table 11.11), though tag questions show no effect. Although none of the input measures are significantly associated with all three auxiliary scores, several attain significance on two and approach significance on the third (the threshold for significance at the .05 level is $r = .349$).

However the most striking aspect of these results is that BGSW's original finding has been reversed. It is now the inverted category of Y/N question which is significantly associated with learning auxiliaries. There is no longer any correlation with the intonation only type. This result, which for the first time replicates NGG and GNG's finding, albeit at a much weaker level, is consistent with the Auxiliary Clarification Hypothesis. Nevertheless, when copula inversions are removed (variable 4), the effect is less robust; the correlation only holds for auxiliary forms, although auxiliary frequency also approaches significance.

Given the lack of any relationship between auxiliary growth and intonation only Y/Ns, the results for the responding categories (Table 11.12) are less surprising. There is no evidence that Y/Ns as part of a responsive style of interaction contribute to auxiliary verb learning.

Table 11.11 *Correlations between Y/Ns (combined discourse roles) and auxiliary gains*

	Aux. gain scores		
Y/N variables	Meanings	Frequency	Forms
1 All Y/Ns (incl. tags)	.32	.45‡	.35*
2 Y/Ns (excl. tags)	.37*	.34	.38*
3 Y/N inversions (excl. tags)	.36*	.32	.42†
4 Aux. inversion only	.30	.32	.38*
5 All tag questions	−.01	.31	.03
6 Aux. tags only	−.16	.21	−.13
7 All intonation only Y/Ns	.17	.18	.12

$*p < .05$; $†p < .02$; $‡p < .01$; $df = 30$; two-tailed.

Table 11.12 *Correlations between responding Y/Ns and auxiliary gains*

	Aux. gain scores		
Y/N response variables	Meanings	Frequency	Forms
8 All responding Y/Ns	−.05	.19	.01
9 Intonation only responses	−.05	.11	−.02
10 All extensions/expansions	.00	.25	.03

All are ns; $df = 30$; two-tailed.

If Y/N responses produce no effects, then it is reasonable to assume that the significant correlations in Table 11.11 were brought about by the contribution of initiating utterances, particularly inversions. There is also the possibility, however, that initiating intonation only Y/Ns, which were seen in Table 11.10 to occur in substantial numbers, are responsible for the relationship between auxiliaries and intonation only Y/Ns found by FNB and BGSW.

Table 11.13 confirms the contribution of initiating Y/Ns (significant across all three auxiliary measures), and initiating inversions (significant for two measures), although once again the effect is less consistent when the contribution of the copula is removed. Intonation only Y/Ns as exchange-initiating utterances show no effect.

Table 11.13 *Correlations between initiating Y/Ns and auxiliary gains*

	Aux. gain scores		
Y/N initiating variables	Meanings	Frequency	Forms
11 All initiating Y/Ns	.39*	.37*	.39*
12 Initiating Y/Ns (excl. tags)	.41†	.24	.39*
13 Initiating inversions (excl. tags)	.37*	.24	.41*
14 Initiating aux. inversion only			
(excl. tags)	.29	.32	.37*
15 Initiating intonation only	.27	.13	.16

*$p < .05$; †$p < .02$; $df = 30$; two-tailed.

11.4.3 Summary of results

It was found that Y/N inversions usually initiate exchanges, while intonation Y/Ns equally respond and initiate. Responding Y/Ns usually omit the operator. Nevertheless, the Responsive Style Hypothesis has to be rejected. Neither intonation only, nor responding Y/Ns predict rate of auxiliary learning. Instead, Y/N inversions, especially the combined auxiliary and copula category facilitate auxiliary growth.

Clearly this brings us no closer to an explanation for BGSW's result, but a further hypothesis will be tested in the next section. Then, in Section 11.6, results will be evaluated in greater detail for their compatibility with the Auxiliary Clarification Hypothesis.

11.5 The statistical effect of intonation only Y/Ns: an alternative hypothesis

Even though a relationship between intonation only Y/Ns and auxiliary learning was absent from the reanalysis of BGSW's data, their original finding cannot be dismissed as uninteresting, especially as FNB had an identical result. Initially, it had been suspected that adult interlocutors were responding to the child's auxiliary development, or that correlations were spurious because Y/Ns which retained and dropped the auxiliary were themselves correlated. These explanations were easily rejected on the evidence available. However, another type of spuriousness is also possible. This could occur if two variables, which were not correlated at T1, become related at a later stage. A finding by Wells (1985) suggests a way in which this might happen.

Wells plotted the pooled input frequencies of five auxiliaries against the age of sixty children. These included BGSW's thirty-two subjects. Wells found that the median age of emergence of each form for the children was preceded by an increase in the input frequency of that form and eventually followed by a decline in frequency (Wells, 1985, p. 375). A similar phenomenon can be observed in the development of sentence meaning relations (p. 376). Wells interprets this as a process of linguistic 'fine-tuning'. This is a strong claim, though there is evidence of adjustments in maternal auxiliaries/verb phrase to child auxiliary development from the Fiffin Project (K. E. Nelson et al., 1984). Whatever the reasons, however, its existence provokes questions about the possible role of Y/Ns in this 'tuning'. Interestingly the rise in auxiliaries in input in Wells' graph takes place when the average child in the BGSW study is between T1 and T2, and for four of the five auxiliaries analysed by Wells the median age of emergence occurs before the median age at T2. Is it possible, then, that over the period covered by the BGSW study, there is a trend for Y/Ns to omit the auxiliary less and less? If this is the case, a proportion of intonation only Y/Ns at T1 would be replaced by inversions by T2. This trend might then be responsible for an indirect relationship between intonation only Y/Ns at T1 and rate of auxiliary verb development by T2. If this explanation is true, then within Y/Ns one would expect a falling trend for the intonation category and a rising trend for inversions.

This hypothesis was tested on ten children chosen at random. Using BGSW's definition of input, Y/Ns were coded for the four recordings which span the period T1 to T2. Copula and auxiliary inversions were pooled.

11.5.1 Trends in Y/N input frequency

As can be seen from Table 11.14, the pooled frequencies for the ten children over four occasions suggest trends consistent with the above hypotheses.

It appears from these figures that increases in Y/Ns which retain the auxiliary are accompanied by a decrease in those which do not. There is also a suggestion that this pattern is repeated within initiating Y/Ns and within Y/N responses. However, trends in pooled frequencies do not necessarily reflect trends which are valid for individuals. In order to check that these trends are real, therefore, Page's L Test (Page, 1963) was applied to those trends where a frequency of over 10% was attained (Table 11.15).

The significance tests confirm the reality of upward and downward trends in inversions and intonation only Y/Ns. Within response and initiating categories, however, this pattern is less clear. Nevertheless, the results are broadly consistent with the possibility of an indirect association as outlined above,

Table 11.14 *Trends over four recordings of selected Y/N types as a proportion of all Y/Ns (incl. tags)*

	Recording			
Y/N input variable	1(T1) (%)	2 (%)	3 (%)	4(T2) (%)
Y/N inversions (excl. tags)	23.0	25.4	40.4	43.4
Intonation only Y/Ns	39.3	28.4	27.1	26.5
Non-inverted Y/Ns	1.6	1.8	2.1	2.6
Intonation only responses	22.4	18.3	11.7	13.5
Intonation only initiating	16.9	10.1	15.4	13.0
Initiating inversions	20.8	18.3	32.4	31.7
Responding inversions	2.2	7.1	8.0	11.7

Table 11.15 *Significance and direction of trends identified in Table 11.14*

Y/N input variables	Direction	Significance*
Y/N inversion (excl. tags)	up	$p < .01$
Intonation only Y/Ns	down	$p < .05$
Intonation only responses	down	ns
Intonation only initiating	down	$p < .05$
Initiating inversions	up	ns
Responding inversions	up	$p < .05$

*Subjects: 10; Conditions: 4.

even though they are a long way from demonstrating that the significant increases and decreases in frequency are related. This is shown by the fact that if we look at correlations for the ten children between intonation only Y/Ns at T1 (Rec.1), and Y/N inversions in the remaining three recordings, we only find a significant association with Y/N inversions at Recording 2 ($r = .66$; $df = 8$; $p < .05$; two-tailed). There is no relationship with inversions at Recording 3 ($r = -.17$) or Recording 4 ($r = .32$). Interestingly, though, the correlation between intonation only and inverted Y/Ns at T1 ($r = .55$) approaches significance for this subsample of children. Since the corresponding figure for all thirty-two children was $r = -.02$, there seem to be individual differences in the way that subsections of the Y/N system relate to each other.

11.5.2 Discussion of Y/N trends

The existence of significant trends in favour of more frequent auxiliary inclusion in input raises some interesting questions about tuning. Wells (1985) argues convincingly for a form of linguistic fine-tuning in which adults respond to the child's current level of comprehension. This explanation has some appeal because it is consistent with Wells' results from both the analysis of auxiliaries, and of sentence meaning relations. If, on the other hand, we consider the auxiliary forms in isolation, an equally viable explanation presents itself.

Wells studied five forms (DO, WILL, BE + ING, HAVE + EN, HAVE + GOT), and four of these are verbs for which obligatory, or at least probable contexts are relatively easy to identify. We know that children learn to produce contexts such as # 'Man going', # 'Daddy got new car', # 'I got to go bed', and # 'I have tea now' before they produce equivalent utterances containing an auxiliary (see Chapters 5 and 6). It is possible therefore that child-directed speech is sensitive to the production of contexts into which an appropriate auxiliary can be inserted without changing meaning or function. In the case of the fifth auxiliary, DO, whose role is purely as a syntactic operator, it is inappropriate to invoke explanations which depend on comprehension of auxiliary meanings. At the most, adult interlocutors may be responding to the syntactic functions of negation, interrogation, and emphasis. On the other hand, the child has other means such as negative particles, intonation, and stress for performing these syntactic functions before DO develops, and it may be the development of these which triggers changes in the child's conversation partners.

Two explanations for trends in the frequency of auxiliaries addressed to children, one based on the child's comprehension, one on production, have been considered. Both accounts imply a degree of monitoring, conscious or unconscious, which is difficult to explain, so it is also worth considering other, nonlinguistic explanations such as 'rough tuning' to the child's age, or developing behaviour patterns. Between the ages of two and three, one can imagine that physical and social developments cause significant changes in the quality of interaction between child and caregiver which are realised in the linguistic systems of child-directed speech. As the child becomes physically less dependent, more mobile and more autonomous, it is not inconceivable that a system such as the auxiliary, with its potential for performative usage, plays a major part in the linguistic response to such developments.

Of the above explanations it is the nonlinguistic one which can most easily be reconciled with the hypothesis that the relationship between intonation only Y/Ns and auxiliary learning is mediated by auxiliary inversions. If the trends in Y/Ns were a response to the child's developing auxiliary system, it could not also be the cause of those developments unless we posit a complex series of developments and reactions. However, one way such a process could unfold is as follows:

1. Some children's conversational partners at T1 use a high proportion of Y/Ns. Many contain no operator. They are as yet unrelated to the child's auxiliary development.
2. Children develop understanding of, and obligatory contexts for, usage of auxiliaries.
3. In response, Y/Ns in child-directed speech increasingly include the auxiliary. High Y/N producers at T1 continue to be high producers.
4. The effect of 3. is to increase the frequency of clarified Y/N-initial auxiliaries sufficiently to facilitate further auxiliary learning.
5. These developments return us to 3., after which the cycle continues until the child's auxiliary development levels off.

This account is, of course, highly speculative. But whatever the reason for trends towards greater use of auxiliaries in the language addressed to children, the results which have been obtained thus far are consistent with the hypothesis that auxiliary learning is made easier by hearing Y/N inversions.

11.6 Re-evaluation of the Auxiliary Clarification Hypothesis

Now that we have results which support the view that Y/N inversions contribute to learning auxiliaries, we need to establish whether auxiliaries in Y/Ns really are clarified in the way GNG suppose, and whether they are the same forms as those being acquired by the children between T1 and T2. These points will be examined in the next two sections.

11.6.1 Clarification of the auxiliary

Figure 11.6 shows how the phonological features of the initial auxiliary or copula in Y/Ns might be expected to increase its salience. The most useful combination would be Cell 1 (Stressed + Full form), and the least helpful would be Cell 4 (Unstressed + Reduced). Since heavily stressed forms also tend to be nonreduced and noncontracted, and unstressed forms are associated with reduction and contraction, it was predicted that most initial auxiliaries would fall into Cells 1 and 4. To be consistent with GNG's hypothesis a substantial proportion of auxiliaries would have to appear in Cell 1.

	Full	Reduced
Stressed	(1)	(2)
Unstressed	(3)	(4)

Fig. 11.6 Model of salience of the operator in Y/N inversions

Patterns of stress and reduction were analysed for half the subjects in the sample (seven boys and nine girls), only selecting children whose T1 recordings were of high acoustic quality. A total of 128 Y/N inversions (excluding tags) were retranscribed, marked for stress patterns,[2] and the operator given a phonetic transcription. Operators carrying primary or secondary stress were coded as stressed. Each case was then assigned to one of the four cells in Figure 11.6:

1. /'hæv/ (= have) you 'eaten the 'others? (*Benjamin, 1;9*): Full + Stressed.
2. /'kə/ (= can) you . "see 'yourself in the 'mirror? (*Gerald, 1;9*): Reduced + Stressed.
3. /wɪl'ju:/ (= will you) 'sit 'up at the 'table 'properly? (*Debbie, 2;3*): Full + Unstressed.
4. /ʃl'aɪ/ (shall I) 'eat it? (*Benjamin, 1;9*): Reduced + Unstressed.

Sometimes a consonant was dropped without affecting the length or quality of a vowel: /'dɪjʊ/ (= did you) and this was also classed as reduction. On the other hand, the quality of a terminal vowel can change without reduction due to assimilation to the sound of the following pronoun: /di:jʊ/ (= do you). This is an additional dimension not allowed for in the model. Such cases, which were rare, were coded as full forms, but their existence draws attention to a third source of variation which must surely make the child's task of segmentation and identification of related forms all the more difficult. In the pronunciation of 'Do you?' the more common versions were /dju:/ or /djʊ/, sounds which also have no obvious point of segmentation. In fact this analysis further illustrates the variation in the properties of Y/N-initial auxiliaries discussed by Fletcher (1983; 1985) and Malan (1983). A good example is the verb 'shall' which in sixteen occurrences at the beginning of Y/Ns received eight different pronunciations. More importantly, it was often the *same* child who was exposed to different versions:

/ʃlaɪ/	= Shall I?	(*Martin, 2;0*)
/ʃəwɪ/	= Shall we?	(*Martin, 2;0*)
/ʃæl dædɪ/	= Shall Daddy?	(*Jonathan, 1;9*)
/ʃʊwɪ/	= Shall we?	(*Jonathan, 1;9*)
/ʃəlaɪ/	= Shall I?	(*Neville, 2;0*)
/ʃaɪ/	= Shall I?	(*Elspeth, 2;0*)
/ʃə/	= Shall I?	(*Elspeth, 2;0*)
/laɪ/	= Shall I?	(*Benjamin, 1;9*)

As predicted, when the codings of stress and reduction were related to the four cells in Figure 11.6, the majority of cases (78%) were allocated to Cells 1 and 4. These were the cells hypothesised to be most and least facilitative respectively. The combined analysis for copula and auxiliary is shown in Table 11.16 and separate figures for the auxiliary are given in Table 11.17.

Table 11.16 *Salience of the operator in 128 Y/N inversions*

	Full (%)	Reduced (%)	Total (%)
Stressed	28.1	14.8	42.9
Unstressed	7.0	50.0	57.0
Total	35.1	64.8	99.9

Table 11.17 *Salience of the auxiliary in 94 Y/N inversions*

	Full (%)	Reduced (%)	Total (%)
Stressed	24.5	16.0	40.5
Unstressed	6.4	53.2	59.6
Total	30.9	69.2	100.1

From these figures it appears that in half the cases the operator is not 'clarified' by either stress or nonreduction (Cell 4) and only a quarter of Y/Ns are both stressed and nonreduced.

It is interesting to compare these results with those of Malan (1983) who coded Y/Ns addressed to one child, Sophie, for stress and 'contraction'. Malan included tag questions, but Table 11.18 combines her data for ellipsed and non-ellipsed Y/Ns in a way which makes it comparable with Table 11.16.

Table 11.18 *Salience of the operator in Malan's[a] analysis (N = 66)*

	Full (%)	Reduced (%)	Total (%)
Stressed	22.7	3.0	25.7
Unstressed	15.2	59.1	74.3
Total	37.9	62.1	100.0

[a] Figures obtained by combining tables for ellipsed and 'full' Y/Ns (Malan, 1983, p. 30).

Although the Y/Ns addressed to the Bristol children appear to be slightly more helpful in their clarification of the operator than those addressed to Malan's subject, both analyses place at least half the tokens in the least clarified category. It should perhaps be noted that Sophie was older (2;4) and linguistically more advanced (MLU = 2.53) than the Bristol children when this aspect of input was coded.

These results demonstrate that, even in data where Y/N inversions are significantly correlated with rate of auxiliary development, they do not clarify the auxiliary to anything like the extent claimed by GNG. This raises two possibilities which will be addressed in section 11.7: either the auxiliary becomes more salient in Y/N questions for quite different reasons, or the low frequency of fully or partially clarified cases is nevertheless sufficient to bring about the effect.

11.6.2 A comparison of auxiliaries heard at T1 and children's auxiliaries used by T2

This part of the investigation re-uses the data from Section 11.6.1. Firstly, the ninety-four auxiliaries in Y/N inversions were classified according to form. Secondly, the forms which emerged in the two recordings between T1 and T2, and at T2 were extracted and a comparison was made between the two sets of auxiliary forms.

As can be seen from Table 11.19, the most striking feature of the Y/N-initial auxiliaries heard by the child is the preponderance of DO forms, particularly 'do', due to the frequency of the 'Do you . . .?' format. 'Shall' also appears frequently and reflects the use of 'Shall we . . .?' as a suggestion for activity, or as a weak request.

Table 11.19 *Frequency of auxiliary forms in Y/N inversions at T1*

	Frequency of forms	
Aux. form	Major form (%)	Subform (%)
DO	41.5	
do		31.9
does		1.1
did		6.4
don't		2.1
HAVE + EN	10.6	
have		7.4
haven't		2.1
hasn't		1.1
BE + ING	10.6	
is		7.4
are		3.2
can	11.7	11.7
will	3.2	3.2
shall	17.0	17.0
could	1.1	1.1
WOULD	4.3	
would		3.2
wouldn't		1.1
Totals	100.0	100.0

On average, 61% of the subforms which each child heard in Y/N inversions at T1 had emerged by T2. If anything, an analysis by subforms underestimates the proportion of forms to emerge because it fails to take into account possible relationships such as 'shall' in input, and ' 'll' used by the child in medial position. The percentage based on major forms is 77.8%, but this is probably an overestimate since it presupposes a relatively advanced degree of analysis of the auxiliary system – it would assume, for example, awareness of the relationship between 'will' and 'won't'.

Using a sign test it is possible to demonstrate ($p < .006$) that for most children more than half the Y/N-initial auxiliaries (major forms, excluding ''ll') subsequently occur for the first time. When this procedure is applied to subforms, however, the relationship is nonsignificant ($p < .212$). This approach is not particularly helpful, therefore, and the most that can be said is that auxiliaries being heard are not different from those emerging. But it is hardly likely that they would be different, since there is only a limited number of auxiliary forms which can emerge. However, another aspect is that there are also forms emerging of which there is no record in Y/N-initial position in the input at T1. If we use the above method to focus on all the subforms which had emerged by T2, we find that just under half (42%) had been sampled in inverted Y/Ns at T1.

In summary, this type of analysis using fairly sparse data from sixteen children has done little more than to draw attention to the distribution of forms in initial position at T1. The strongest claims that can be made from the comparison between T1 and T2 are that forms heard are not different from the forms to develop, and that the forms to develop are not different from the forms heard.

11.7 Discussion

The analyses in this chapter began as an attempt to explain BGSW's finding that intonation only Y/Ns predicted rate of auxiliary learning. After inspecting BGSW's data and rejecting several of the more obvious explanations, it was decided to test the hypothesis that Y/Ns were part of a facilitative responding style of interaction. Since the auxiliary played an important part in the children's language development between T1 and T2, it was felt that auxiliary gain scores might be sensitive to general linguistic development. An analysis of the utterances addressed to the children confirmed that Y/Ns (excluding tags) which responded to the child, tended to omit the operator.

It proved impossible to reproduce BGSW's input frequencies for Y/Ns with sufficient accuracy to guarantee identifying the factors which gave rise to their result. The decision was taken, therefore, to recode all Y/N input on the basis of what was considered to be a more representative sample of the speech addressed to the thirty-two subjects. This also had the fortunate spin-off of enlarging the size of the data base from which input frequencies were calculated.

The result of the new coding was that BGSW's effect disappeared. No category of intonation only Y/Ns nor of responding Y/Ns was associated with auxiliary scores, and the Responsive Style Hypothesis had to be rejected. Instead, a set of correlations was obtained which were more consistent with the Auxiliary Clarification Hypothesis. Inversions and exchange-initiating Y/Ns, which were themselves highly correlated at T1 ($r = .83$), were the categories which predicted development most consistently across the three measures of auxiliary growth. Significant correlations were also found when the contribution of the inverted copula was removed, although these effects were less consistent. Copula inversions and auxiliary inversions were not related at T1 ($r = .18$), but from the point of view of syntactic function the copula is similar to the primary auxiliaries and central modals. All exhibit the NICE properties. At some stage, knowledge of these functions may contribute to the development of a class of *operators* rather than a pure auxiliary class. Initially, however, it is possible that inverted copula BE *and* inverted auxiliary BE play a role in clarifying the various unstressed and contracted BE forms. Work is currently in progress to investigate the contribution of Y/N inversions to the development of the copula.

11.7.1 Why do the results differ in the two analyses?

Why Y/N inversions should appear to be facilitative in one case and not the other is not clear. One possibility is that including all utterances addressed to the child genuinely improved the representativeness of the input sample and produced more valid results. Another possibility lies in the application of coding criteria in the two studies. It was suggested above that variation in the treatment of tags may account for the failure to reproduce BGSW's input frequencies. Formal tag questions were found both in this analysis and in BGSW's unpublished results to make no contribution to auxiliary learning, despite the fact that inversion is an obligatory feature. On the other hand, inversion in tags places the operator at the beginning of its clause and not necessarily at the beginning of the utterance. It may be 'clarified' in terms of stress and noncontraction but still be less salient than most other operators in Y/N-initial position. It is feasible, therefore, that the inclusion by BGSW of some utterances in the Y/N inversion category which would have been coded as tags in the reanalysis could have caused correlations to be attenuated.

Explanations for the difference in the effect of intonation only Y/Ns between the two analyses can also only be speculative. In section 11.5 it was suggested that this effect is an indirect one mediated by a later tendency to include more auxiliaries in Y/Ns. If adult Y/Ns are tuned in some way to behavioural, physical, chronological, or linguistic aspects of child development, then input from siblings and peers may be less sensitive to such changes.

11.7.2 How strong is the evidence for a link between Y/N inversions and auxiliary learning?
It must be remembered that of the correlational investigations reviewed in Chapter 10, there is no published report of a significant correlation with a separate category of auxiliary inversions in Y/Ns. Three studies (HG1, FNB and BGSW) found a relationship with intonation only Y/Ns, although the HG1 correlation was found to be spurious. Nevertheless, as indicated in Section 11.5, these associations are not necessarily inconsistent with an indirect effect through Y/N inversions. Evidence from NGG and GNG, and from blind children (Landau and Gleitman, 1985) attest to the contribution of Y/Ns as a global category, but an experimental study (Shatz et al., 1989) which provided an enriched input of initial auxiliaries was unable to show a faster rate of development than for a control group. On the other hand, it was found that pairs of utterances containing the initial auxiliary were more effective than either pairs of utterances containing the auxiliary in medial position or pairs which contrasted the auxiliary in initial and medial positions.

11.7.3 The Auxiliary Clarification Hypothesis and other explanations
GNG's version of the Auxiliary Clarification Hypothesis has two main strands: positional salience and phonological clarification (full, stressed forms), and a learnability account which depends on input of intermediate complexity (Y/Ns) combined with the child's disposition to reconstruct canonical form. Data of intermediate complexity are required, in the absence of negative evidence, to enable the child to develop rules which not only account for grammatical surface structures but also preclude the production of ungrammatical strings. Canonical form refers to Bellugi's (1967) finding that, in both declaratives and interrogatives, children first use auxiliaries in an uncontracted form in *medial* position (despite the fact that maternal auxiliaries in declaratives are usually contracted).

Despite obtaining a pattern of correlations which are consistent with GNG's explanation, several problems remain. Most seriously, it has been shown that only about 40% of initial Y/N auxiliaries are stressed. Added to this, 69% are phonologically reduced. This means that only a quarter are both full *and* stressed in the way that GNG's argument requires. It has also been shown that initial Y/Ns can exhibit phonological variation to an extent which highlights an additional burden on the child in making use of data of this type. Another piece of evidence which suggests a less than straightforward Y/N–auxiliary association concerns the forms which tend to occur in Y/N inversions. In Section 11.6.2 it was found that DO forms were the operator in over 40% of auxiliary Y/Ns. The overwhelming majority of these are 'do', mainly in a 'Do you . . .?' construction and frequently pronounced in a way which did not obviously indicate a point for the segmentation of auxiliary from pronoun: /dju:/. The next most frequent form was SHALL (17%). That these forms should be the most common is interesting because affirmative DO forms rarely occur medially in declaratives unless for emphasis, or as a feature of certain regional dialects (see Section 8.3). Uncontracted SHALL can occur medially in declaratives, but is more common in Wh- and Y/N inversions; in the transcripts of the thirty-two Bristol children, SHALL had emerged in declaratives for only two children by T2 and in Y/Ns for seven children. There was no record of any child using SHALL in other syntactic frames.

Secondly, GNG's hypothesis can only provide a partial account of auxiliary learning, a theme which will be addressed more fully in Chapter 12. Two claims should be challenged immediately, however. Firstly, the auxiliary does not always appear medially since the initial pronoun is frequently absent from first auxiliary utterances ('can't do it!', 'can't open it', 'can't!', 'can't find it': Alex, Rec. 3, 2;8.3), and there are other language learning processes consistent with this phenomenon which will be considered below. Secondly, there was evidence from the Welsh children that for contractible auxiliaries in medial position in declaratives, it is not the full, canonical form which occurs first, but the contracted form[3] – a form which is even further removed from the Y/N initial form.

In the light of these difficulties it is worth considering alternative explanations for the association between Y/Ns and rate of auxiliary verb development.

Hoff-Ginsberg and Shatz (1982) suggest four ways in which the Y/N–auxiliary correlation might be mediated by characteristics of questions other than the clarification of the auxiliary operator. The first two of these will be considered jointly, followed by a separate consideration of the remaining two points.

It is suggested that a) questioning could be part of a type of interaction which is associated with a faster rate of general language development, or that b) questions, because they attempt to elicit responses, are more salient than other speech acts. The child is therefore more likely to notice any auxiliary which they contain. Such a position receives some support from HG2 – Real Questions (genuine request for information) and Verbal Reflective Questions (usually communication checks) both predict auxiliary verb learning. However, the effect of the latter type would be consistent with the Responding Style Hypothesis which was rejected in the analysis above – Y/N responses were not found to be facilitative. However, many of the Y/N *inversions* could certainly be classified as 'Real Questions'. From Hoff-Ginsberg's results (HG2, Table 4) it can be seen that Y/Ns and Real Questions are correlated ($r = .68; p < .001; df = 20$; two-tailed). Because this is a global Y/N category, we don't know whether the relationship holds true for inversions, but it seems likely that many utterances in Hoff-Ginsberg's Real Question category correspond with the initiating Y/N inversions in the current study. It also seems likely that the effect is produced by the specific syntactic characteristics of Y/Ns rather than by a questioning style as such. Otherwise there would be more evidence of facilitation through Wh- and tag questions. As yet, there is little indication of the usefulness of tags at this stage, while evidence relating to Wh- questions is contradictory. HG1 and HG2 find a correlation between Wh-questions and auxiliary development. However, BGSW, NGG and FNB find no relationship and GNG found a *negative* correlation between Wh-questions and auxiliaries per verb phrase for their intermediate age group, though this result failed to survive their controversial (Furrow and Nelson, 1986) split half reliability test.

Secondly, Hoff-Ginsberg and Shatz look at the influence of Y/Ns on the linguistic forms practised by the child, especially the way in which the child can use the lexis and syntax of the Y/N in formulating a response. This is interesting in the light of the different effect obtained above for initiating and responding Y/Ns. Since a large proportion of the response category in the current investigation are ostensibly communication checks, they may require no more than a nonverbal acknowledgement in reply. Initiating Y/Ns, on the other hand, give the child greater opportunity to engage in the type of practice described by Hoff-Ginsberg and Shatz. Both the Bristol and the Welsh recordings provide many examples of Y/N inversions which allow partial incorporation of elements in the child's response:

> R: did you have it for Christmas?
> C: yes . did
> R: does it make them nice and smooth?
> [asking about her hand cream]
> C: yes does (*Betty, Rec. 7, 2;7.23*)

The child's strategy can be regarded as a means of practising what is in the process of being acquired, or of performing at a level above current competence by repeating or incorporating unanalysed morphemes (see Clark 1974, 1977, 1978, 1980). Nevertheless, it can also be argued that this type of practice will be more likely to occur if the operator *is* clarified, since there is then a greater likelihood that an auxiliary will be included in the reply. Certain routine exchanges of this type are particularly well suited for the acquisition of rote-learned units containing an auxiliary, and even if the child only pays attention to the elements which are acoustically and positionally salient, the result can still be identical to a well-formed declarative:

> M: Can't you do it?
> C: Can't do it (*Alex, Rec. 1, 2;7.6*)

Processes such as these are therefore compatible with aspects of NGG and GNG's account of the role of Y/Ns in auxiliary learning which are not derived from learnability theory: the position and clarification of the operator, and children first using the auxiliary in an uncontracted form in declarative sentences. This might also help to explain the occurrence of auxiliary utterances which omit the initial subject. Future research might include detailed analyses of this type of discourse dependency in conversations with children.

Thirdly, and finally, Hoff-Ginsberg and Shatz consider the contrasting positions of the auxiliary in declaratives and inverted Y/Ns as one of its defining properties. An awareness of this change of position could assist in a distributional analysis as part of the process of developing 'auxiliary' as a form-class. However, the evidence does not seem to support such a hypothesis at this early stage of learning. Shatz et al.'s (1989) experimental manipulation of Y/N input found pairs of Y/Ns which contrasted auxiliary position to be less helpful than pairs of utterances containing the initial auxiliary. In addition, there is no evidence that tag questions are facilitative. One would expect reversed polarity tags which repeat the auxiliary in the matrix clause (# 'You can do it, can't you?') to be particularly useful in displaying no less than three of the four NICE properties (Negation, Interrogation, Code, and Emphatic Affirmation). Yet tags seem to be unhelpful in learning the very items whose behaviour they illustrate so well. What more effective way could there be, for example, of showing the relationship between, say 'will' and 'won't' within the span of a single utterance?

On the other hand, the child may not yet be ready for such complex information. As the analysis of usage of T2 showed, this is still a relatively basic stage of auxiliary development for most of the children and it is too early to think in terms of an integrated system. Hearing a demonstration of the derivation of 'won't' from 'will' may have little value until the child already possesses some knowledge of these forms. There is also the possibility that because of the complexity of tags (see Chapter 7), the difference between the tag and its matrix is so great that the child is overloaded with contrasting information and is unable to develop hypotheses of sufficient complexity to account for the relationship between the two. The advantage of a 'simple' Y/N question compared with a declarative + tag might be similar to that enjoyed by simple recasts (those which make a structural change to only one constituent) over more complex recasts. K. E. Nelson et al. (1984) found that the thirteen children who were most advanced on a composite syntactic growth score at 27 months had received a significantly higher frequency of simple recasts that twelve low scorers five months earlier. The low scorers, on the other hand, had received a higher frequency of complex recasts. Hoff-Ginsberg (HG1) reports a similar finding; in pairs of utterances, changes which affected parts of constituents were correlated with language development, while changes to the whole constituent were not. Nelson's explanation for the effectiveness of recasts is that they enable 'cognitive comparisons' (K. E. Nelson, 1980, 1981) to be made between utterances, particularly between the child's utterance and the adult's recast. But even though the child may be more likely to attend to adjustments to its own productions, there is no reason why cognitive comparisons shouldn't be effected within a single utterance. In fact there may be advantages in receiving contrasting information in this way, in as far as it reduces memory load. If a reversed polarity Declarative + Tag is too complex at a certain stage, an interesting hypothesis would be that auxiliary gains are initially predicted by tags whose polarity is not reversed (#'You can do it, can you?') and only at a later stage by the more complex type. The role of tags of varying complexity in providing evidence of the syntactic properties of the auxiliary is currently being investigated.

Finally, we shall address the question of segmentation and identification of constituent boundaries. Hoff-Ginsberg and Shatz refer to work by Morgan and Newport (1981) on the acquisition of artificial languages by adults. Morgan and Newport showed the importance of properties of the input which draw attention to constituent boundaries. For marking off the auxiliary this might include pairing declaratives with their related interrogative form, a strategy which seems to be less effective than hearing pairs of Y/Ns. Nevertheless, the very fact of the auxiliary being placed initially, rather than medially, is a segmentation problem halved. Interestingly, the other half of the segmentation problem can be solved by another of the unique properties of the auxiliary which this time unequivocally avoids contraction and reduction and increases its salience. This is the use of the auxiliary as a 'stranded operator' (Quirk et al., 1985) in sentences with main verb ellipsis ('You must', 'He does', etc.). Since there is evidence that children attend to the end of words and utterances (Kuczaj, 1979b; Slobin, 1979; Slobin and Welsh; 1973), the auxiliary in final position would also correspond with processing biases discussed by NGG, a primacy effect being replaced by a recency effect. One way in which future research might disentangle saliency and segmentation effects from the effects of question functions might be to investigate relationships between this type of ellipsis in input and children's auxiliary verb learning.

11.8 Summary and conclusion

A number of factors and processes have been identified through which Y/N inversions might facilitate auxiliary development:

1. Questions are salient speech acts and draw attention to auxiliaries they may contain.
2. Y/Ns allow children to incorporate auxiliaries in their replies, allowing practice with the auxiliary and the acquisition of unanalysed or partially analysed functional 'chunks'.
3. Y/N inversions display a combination of at least two characteristics of the syntax of the auxiliary: subject–verb inversion, and either co-occurrence with a main verb or ellipsis. Such information would aid the development of the auxiliary as a form class through a distributional analysis.
4. Medial auxiliaries present a segmentation problem. Y/N inversions reduce this problem by half.

To these we can add aspects of clarification proposed by NGG and GNG:

5. The salience of sentence-initial position.
6. Stress and noncontraction of the initial auxiliary.

Of these factors only 5. is unassailable. Evidence from the phonetic transcriptions suggests that even 4. would still leave the child with the problem of classifying the various allophones of the sentence-initial auxiliary. As far as 1. is concerned, other questions which contain an auxiliary such as Wh-s and tags do not appear to be facilitative. In 2. practice, incorporation, and rote learning from Y/Ns cannot account for the child's learning to use medial unstressed affirmative DO forms or early declarative usage of contracted forms. In 3., since earlier chapters have shown that much of the auxiliary system seems to be developed piecemeal, considerable knowledge of discrete parts of the system will have to be acquired before one can speak of a form class based on more complex syntactic features such as inversion. This is a hypothesis which would apply more to the later stages of auxiliary learning, possibly after T2. Finally, with regard to 6., it has been shown that initial auxiliaries are not usually stressed and unreduced.

One solution may lie in a consideration of the very nature of this type of research into individual differences in which the frequencies of input variables are all-important. This is based on the More-the-Merrier Principle, the assumption of a roughly linear relationship between quantity and usefulness. However, Nelson (K. E. Nelson et al., 1973) has produced evidence which indicates that rapid grammatical developments can be triggered by a low frequency of recasts (K. E. Nelson, 1980). The proviso is that the child attends to the new syntactic information presented, and encodes it in some way. What may be happening with Y/Ns is that the occasions on which the auxiliary is phonologically clarified conspire with other characteristics of questions in general, and Y/N questions in particular (such as position of the operator), to produce a synergistic effect. None of the six factors discussed above may, on its own, be sufficient to account for auxiliary learning, but they may combine in different ways and at different stages to accelerate rate of development. A higher frequency of Y/Ns in the input may simply act as a way of raising the incidence of 'rare events' (K. E. Nelson, 1980) to the threshold required to effect changes.

Two interesting questions arise from such a multifactor hypothesis. Firstly, there is a suggestion in the data analysed in this chapter that the admittedly small number of Y/Ns which function as indirect requests clarify the auxiliary in the majority of cases. Hoff-Ginsberg and Shatz (1982) emphasise the salience of questions compared with statements. If this is true, then questions which also regulate the behaviour of the child may be even more salient. One thing we do know is that children are surprisingly adept at understanding indirect requests, despite their apparent syntactic complexity and the discrepancy between their form and function (Shatz, 1978). This is a feature of input which is worthy of further investigation as a potential facilitator of auxiliary verb learning. However, it must be stressed that in the current study the number of indirect requests was very small: only thirty-one tokens from all utterances addressed to thirty-two children. Of these, just thirteen were Y/N inversions, while two were intonation only Y/Ns, and sixteen were tags. If such low frequencies are typical, then this question can only be addressed experimentally.

Secondly, in the analysis of the discourse role of Y/Ns it was found that contingent responses tended to omit the auxiliary. As a result, it was the initiating Y/Ns which predicted child auxiliary growth. One hypothesis would be that if they could occur with greater frequency, responding Y/Ns which contained the operator would be even more useful to the child. They could then combine the factors of auxiliary salience and phonological clarification with the type of feedback which allowed cognitive comparisons between utterance pairs and made use of those characteristics of child directed speech which motivate (Howe, 1981; Nelson, 1973) and facilitate (McDonald and Pien, 1982) participation in discourse.

12 Conclusion

12.1 Summary of main findings

The research reported in this volume set out to study individual differences in rate and style of auxiliary verb learning. In the three main sections these have been related to age and stage of emergence, variation in analytic and holistic tendencies, and the facilitative role of child-directed speech.

12.1.1 Part I
Chapter 2 investigated the extent to which rate of auxiliary verb learning as measured by Wells (1979a) was attributable to syntactic rule-learning ability. It was found that measuring the time from emergence to a criterion of proficiency confounded age and stage of emergence with rate of development. Nevertheless, the analysis drew attention to broad variation in the stage of syntactic development at which the first auxiliaries are recorded. This variation was interpreted as being due to differences in children's use of rote-learning strategies at a low MLU. An additional factor, possibly related to syntactic rule-learning ability and age/stage of emergence, was an indication that a minority of children are rapid piecemeal learners. This phenomenon is of methodological interest to any research which uses the auxiliary as an index of development. Children who satisfy functional requirements in this way may give a misleading impression of syntactic maturity.

Redefining 'auxiliary' to comprise a more homogeneous set of forms reduced differences in the stage (as measured by MLUS) at which a new criterion was reached. It was concluded that there is a reciprocal relationship between general syntactic development and the auxiliary; variation in rate of auxiliary learning cannot be considered in isolation from other aspects of the development of syntax.

12.1.2 Part II
The more detailed longitudinal study of seven children produced clearer evidence of extensive variation in the rate of development of auxiliaries. 'Across

the board' developments did not occur, though there were periods of rapid development for some children. Instead, progress was typified by piecemeal additions to the range of forms and the range of linguistic contexts and syntactic frames in which they were used. The elicitation task tested the hypothesis that some children would rapidly be able to generalise a rule for auxiliary inclusion across a wide spectrum of forms. This hypothesis had to be rejected. The evidence suggested that even when the model sentences contained familiar concepts, the perceived modal meaning influenced the form of the response, including the presence or absence of the auxiliary. An attempt to compare the rate at which children learn to fill obligatory contexts for the auxiliary failed because of insufficient data to identify clear developmental trends.

The sequence of emergence of auxiliaries in various syntactic contexts was investigated. In all cases except one, order of emergence for the group as a whole corresponded with the complexity of the frames in which they occurred. The exception to the Complexity Principle was the tendency of contracted auxiliary subforms to appear before their noncontracted counterparts. Elsewhere, violations of the Complexity Principle were used to identify rote-learned or partially analysed usage by individual children. It was not possible to show consistent tendencies across the systems analysed, but when children were ranked on each system for the number of violations, and the ranks totalled for each child, the extreme analytic and holistic positions were occupied by Gemma and Alex respectively. This was consistent with other features of the data from these two children.

An analysis of the development of tag questions followed up indications of holistic learning and two children (Alex and Clare) had been identified as children for whom auxiliaries emerged in tags surprisingly early. The analysis which followed indicated that this finding was not attributable to error in the sampling of auxiliary forms, but characteristic of a style of development typified by the gradual appearance of auxiliaries in a slowly increasing range of unanalysed tags. By contrast, three other children (Betty, Eric, and Fleur) developed tags in a more analytic sequence in which tags integrated previously acquired syntactic operations. Elsewhere, child language research has considered the late emergence of tags in terms of their syntactic complexity. However, the fact that the youngest of the Welsh children (Gemma) never developed tags, despite being the most advanced in respect of syntax, suggests that an understanding of the discourse role of tags and their place in the system of modality is a necessary condition for their emergence.

In the development of auxiliary DO, six children developed redundant unstressed DO forms. In one case (Gemma) this was of particular interest because no such forms could be detected in the language addressed to her, and their occurrence suggests the use of analytical strategies which depend on the observed syntactic behaviour of auxiliaries. The significance of this phenomenon will be discussed below, but the function of Gemma's declarative unstressed 'did' appeared to be to regularise past time reference.

Both DO and CAN were examined for developments in the range of main verbs with which they co-occurred. In general, it was not possible to discriminate between children in this way but the analysis showed contrasting patterns in the development of 'can' and 'can't'. 'Can't' increases the range more gradually, and usage is stereotyped during early recordings. 'Can', on the other hand, shows no evidence of repetitive usage for any child, and shows a stage for Clare, Fleur, and Gemma during which there are clearly identifiable increases in range of contexts. Like 'can't', usage of 'don't', the most common DO form, was relatively stereotyped, the highest frequencies of co-occurrence being with 'know', 'like', 'want', and 'want to'. These usually had a first person singular subject orientation and conveyed a performative meaning. The contexts in which both 'don't' and 'can't' occurred were particularly repetitive for Fleur. In the latter case this was associated with her usage of 'can't' to express performative meanings.

Both Fleur and Alex produced an exceptionally high number of performatives containing CAN. However, the modal meanings on which they were predicated and the nature of their interpersonal function were shown to be different for each child. Alex used declarative 'can't' (Permission) and declarative and Y/N 'can' (Permission), and, as a way of refusing to comply with requests, 'can't' (Ability). By contrast, Fleur, who never produced Y/Ns containing CAN, discovered that 'can't' (Ability) was an efficient way of getting her adult interlocutors to carry out her wishes.

One child (Gemma) uniquely used 'can' before 'can't' and uniquely showed a continuing preference for the affirmative form. This marked difference between Gemma and the other six children could not be attributed to the use of the affirmative to convey performative meanings. Instead, Gemma showed an orientation towards expressing affirmative Ability meanings with a representational function. The extent to which Gemma and others can be said to exhibit distinctive *styles* of development will be considered in section 12.2.

12.1.3 Part III
In Chapter 11, hypotheses were tested to explain relationships reported in the literature between rate of auxiliary verb development and Y/N questions

addressed to children. It was pointed out that the conventional explanation (that Y/Ns clarify the auxiliary) could not account for correlations reported with subcategories of Y/Ns, and a reanalysis of Barnes et al. (BGSW, 1983) was undertaken in an attempt to explain the relationship in their findings (and those of Furrow et al., 1979) with Y/Ns which contain no auxiliary. Having rejected several explanations for a possibly spurious correlation, the hypothesis was tested that the effect was caused by the role of intonation only Y/Ns in a facilitative responding style of interaction. Recoding the input confirmed that Y/Ns as responses tended to omit the operator. However, extending the definition of 'input' to include all utterances addressed to the child, and possibly the application of slightly different coding criteria, reversed the pattern of correlations obtained by BGSW. It was now Y/N inversions (and exchange-initiating Y/Ns) which entered into significant correlations. Tag questions, Y/Ns as responses, and intonation only Y/Ns were not associated with any auxiliary measure.

These results showed that a Responsive Style Hypothesis could not account for correlations obtained either with intonation only Y/Ns for BGSW, or with Y/N inversions in the reanalysis reported here. In a further attempt to explain BGSW's finding, trends in the development of Y/Ns between T1 and T2 were analysed for a subsample of ten children. The analysis showed that within Y/Ns, a decrease over time in the proportional frequency of the intonation only type was accompanied by an increase in Y/N inversions. This trend was consistent with the interpretation that the apparent effect of intonation only Y/Ns was actually brought about by a tendency to include the auxiliary with greater frequency during the period leading up to T2.

If the above interpretation is correct, the findings of both BGSW and the reanalysis reported here could be interpreted within the framework of the Auxiliary Clarification Hypothesis. Two essential aspects of this hypothesis were therefore addressed. Firstly, the extent to which the operator was stressed and unreduced was investigated. It was found that 40% of auxiliary operators in Y/N inversions were stressed, 31% were phonologically unreduced, but only 23% were both stressed and unreduced. Although this suggested that the role of Y/Ns in clarifying the auxiliary is less consistent than is assumed by NGG and GNG, it was argued that clarification may nevertheless occur with sufficient frequency to be effective. Secondly, the auxiliary forms that children heard at T1 were compared with those which had emerged by T2. The most that could be claimed here was that no difference could be shown between forms heard and forms emerging.

12.2 Styles of development in the seven Welsh children

In the analysis of tag questions it was noted that, while distinct styles of development could be identified, they tended to be a matter of degree rather than mutually exclusive dichotomies. Children used different strategies at different stages, and the same can be said of the overall auxiliary verb development of the seven children. At the extremes, certain children stand out because they exhibit a cluster of characteristics which are consistent with one or other style reported in the literature, but characteristics of an alternative style are not precluded and most children defy simple classification.

One child who stands apart on a number of dimensions is Gemma, described in Chapter 4 as an Early Fast Developer. Despite being more than three months younger than any other child, and nine months younger than the oldest child, Gemma's MLUS at Recording 1 was the second highest for the group and regardless of how gains are calculated, the subsequent development of her MLUS proceeded at a faster rate than for any other child. By the end of the study, therefore, Gemma had the highest recorded figures for both MLUS and MLUL. She was also the only child whose MLUS differed by more than one standard deviation from the mean for the sixty Bristol children. On measures of the auxiliary, Gemma only produced a single token in the first recording, showing less knowledge of the auxiliary than most other children. Nevertheless, her auxiliary subforms emerged at the fastest rate both in spontaneous speech and in the imitation test, and by her last recording she ranked second both on the range of subforms/100 structured utterances, and on the total number of subforms to have emerged.

Apart from her rate of learning, two features typify Gemma's approach to the auxiliary. The first is the absence of stereotyped usage, and the second, probably related, feature is the analytical sequence in which utterances containing the auxiliary emerged. As far as the first feature is concerned, developments in auxiliary frequency were, without exception, accompanied by an increase in the range of subforms being used. Similarly, there is no evidence from the analysis of 'don't' and C A N that Gemma used any co-occurrence of an auxiliary form with a single lexical verb as a multipurpose strategy in different situations. With regard to sequence, the pattern is one of proceeding from simple to complex structures. In the development of C A N, for example, Gemma is the only child for whom emergence and development clearly proceeded from affirmative to negative in declarative sentences, and then to affirmative Y/N inversion. The smallest number of violations of the Complexity Principle were recorded for Gemma and she is the only child for whom, in the comparison of emergence of contracted and noncontracted pairs, the majority of full forms emerge first.

In almost direct contrast with Gemma is Alex, the oldest child in the sample. Alex was three months older than any other child and nine months older than Gemma. At the first recording he ranked fifth on MLUS, and was below the mean for the Bristol children at a comparable age. Development of MLUS was the slowest for the group (equal with Fleur), but on indices based on the auxiliary the picture is more confused. In spontaneous speech Alex ranked fifth, but on the imitation test his progress was more typical of the group as a whole. Alex's style of auxiliary verb learning is characterised by two features. Firstly, there was a tendency for auxiliaries to appear early in complex structures, the most extreme example being the emergence of tag questions before the separate syntactic processes required for tag production had been mastered. Similarly, an examination of CAN showed simultaneous, rather than consecutive development of 'can' in declarative and Y/N frames, both of which followed the emergence and development of 'can't'. Alex also produced the largest number of violations of the Complexity Principle. Secondly, Alex (together with Fleur) produced an exceptionally high proportion of Performative utterances containing CAN forms, especially 'can't'.

If Alex and Gemma represent the extremes of an analytic/holistic continuum, two other children show characteristics which suggest a similar classification. Clare is similar to Alex in her early use of unanalysed tags and is above the median for violations of the Complexity Principle. Early developments in auxiliary usage are typified by very low frequencies accompanied by a comparatively wide range of auxiliaries, suggesting a repertoire of rote-learned forms. Towards the other end of the continuum, Betty shows the most analytic approach to learning tag questions: the correspondence between order of emergence and syntactic complexity being almost perfect. She also ranks low on violations of the Complexity Principle.

The remaining three children (Daisy, Eric, and Fleur) show a combination of the characteristics which form the basis of the contrasts identified above. Eric develops tags in a mainly analytic sequence, but ranks second highest on the number of complex structures which precede simple structures. Fleur's general syntactic progress, and her auxiliary verb development in spontaneous and elicited speech, is the slowest, or equal slowest of the group. Her structures containing auxiliaries are highly stereotyped and, from evidence relating to 'don't' and CAN, usage is extremely high in Performatives. Nevertheless, no child other than Gemma has fewer violations of the Complexity Principle.

It would be tempting to equate Gemma with an 'ideal type' of referential/ analytic child. After all, she does embody many of the characteristics exhibited by children who have been thus described (see Chapter 1): female, only child, well-educated middle-class parents; child-centred upbringing – spends much of the day at home with her mother who engages her in structured 'formats' (Bruner, 1983), particularly being read to; rapid linguistic development; little evidence of unanalysed or repetitive usage; production of lengthy novel utterances through creative combinations of discrete units; analysis of the distributional characteristics of the auxiliary enabling her to overgeneralise the affirmative declarative function to unstressed DO.

Equally, it might be possible to see Alex as the expressive/holistic child: the sometimes repetitive use of early unanalysed, or partially analysed, 'chunks'; the high proportion of Performatives possibly indicative of a personal–social orientation. Such a classification would, however, ignore features which Alex and Gemma have in common. There was no evidence, for example, that Gemma used language for interpersonal functions any less than most other children in the study. In fact, in the analysis of CAN, the proportion of Performatives for all children except Alex and Fleur was remarkably similar. Neither is there any indication that Alex was less skilled or less well motivated to use language for referential functions than Gemma. Both children enjoyed giving accounts of significant events which had happened since the last visit.

It is easy to see why a high frequency of Performatives might be accompanied by stereotyped usage and unanalysed units if a child frequently uses a small number of rote-learned structures as a strategy to accomplish interpersonal goals. But even though Alex does produce utterances which are Performative, unanalysed, or used with a high frequency in an invariable form, there could be no justification for regarding these three variables as part of a single dimension. Alex's auxiliary usage is less stereotyped than Fleur's, and no more stereotyped than for the other children in the later phases; his Performative utterances, especially those predicated on Permission, employ auxiliary CAN in a variety of linguistic contexts. Finally, it is not the case that unanalysed structures were used mainly as Performatives. Neither is it always the case that such structures were used with a high frequency in an invariable form.

The clearest dimension on which to characterise the differences in style between Alex and Gemma is sequence of development. It is probably no coincidence that the children who represented the most extreme differences were the oldest and youngest in the sample, and that compared with Gemma,

Alex, because of age and family circumstances, had a wider range of conversational experience. Despite an age difference of nine months, these two children were not vastly different at the beginning of the study in their level of syntax. Whereas Gemma made rapid advances, however, Alex's progress was much slower. It has been noted that Gemma never developed tag questions, despite knowledge of the necessary syntax and a plentiful supply of examples. It was suggested that she would only be able to produce tags when her understanding of their role in discourse matched her knowledge of their syntax. At the other end of the spectrum, Alex apparently developed at least a partial understanding of the semantic and discourse characteristics of tags at a stage when his syntax was inadequate for an analytic approach to their production. As a result, the use of semi-analysed structures can be seen as a performance strategy to compensate for lack of linguistic competence. For such children, therefore, contrasting styles become apparent when the development of different linguistic systems (for example syntax and pragmatics) are out of phase.

12.3 Evaluation and recommendations for further research

The observations which follow fall into three areas: defining the auxiliary, measuring auxiliary development, and the correlational analysis.

12.3.1 Definition of 'auxiliary'

In child language research into the auxiliary, it has been customary to introduce the set of verbs to be studied by referring to a version of Chomsky's (1965) auxiliary expansion rule, or some derivation thereof. Thus, although the notation may vary slightly, Fletcher (1985), Major (1974), and Wells (1979a) all quote:

$$\text{Aux} \rightarrow \text{Tense (Modal)} \, (\text{HAVE} + \text{EN}) \, (\text{BE} + \text{ING})$$

Essentially, this is a phrase structure rule which summarises the ways in which auxiliary elements can co-occur. It accounts for the ordering of those elements but precludes selecting items from each bracketed option more than once. In this way we can generate the grammatical sentence: # 'They might have been stealing', but not the ungrammatical: * # 'They have might been stealing', or * # 'They should can do that'.

Despite the appeal of the expansion rule in describing syntactic regularities for mature speakers, the vital question to ask is how relevant it is to child language. Even a cursory glance shows up two aspects of auxiliary usage

included in child studies which do not fall within its scope. These are dummy
DO and the passive. Kypriotaki (1974) solves the latter problem by using
an extended version of the rule which includes (BE + EN) as a final optional
element. This allows the inclusion of structures such as 'The lady next door
could have been hurt' (Kypriotaki, 1974, p. 89). Wells (1979a) fails to account
for the passive in his theoretical framework, but covers the behaviour of
DO by reference to the NICE properties.

Two further problems now arise. Firstly, if the researcher includes catenatives ('wanna') or any of the semi-auxiliaries ('be able to', 'have to', 'be
going to', etc.), then these fall outside the frame of reference offered by
the expansion rule. The reason for this is the ability of semi-auxiliaries and
concatenatives to co-occur with the central modals:

> * # They should can do that
> # They should be able to do that

Neither can the NICE properties bring these additional forms into a homogeneous group with the primary auxiliaries and central modals. A definition
based on the NICE properties excludes marginal modals, modal idioms,
semi-auxiliaries and catenatives.

The second problem is that an auxiliary expansion rule can only be of
relevance if the subjects under investigation are at a stage of development
when the auxiliary constituent is being 'expanded'; in other words, if more
than one auxiliary element is present in the verb phrase. Research into
sequence of acquisition (Brown, 1973; Brown and Hanlon, 1970) and emergence (Wells, 1985) suggests that the inclusion of more than one auxiliary
is a relatively late development, and this prediction is borne out both by
the Bristol data analysed in Chapter 2 and by the Welsh children. If we
exclude instances containing semi-auxiliaries, expansions were almost totally
absent (only ten tokens for thirty-three Bristol children between 1;3 and 3;6).
Instead, auxiliary verb development during the period under investigation
is characterised by three features: the acquisition of unanalysed or semi-
analysed units, the introduction of single forms into declarative utterances,
and the development of auxiliaries as operators in negation, interrogation,
ellipsis and contrastive emphasis. Only later can we observe expansion of
the auxiliary constituent.

The point of the above exposition is to demonstrate the frequent lack of
congruence between what Chomsky (e.g. 1977/1979, p. 50) calls the 'model
of competence' and the set of items which comprise the system to be studied.
If the aim of such research is purely descriptive, then the consequences need

not be serious provided that membership of the category is fully documented. If, on the other hand, the aim is to test hypotheses about the development of syntax or semantics, then the class must be syntactically or semantically homogeneous. Nowhere is this more relevant than to the type of correlational research reviewed in Chapter 10. Newport et al. (NGG, 1977) reported a significant correlation between a global Y/N category (which included a number of copula inversions) and a heterogeneous category of auxiliaries. Whether their result was predicted, or whether it arose from the exploratory pairing of 'motherese' characteristics with a set of child indices, is not known. Nevertheless, NGG provide a coherent explanation for their finding, an explanation which is an appealing integration of psychological and linguistic theory, and which at first sight (Fletcher, 1983) seems to offer hope of remediation for children who have difficulty in learning the auxiliary. It would have seemed logical therefore for subsequent research to delve more deeply into the Y/N–auxiliary relationship by testing hypotheses derived from NGG's explanation. In so far as later studies make a limited subdivision of Y/Ns, this process has already begun, though the reasons for these subdivisions have not always been articulated. However, no one has yet demonstrated that auxiliary Y/N inversions heard by children are associated with the rate of development of the class of auxiliaries which are capable of inversion in Y/Ns. This is an omission which we are currently addressing in a new study.

In Parts I and II of this volume a definition of 'auxiliary' was adopted which was consistent with the syntactic features hypothesised to facilitate its acquisition. One consequence in Chapter 2 was greater consistency in the stage at which children attained a criterion of development. This might be taken as an indication that the set of auxiliaries analysed had greater psychological coherence than a set which allowed the inclusion of semi-auxiliaries.

In Part III a larger set of verbs was used. Here, the motivation was to find an explanation for results obtained by Furrow et al. (FNB, 1979) and Barnes et al. (BGSW, 1983). Both studies had found a relationship between auxiliary growth and intonation only Y/Ns, rather than with Y/N inversions. BGSW's input data were recoded in order to explain this relationship and their original auxiliary gain scores were re-used in computing correlations with the new set of independent variables. Although results were now consistent with NGG's hypothesis, the child auxiliary scores were based on Wells' (1979a) heterogeneous set of forms, to which Y/N inversions can only be partially relevant.

It was found in Chapter 11 that the relationship between Y/N inversions and the auxiliary was weaker if copula inversions were excluded. Potentially this is a problem for the Auxiliary Clarification Hypothesis, unless the development of auxiliary and copula BE are interrelated. The copula, while unable to co-occur with other verbs, also exhibits the NICE properties. The existence for children of an undifferentiated class of operators which includes both primary auxiliaries and central modals, and the copula is therefore possible. Since the NGG and GNG accounts of auxiliary learning are equally applicable to copula BE, current research is testing the hypothesis that Y/N copula inversions addressed to children will predict development of the copula.

12.3.2 Auxiliary indices and criteria of acquisition

In Chapter 2 attempts were made to find a criterion which guaranteed syntactic knowledge of the auxiliary class. In order to make the criterion objective and appropriate to the data available, the number of auxiliary forms to have emerged was used as a basis. Although a criterion was found which ensured that most children had demonstrated usage of key properties of auxiliaries, it was found that criteria based on these principles encompass considerable variation in the syntactic knowledge of the children who attain them. Without more information about sequence of development and range of linguistic contexts it is impossible to make adequate judgements about the productivity of the forms which enable a child to fulfil such a criterion.

Another possible criterion was originally thought to be the emergence of auxiliaries in tag questions. It was pointed out that the most common variety of tag combines three of the defining characteristics of the auxiliary. Tags could also tell us that some of the less obvious relationships between full and contracted forms (''d' and 'wouldn't'), or between affirmative and negative forms ('will' and 'won't') had been understood. However, it was also pointed out that since the reversed polarity tag represents an accumulation of these features, their occurrence would have to be regarded as more than sufficient evidence for the existence of 'auxiliary' as a form-class. Even so, the existence of children who use a small repertoire of tags which are not fully productive necessitates a revision of this view and even at a later stage the status of some tags is doubtful since they frequently follow a matrix which omits the auxiliary. There are at least three possible explanations for this. Firstly, children may acquire a tag as a single (syntactically) unanalysed unit, but understand enough about the contexts in which it occurs to be able to apply it appropriately. Secondly, the tag may be productive but the dialect of the child's interlocutors may frequently drop redundant auxiliaries in declarative sentences. Thirdly, the tag may be productive, but the burden of processing the tag in addition to the matrix clause causes the element which adds least meaning to be dropped. Any one of these explanations could account for Alex's: 'You got cars in there haven't you?' (Rec.6, 2;10.6). This is an issue which raises theoretical questions about the derivation of tags, but even though the phenomena of auxiliaries missing from the matrix, and of errors of matching auxiliaries in tag and matrix have been reported elsewhere, no serious attempt has been made to explain them. In the meantime caution should be exercised before interpreting the emergence of auxiliary tags as evidence for the reality of 'auxiliary' as a form-class.

Frequently, acquisition has been defined in terms of the percentage of cases in which an item is included in its obligatory context. Cazden (1968) and Brown (1973) set criteria at a 90% inclusion rate. In Section 5.2, Brown's procedures were applied to an analysis of the rate at which children developed two auxiliaries (BE and HAVE + got) in obligatory contexts. Unfortunately, this approach failed to discriminate between the children. No child consistently reached an inclusion rate high enough to justify the term 'acquisition'. In addition, development was so erratic that upward trends were hardly discernible. A number of factors could account for this. Firstly, the analysis pooled the subforms of each auxiliary, and as there is no guarantee that subforms develop in parallel, it is possible that different developmental patterns have been confounded. Secondly, since analysis was confined to contractible contexts, early cases of auxiliary inclusion may have consisted of Subject + Contracted Auxiliary functioning as single lexical items. This would boost early inclusion rates and prevent the analysed development of the relevant auxiliary appearing as a linear process. Thirdly, as was pointed out above, in Declarative + Tag utterances the auxiliary is frequently omitted from the matrix. This can occur even when the auxiliary is productive. It is possible, therefore, that some children possessed greater competence than was apparent from the proportion of obligatory contexts in which the relevant form was supplied. In the current study there was no way of avoiding these problems. Only a larger data base would have allowed a separate analysis of different subforms. The question of contracted forms functioning as single units only arises from an analysis of contractible contexts. Although others (Brown, 1973; De Villiers and De Villiers, 1973; Kuczaj, 1979a) have coded both contractible and noncontractible contexts, it was found in Section 5.2 that empty noncontractible obligatory contexts could not be identified reliably, which inevitably leads to a bias towards a higher proportion of filled obligatory contexts. Since these were relatively infrequent in comparison with their contractible counterparts, there were insufficient data to justify an attempt to compare children on this variable. Because of these factors, and because no child even approached a consistent 90% inclusion level on the analysis that was carried out, it seems likely that this procedure would be more suitable at a late stage.

One way of assessing competence on a closed set of items, such as auxiliary forms, which removes the element of chance in spontaneous speech sampling, is to use an elicitation task. The imitation test used in Part II succeeded in discriminating between the seven children on rate of development in a way which was consistent with other analyses, and useful data were obtained which informed the analysis of spontaneous speech. Some success was obtained in gaining and sustaining the co-operation of subjects, but there was a delay in most cases before children understood what was required, or felt at ease with the experimenter. In addition, keeping children interested was at the expense of a standardised form of administration, and even this could not prevent fluctuations in the children's willingness to participate. Nevertheless, such problems are likely with any group of children of this age, and it is difficult to see how they can be avoided.

In Section 4.4 it was found that children had difficulty imitating the item containing affirmative 'can'. It was suggested that the linguistic and pictorial context of the item was responsible for a mismatch between the intended Ability meaning and the meaning perceived by the child. Since modality is an area which is likely to be particularly prone to this type of misinterpretation, this serves as a useful lesson for the construction of test items. There are two other questions about the validity of the imitation test. One is the question of whether the models were really being processed, and the second is whether children were learning the items through repeated administration. Randomising order of presentation and increasing the length of the model from five to seven morphemes were ways of minimising such effects. That the model sentences were still being 'recoded' during the final administration is reassurance that these measures were largely successful. However, the effect of the children's gradually increasing familiarity with the test is unknown, and increasing the length of items had an unfortunate effect on one child (Fleur) who was unable to cope with the increase and whose performance later deteriorated even on the five-morpheme version. One way of ensuring greater confidence in the validity of similar tasks which elicit auxiliaries would be to balance items which require verbatim repetition against ungrammatical models which require normalisation. This is the approach used by Kuczaj and Maratsos (1975) in their work on C A N and W I L L where ungrammatical sentences contained the auxiliary in the wrong position. With the Welsh children such an approach was rejected because it had been difficult enough to devise situations in which repeating sentences made sense. Nevertheless, future attempts might include sentences which omit auxiliaries from an obligatory context to see if they would also be normalised.

In the spontaneous speech of the seven children, analysing trends in auxiliary verb development was approached in three ways for the seven children in Part II. The number of structured utterances in each recording was related firstly to auxiliary tokens, and secondly to auxiliary types. Children's development usually showed a similar pattern on these two measures, but some interesting discrepancies suggested either stereotyped usage in some cases or rapid piecemeal learning in others. An additional measure, a version of which had formed the basis of one of BGSW's residual gain scores, was cumulative range of auxiliary forms. In Chapter 11 BGSW's original scores on this measure were re-used, together with auxiliary frequency and cumulative range of auxiliary meanings. Elsewhere correlational studies have used an index of frequency as the only dependent variable for the auxiliary. However, frequency does not discriminate between stereotyped and diverse usage, and if the measure is auxiliaries per verb phrase, children who tend to use unanalysed utterances containing auxiliaries obtain a misleadingly high value if verb phrases are not yet a regular feature of their speech. Indices using cumulative range cannot be subjected to these criticisms. There is, however, the proviso that they are likely to be influenced by variation in the size of speech sample. In Part II, care was taken to ensure that the cumulative range of subforms was derived from an equal number of samples from each child and if figures were not obtained from an identical number of utterances it was not a serious problem because results were interpreted in the light of a wealth of other data, both elicited and spontaneous. If, however, such values are used in correlational analyses, they should in future be adjusted for the size of sample from which they are obtained.

12.3.3 The correlational analysis: further considerations
The previous section touched on two aspects of the work described in Chapter 11 which are not totally consistent with explanations for the correlations obtained. These are the definition of the auxiliary class, and the appropriateness of the dependent variables.

One other criticism needs to be evaluated. In the methodological debate about correlational input studies (see Chapter 10) there is a consensus that it is necessary to guard against two possible effects. These are the effect of 'the child on the child', and the effect of the child on the interlocutor(s) (GNG, 1984, p.46). The former can arise if child growth scores are calculated simply by subtracting the value for the dependent variable at T1 from the value at T2. If all the children in the sample have identical values at T1, gain scores calculated in this way will be meaningful. If, however, as is usually the case, children are not well matched, it can be predicted that gains will be negatively influenced by the magnitude of T1 values. O'Connor (1972, p.73) illustrates the point as follows: if we studied athletes training to run the mile, we would expect times to improve more for eight-minute milers than for four-minute milers. It would therefore be naive to assume that the trainer of the eight-minute milers was more effective than the trainer of the four-minute milers.

The second effect is the influence of the child's age and stage of language development on the speech of the interlocutor. Spurious correlations can arise from either or both of these effects (see Yoder and Kaiser, 1989, for a discussion of possible child-driven effects). One solution, provided that initial differences are not so great as to confound different effects at different stages of development, is to partial out the children's age and initial status on each dependent variable. This was the procedure adopted by NGG.

With regard to the BGSW study (and consequently to the reanalysis in Chapter 11), it has been claimed (GNG, 1984, footnote p. 50) that procedures failed to match children adequately, and that for this reason their results may be spurious. It is important to consider whether this criticism is justified.

BGSW attempted to match children at T1 by selecting the occasion of recording on which the child's MLUS was closest to 1.5 morphemes. In practice, children still varied quite extensively in age (1;6–2;9) and MLUS (1.0–2.21). Since there was no adjustment for the possible effects of this variation on the children's interlocutors, there may be some grounds for GNG's criticism. On the other hand, BGSW use residual gain scores to adjust for the effect of initial status on the child's progress. Residual gain scores are calculated from the difference between the child's actual score at T2 and the predicted score estimated from the regression of T2 scores on T1 scores (see BGSW, 1983; O'Connor, 1972). They therefore at least partially meet GNG's objections.

The extent to which results were affected by the failure to match children more closely is difficult to judge. There are clearly methodological flaws in all the correlational input studies (see Furrow and Nelson, 1986; Schwartz and Camarata, 1985), and, as was shown in Section 11.1.1, the work by BGSW has points in its favour which are not enjoyed by similar studies. With specific regard to the apparent environmental influences on the auxiliary verb, this is one of the few areas where there are viable explanatory hypotheses for the results obtained (Fletcher, 1983), and where results, if not identical, can at least be interpreted in a way which is consistent with those hypotheses. Nevertheless, this chapter has pointed out several potential sources of error, and until results have been replicated in a study which eliminates them, it would be rash to claim at this stage that relationships between Y/Ns and auxiliary verb development have been adequately understood.

12.4 Learning the auxiliary: an attempt at integration

In this final section an attempt will be made to relate our knowledge of individual differences to more general principles of auxiliary verb learning. In doing so two issues have to be addressed: firstly, how we reconcile apparently incompatible features of development such as the facilitative role of the uncontracted auxiliary in Y/N inversions, and the fact that it is the contracted auxiliary which tends to emerge first; secondly, whether the data collected for research into individual differences, and the methodology appropriate for the study of individual differences can illuminate universal aspects of development.

The second of these issues has been approached with particular clarity by Plomin and DeFries. They argue as follows: 'it should be noted that data collected for the purpose of conducting individual-differences analyses are just as useful for studying normative questions . . . . However, data collected solely for the purpose of studying normative issues are not often applicable to the study of individual differences' (Plomin and DeFries, 1985, p.7). What does not follow, however, is that the results gained from analytical procedures suited to individual differences research tell us about necessary or sufficient conditions for development. This point is also made by Plomin and DeFries, and their example is one which is particularly relevant to the research discussed here:

> Researchers attempting to disprove Chomsky's theory [of innate linguistic knowledge] have demonstrated that individual differences in infants' rates of language acquisition are related to differences in the infants' language-learning environments. However, these results have no bearing on the issue of the origin of our species' universal propensity to use language (Hardy-Brown, 1983). As a specific example, consider the finding that individual differences in infants [sic] communicative competence are related to mothers' contingent vocalizations (Hardy-Brown, Plomin & DeFries, 1981). This finding does not imply that contingent vocal responding is necessary for the modal development of human language. (*Plomin and DeFries, 1985, p.4*)

We must be wary, therefore, of interpreting the Y/N–auxiliary relationship as indicating that it is solely or even primarily from Y/Ns that children learn auxiliaries, or that Y/Ns are even necessary. Neither would such a position be a fair representation of the accounts given in NGG and GNG. Y/Ns are described as 'useful input data for noticing auxiliaries' (GNG, 1984, p. 74), and it is acknowledged that other properties of input will be needed before we can account for the appearance of auxiliaries in canonical sentences in the child's speech. What seems to be wrong with the line of argument developed by GNG is their assumption about the *relative* contribution of declaratives and auxiliaries in other syntactic frames. NGG pointed out that auxiliary growth is predicted by auxiliaries in Y/Ns, but not by the total frequency of auxiliaries in all positions. However, GNG, in explaining the fact that auxiliaries first appear medially in declaratives, conclude:

> He [the child] thereby begins to reconstruct the canonical positions from which movement and stress features are derived. This, we conjecture, is an interim characterization of the facts (puzzling taken together) that the child learns primarily FROM certain forms (the *yes/no*-questions more than the declaratives) but learns ABOUT other forms (the canonical declaratives earlier than the *yes/no*-questions). (*GNG, 1984, p. 75*)

In the light of the discussion above it is clear that the argument here is flawed. The evidence does not necessarily support the view that children learn *more* from one source than another. The pattern of correlations could simply mean that the *variation* in Y/N frequency was sufficient to be related to *variation* in rate of auxiliary growth, while the degree of variation in auxiliary frequency in declaratives was insufficient, perhaps because input was above some facilitative threshold for all children. GNG themselves admit that declaratives will also be necessary for the child to be able to 'construct . . . the canonical position of auxiliaries' (p. 75). If so, they must be regarded as at least equally important.

We therefore have to regard Y/Ns as data which at the right stage can *facilitate* development, but which are not the only source of phonological information about auxiliary forms, nor the only type of auxiliary verb structure which can assist with segmentation or demonstrate the relationship between the syntactic frames in which the auxiliary participates. The strength of the Y/N inversion is that it is one of two syntactic frames which combines these features with placing the auxiliary on a boundary where it has particular salience. The other frame which does this, as was pointed out in Chapter 11, is the use of the auxiliary as a residual operator in ellipsis.

Let us for a moment forget the caveats which have been expressed about methodology, and, for the sake of argument, accept unreservedly that Y/Ns clarify the auxiliary and facilitate its development as claimed. Having done so, we can now evaluate GNG's account of how it is that the auxiliaries heard in Y/Ns subsequently appear in medial position in declaratives. This is explained in terms of the child's predisposition to reconstruct canonical form. In Chapter 11 it was not possible to prove or disprove that the auxiliaries heard at T1 were the same as those to have emerged by T2, although it has been possible to confirm that forms tend to occur first in declaratives. However, analyses of utterances from both the Welsh children and the Bristol children show that for contractible subforms it is *not* the canonical form which first emerges, but the contracted form. It has been assumed throughout this volume that the emergence of contractions before corresponding full forms is evidence of rote learning. And if these contractions are rote learned, then Y/Ns are irrelevant to their acquisition. In most cases their source will be declarative sentences. If this is so, how do Y/Ns come to be correlated with auxiliary verb development? Of course, not all auxiliary subforms are capable of contraction, but it is worth recalling some evidence which was introduced in Chapter 1. Fletcher (1983) reports that the auxiliaries which discriminate between normal and language-impaired children are the modals, DO, and the noncontracted forms of HAVE and BE. The frequency of *contracted* forms did not differ significantly between the two groups. It is possible, therefore, that within groups of normally developing children, the source of variation is the noncontracted, rather than the contracted auxiliary. This would explain the lack of significant correlations with overall auxiliary frequency but would be consistent with the Y/N–auxiliary relationship.

Such a view suggests two contrasting processes in the development of the auxiliary: a holistic process by which contracted forms are rote learned from declaratives, and an analytic process by which knowledge of noncontracted forms is gained from utterances which display the grammatical and phonetic properties of auxiliaries in non-declarative syntactic frames.

Although the existence of unanalysed contracted auxiliaries is acknowledged in the literature (Kuczaj, 1981b), it is possible that they are far more common than has been supposed. If this is the case, or if this is a route to learning the auxiliary which some children rely on more than others, we still have to explain the processes by which analysis and segmentation are subsequently effected. Here too, it can be hypothesised that Y/Ns play a role, though predominantly at a later stage. Two categories of Y/N might be expected to contribute to this process. The first is Declarative Contracted Auxiliary + Auxiliary Tag. Because these adequately perform the clarification and segmentation function without presenting additional and potentially confusing

information about negated forms (see Chapter 11), we can speculate that
the *matched* polarity tag will be particularly useful, as in the following
example:

> \# You're going out are you?

A second type of Y/N is contingent on the child's use of a contracted auxiliary,
and might therefore offer a higher probability of the discrepancy between
contracted and noncontracted forms being encoded:

> Child: \# It's raining
> Response: \# Is it?

Nevertheless, it should be noted that where pronoun-switching occurs such
exchanges may be less helpful:

> Child: \# I'll do it
> Response: \# Will you?

or even unhelpful:

> Child: \# I'm eating it
> Response: \# Are you?

The evidence for the acquisition of auxiliary forms as unanalysed units
seems to be fairly strong, but what direct (other than correlational) evidence
do we have of a generalisation from initial Y/N to medial declarative? In
Section 8.3 it was found that several children produced unstressed DO in
medial position in declaratives (UDAs). It was also noted that this phenomenon occurred at an early stage in the development of the auxiliary. The problem
with interpreting this finding is that although such usage is ungrammatical
in standard British and American English, it was a feature of the dialect
of the area in which the data were collected. Only for one child (Gemma)
could it be claimed with any certainty that using declarative unstressed 'did'
was not directly modelled on the speech addressed to her. Elsewhere, however,
Fletcher (1979) also reports unstressed 'did' in the speech of one child, as
does Menyuk (1969). This raises the interesting question of whether UDAs
occur frequently in the speech of children learning standard English. Even
though they have received little attention in the literature, it is possible that
they are a normal stage in the development of the auxiliary.

A search through the diaries of W.F. Leopold (Leopold, 1949a, 1949b)
reveals that no unstressed DO forms were recorded for Hildegard, but that
at the age of 2, Karla had 'an analytic past tense ... namely, the auxiliary
did followed by the infinitive: *I did fall*, etc.' (Leopold, 1949a, section 586,
note 53; see also Leopold, 1949b, section 984). Since Leopold's children

were being brought up in a bilingual English/German environment, it is still possible that this speech pattern was the result of interference from colloquial German usage of main verb TUN (= DO) as an auxiliary (see Section 8.3.2). However, from checking the dates for Karla against the greater detail given in the entries for Hildegard, it appears that Karla's only source of German up to this point had been her father who was concerned to shield his children from dialect and colloquialisms (e.g. Leopold, 1949b, section 929). It will be noted that the unstressed forms produced by Gemma (Chapter 8), Daniel (Fletcher, 1979), and Karla Leopold were all 'did'. In Gemma this was interpreted as a means of regularising reference to the past. Pinker (1984), on the other hand, finds two present tense examples in the transcripts of Adam (Brown, 1973), but emphasises the rarity of both types of error given the frequency of the linguistic contexts in which they could occur. But the apparent rarity might simply be a function of the length of the period during which these errors are produced. And if one really starts to hunt for examples, it may be surprising how many UDAs turn up. In recordings of this author's daughter, for example, the following monologue was found:

> I eat my dress . . . [Playing alone: chewing her dress]
> my dress .
> I did [unstressed] eat it [laughs]
> /ə/ don't eat 'dresses .
> no-o
> I do [unstressed] eat this dress
> mm (*Fiona, 2;4*)

Although there is some doubt about the frequency with which U D As occur for children whose linguistic environment does not include them, they do show that generalisations are made on the basis of the distributional properties of auxiliaries. That Y/N inversion is one of those properties suggests that, in addition to their potential role of clarifying phonetic features and segmentation boundaries, they can make a contribution to generalisations which enable other uncontracted auxiliary forms to occupy medial position in declarative sentences.

12.5 Conclusion

Evidence has been produced which suggests that both analytic and holistic processes make a significant contribution to the development of the auxiliary. It also appears that children vary in the degree of emphasis they place on each of these processes. At the same time, research has been quoted that children with certain kinds of language-learning difficulty are overdependent on rote-learning strategies. Given the optimism that the results of correlational studies of input can provide effective techniques for language intervention (see, for example, Cromer, 1981), it is tempting to think of Y/N inversions as part of such techniques (Fletcher, 1983) both for facilitating the development of new forms and for breaking down and analysing forms which have been acquired as contractions. The view taken here, however, in the light of suggestions for further research made earlier in this chapter, is that until the results which have raised such interest and controversy have been replicated in a way which avoids the more obvious methodological pitfalls, and until further related hypotheses have been tested, it would be premature to recommend the application of such techniques in intervention programmes.

Notes

1. The auxiliary and the young language learner

1. An important distinction will be between the auxiliary itself and the various forms which belong to its paradigm. These have sometimes been described as allomorphs (e.g. Brown, 1973). However, allomorphs are usually regarded as variations of a form which are semantically identical (Crystal, 1980), and in the analyses described here, semantically contrasting forms such as 'is' and 'isn't' are treated as separate forms belonging to the paradigm of auxiliary BE. To avoid confusion, these forms are referred to as *subforms*, and will appear in lower case in inverted commas ('am', 'are', 'is', 'aren't', etc.). Where the name of the auxiliary to which subforms belong is being referred to, this is printed in upper case (CAN, BE, HAVE, DO, etc.). Where ambiguity is likely, these will be called 'major forms'.
2. The work of both Katherine Nelson and Keith Nelson is referred to. To distinguish between them, Keith Nelson will be cited in references as K. E. Nelson.
3. Labels such as 'style', 'strategy', and 'route' occur frequently in the literature on individual differences. Though 'sequence' is preferred to 'route' here, the terms 'style' and 'strategy' are used. However, there has been some controversy about the use of these terms (see for example Wells, 1986, on the appropriateness of 'style', and Kuczaj, 1982a, and Ramer, 1976, on the distinction between 'style' and 'strategy'). It is important, therefore, to explain what is implied by their use here. 'Strategies' describes *alternative* language learning processes, but there is no implication that they are conscious or intentional. 'Style' indicates a group of features of usage or development which suggest a qualitative contrast between individuals or groups. It does not necessarily imply any correspondence with the referential-expressive contrast.

2. Rate of auxiliary learning in thirty-three children

1. Because marginal auxiliaries were included by Wells but are excluded here, it was possible for the number of subforms to be less than five at Wells' criterion.

7. Individual differences and the development of auxiliaries in tag questions

1. An earlier version of this chapter (Richards, 1988) was delivered at the Child Language Seminar, University of Warwick, 1988.

10. Previous research

1. A shorter version of this chapter (Richards, 1986) and preliminary results from Chapter 11 were presented at the Child Language Seminar, University of Durham, 1986.
2. Both GNG and this author in an earlier treatment (Richards, 1986) have exclusively discussed 'contractibility', though GNG also use the term 'cliticization'. This fails to make the distinction between phonological *reduction* (change in the length and quality of a vowel) and *contraction* (the fusion of adjacent forms following reduction). The difference is an important one because while some auxiliaries in medial position contract (e.g. 'I've'), others only reduce (e.g. /kən/ or /kn/ = 'can'). While the auxiliary in initial position cannot contract, it will be shown that varying degrees of reduction are still possible.
3. My thanks to Mary Gutfreund for spotting this possibility and for providing examples of catenatives in initial Y/N position.

11. Yes/No questions and rate of auxiliary learning for thirty-two children

1. As can be seen from the range in Table 11.1, this is not the conventional auxiliaries/ verb phrase, but a proportional frequency based on utterances rather than verb phrases.
2. Thanks are due to Bencie Woll for her invaluable advice and help with the transcription of stress.
3. Because this finding runs counter to accepted wisdom, the analysis was repeated on the thirty-two Bristol children. The procedure was identical, but the larger number of subjects made it possible to carry out separate significance tests for six of the seven full/contracted pairings. The exception, the 'would/'d' pair, occurred because declarative WOULD was a form which had only emerged for seven children by the last recording at 3;6. The result was identical to the finding from the Welsh children and was statistically significant on a sign test for all six pairs of contracted and noncontracted auxiliary forms (have/'ve: $p < .001$; has/'s: $p < .002$; am/'m: $p < .001$; are/'re: $p < .05$; is/'s: $p < .001$; will & shall/ 'll: $p < .002$).

References

Akmajian, A., Steele, S., & Wasow, T. 1979. The category AUX in universal grammar. *Linguistic Inquiry*, *10*, 1–64

Anderson, E. S. 1975. Cups and glasses: learning that boundaries are vague. *Journal of Child Language*, *2*, 79–103

Armagost, J. L. 1972. *English declarative tags, intonation tags, and tag questions*. Studies in Linguistics and Language Learning (vol. 10). Seattle: University of Washington

Austin, J. L. 1962. *How to do things with words*. Oxford: Clarendon Press

Baker, N. D., & Nelson, K. E. 1984. Recasting and related conversational techniques for triggering syntactic advances in young children. *First Language*, *5*, 3–22

Barnes, S. B. 1984. *Language variation in young children*. Unpublished M.Phil. dissertation, Open University

Barnes, S. B., Gutfreund, M., Satterly, D., & Wells, G. 1983. Characteristics of adult speech which predict children's language development. *Journal of Child Language*, *10*, 65–84 (BGSW)

Bates, E., Bretherton, I., & Snyder, L. 1988. *From first words to grammar: individual differences and dissociable mechanisms*. Cambridge: Cambridge University Press

Bellugi, U. 1967. *The acquisition of negation*. Unpublished doctoral dissertation, Harvard University

Bellugi, U. 1971. Simplification in children's language. In R. Huxley & E. Ingram (eds.), *Language acquisition: models and methods*. London: Academic Press

Berger, D., Drosdowski, G., Grebe, P., & Müller, W. (eds.). 1972. *Duden Band 9: Zweifelsfälle der deutschen Sprache: Wörterbuch der sprachlichen Hauptschwierigkeiten* (2nd edn). Mannheim: Dudenverlag

Berninger, G., & Garvey, C. 1982. Tag constructions: structure and function in child speech. *Journal of Child Language*, *9*, 151–8

Block, E. M., & Kessel, F. S. 1980. Determinants of the acquisition order of grammatical morphemes: a re-analysis and re-interpretation. *Journal of Child Language*, *7*, 181–8

Bloom, L. 1970. *Language development: form and function in emerging grammars*. Cambridge, Mass.: MIT Press

Bloom, L. 1974. Talking, understanding and thinking. In R. L. Schiefelbusch & L. L. Lloyd (eds.), *Language perspectives – acquisition, retardation and intervention*. New York: Macmillan

Bloom, L., Lightbown, P., & Hood, L. 1975. Structure and variation in child language. *Monographs of the Society for Research in Child Development*, *40* (2, serial no. 160)

Blount, B. G. 1972. Parental speech and language acquisition: some Luo and Samoan examples. *Anthropological Linguistics*, *14*, 119–30

Bonvillian, J. D., Raeburn, V. P., & Horan, E. A. 1979. Talking to children: the effect of rate, intonation, and length on children's sentence imitation. *Journal of Child Language*, *6*, 459–67

Boyd, J., & Thorne, J. P. 1969. The semantics of modal verbs. *Journal of Linguistics*, *5*, 57–74

Bretherton, I., McNew, S., Snyder, L., & Bates, E. 1983. Individual differences at 20 months: analytic and holistic strategies in language acquisition. *Journal of Child Language*, *10*, 293–320

Broen, P. 1972. *The verbal environment of the language-learning child*. Monograph of the American Speech and Hearing Association, 17

Brown, R. 1973. *A first language: the early stages*. London: Allen & Unwin

Brown, R. 1977. Introduction. In C. Snow & C. A. Ferguson (eds.), *Talking to children: language input and acquisition*. Cambridge: Cambridge University Press

Brown, R., & Bellugi, U. 1964. Three processes in the child's acquisition of syntax. *Harvard Educational Review*, *34*, 133–51

Brown, R., Cazden, C., & Bellugi, U. 1969. The child's grammar from I to III. In J. P. Hill (ed.), *Minnesota symposia on child psychology* (vol. 2). Minneapolis: University of Minnesota Press

Brown, R., & Fraser, C. 1963. The acquisition of syntax. In C. N. Cofer & B. S. Musgrave (eds.), *Verbal behaviour and learning*. New York: McGraw-Hill

Brown, R., & Hanlon, C. 1970. Derivational cumulative complexity and order of acquisition in child speech. In J. R. Hayes (ed.), *Cognition and the development of language*. New York: Wiley

Bruner, J. 1983. *Child's talk*. Oxford: Oxford University Press

Cattell, R. 1973. Negative transportation and tag questions. *Language*, *49*, 612–19

Cazden, C. 1965. *Environmental assistance to the child's acquisition of grammar*. Unpublished doctoral dissertation, Harvard University

Cazden, C. 1968. The acquisition of noun and verb inflections. *Child Development*, *39*, 433–8

Chomsky, N. 1964. Formal discussion of W. Miller and S. Ervin: The development of grammar in child language. In U. Bellugi & R. Brown (eds.), The acquisition of language. *Monographs of the Society for Research in Child Development*, *29* (no. 1)

Chomsky, N. 1965. *Aspects of the theory of syntax*. Cambridge, Mass.: MIT Press

Chomsky, N. 1979. [*Language and Responsibility*]. Hassocks, Sussex: The Harvester Press (originally published, 1977)

Clark, R. 1974. Performing without competence. *Journal of Child Language*, *1*, 1–10

Clark, R. 1977. What's the use of imitation? *Journal of Child Language*, *4*, 341–58

Clark, R. 1978. Some even simpler ways to learn to talk. In N. Waterson & C. Snow (eds.), *The development of communication*. Chichester: Wiley

Clark, R. 1980. Errors in talking to learn. *First Language*, *1*, 7–32

Coates, J. 1983. *The semantics of the modal auxiliaries*. London: Croom Helm

Colmar, S., & Wheldall, K. 1985. Behavioural language teaching: using the natural language environment. *Child Language Teaching and Therapy*, *1*, 199–216

Cromer, R. 1981. Reconceptualizing language acquisition and cognitive development. In R. L. Schiefelbusch & D. D. Bricker (eds.), *Early language: acquisition and intervention*. Baltimore: University Park Press

Cross, T. G. 1977. Mothers' speech adjustments: the contribution of selected child listener variables. In C. Snow & C. A. Ferguson (eds.), *Talking to children: language input and acquisition*. Cambridge: Cambridge University Press

Cross, T. G. 1978. Mothers' speech and its association with rate of linguistic development in young children. In N. Waterson & C. Snow (eds.), *The development of communication*. Chichester: Wiley

Crystal, D. 1980. *A first dictionary of linguistics and phonetics*. London: Deutsch

Dawson, E. 1981. Psycholinguistic processes in prelingually deaf adolescents. In B. Woll, J. Kyle & M. Deuchar. *Perspectives on British sign language and deafness*. London: Croom Helm

De Villiers, J., & De Villiers, P. 1973. A cross-sectional study of the acquisition of grammatical morphemes. *Journal of Psycholinguistic Research*, *2*, 267–78

De Villiers, J., & De Villiers, P. 1978. *Language acquisition*. Cambridge, Mass.: Harvard University Press

De Villiers, J., & De Villiers, P. 1979. *Early language*. London: Fontana/Open Books

D'Odorico, L., & Franco, F. 1985. The determinants of baby talk: relationship to context. *Journal of Child Language*, *12*, 567–86

Donaldson, M. 1978. *Children's minds*. Glasgow: Fontana/Collins

Drach, K. M. 1969. The language of the parent: a pilot study. In K. M. Drach, B. Kobashigawa, C. Pfuderer & D. Slobin, *The structure of linguistic input to children* (Working Paper, no. 14). Berkeley, Calif.: Language-Behavior Research Laboratory

Ehrman, M. 1966. *The meanings of the modals in present-day English*. The Hague: Mouton

Ellis, R., & Wells, C. G. 1980. Enabling factors in adult-child discourse. *First Language*, *1*, 46–62

Ervin, S. 1964. Imitation and structural change in children's language. In E. H. Lenneberg (ed.), *New directions in the study of language*. Cambridge, Mass.: MIT Press

Ervin-Tripp, S. 1973. Some strategies for the first years. In T. E. Moore (ed.), *Cognition and the acquisition of language*. New York: Academic Press

Fletcher, P. 1979. The development of the verb phrase. In P. Fletcher & M. Garman (eds.), *Language acquisition*. Cambridge: Cambridge University Press

Fletcher, P. 1981. Description and exploration in the acquisition of verb forms. *Journal of Child Language*, *8*, 93–108

Fletcher, P. 1982. On grammars and language acquisition. In D. Crystal (ed.), *Linguistic controversies: essays in linguistic theory and practice in honour of F. R. Palmer*. London: Arnold

Fletcher, P. 1983. *From sound to syntax: a learner's guide*. Keynote address to the Fourth Annual Wisconsin Symposium on Research in Child Language Disorders

Fletcher, P. 1985. *A child's learning of English*. Oxford: Blackwell

Furrow, D., & Nelson, K. 1986. A further look at the motherese hypothesis: a reply to Gleitman, Newport & Gleitman. *Journal of Child Language*, *13*, 163–76

Furrow, D., Nelson, K., & Benedict, H. 1979. Mothers' speech to children and syntactic development: some simple relationships. *Journal of Child Language*, *6*, 423–42 (FNB)

Garvey, C. 1977. The contingent query: a dependent act in conversation. In M. Lewis & L. A. Rosenbaum, *Interaction, conversation, and the development of language*. New York: Wiley

Gathercole, V. C. 1986. The acquisition of the present perfect: explaining differences in the speech of Scottish and American children. *Journal of Child Language*, *13*, 537–60

Gleason, J. 1977. Talking to children: some notes on feedback. In C. Snow & C. A. Ferguson (eds.), *Talking to children: language input and acquisition*. Cambridge: Cambridge University Press

Gleason, J. B., & Weintraub, S. 1978. Input language and the acquisition of communicative competence. In K. E. Nelson (ed.), *Children's Language* (vol. 1). New York: Gardner Press

Gleitman, L. R., Newport, E. L. & Gleitman, H. 1984. The current status of the motherese hypothesis. *Journal of Child Language*, *11*, 43–79 (GNG)

Gleitman, L. R. & Wanner, E. 1982. Language acquisition: the state of the art. In E. Wanner & L. R. Gleitman (eds.), *Language acquisition: the state of the art*. Cambridge: Cambridge University Press

Grebe, P. (ed.) 1966. Duden Band 4: *Grammatik der deutschen Gegenwartssprache* (2nd edn). Mannheim: Dudenverlag

Groenendijk, J., & Stokhof, M. 1975. Modality and conversational information. *Theoretical Linguistics*, *2*, 61–112

Gutfreund, M., Harrison, M., & Wells, G. 1989. *Bristol language development scales*. Windsor: NFER–Nelson

Haber, L. R. 1981. A syntactic analysis of language delay and language impairment. In P. S. Dale & D. Ingram (eds.), *Child language – an international perspective*. Baltimore: University Park Press

Haber, L. R. 1982. An analysis of linguistic deviance. In K. E. Nelson (ed.), *Children's language* (vol. 3). Hillsdale, NJ: Erlbaum

Haegeman, L. M. V. 1983. *The semantics of* will *in present-day British English: a unified account*. Brussels: Verhandeling Letteren, jrg. 45, nr. 103

Halliday, M. A. K. 1970. Functional diversity in language as seen from a consideration of modality and mood in English. *Foundations of Language*, *6*, 322–65

Halliday, M. A. K. 1984. Language as code and language as behaviour: a systemic-functional interpretation of the nature and ontogenesis of dialogue. In R. P. Fawcett, M. A. K. Halliday, S. M. Lamb & A. Makkai (eds.), *The semiotics of culture and language* (vol. 1: Language as a social semiotic). London: Pinter

Halliday, M. A. K. 1985. *An introduction to functional grammar*. London: Arnold

Hardy-Brown, K. 1983. Universals and individual differences: disentangling two approaches to the study of language acquisition. *Developmental Psychology, 19,* 610–24

Hardy-Brown, K., Plomin, R., & DeFries, J. C. 1981. Genetic and environmental influences on the rate of communicative development in the first year of life. *Developmental Psychology, 6,* 704–17

Heny, F., & Richards, B. 1983. *Linguistic categories: auxiliaries and related puzzles* (vol. 2: The scope, order, and distribution of English auxiliary verbs). Dordrecht, Holland: D. Reidel

Hirst, W., & Weil, J. 1982. Acquisition of epistemic and deontic meaning of modals. *Journal of Child Language, 9,* 659–66

Hoff-Ginsberg, E. 1985. Some contributions of mothers' speech to their children's syntactic growth. *Journal of Child Language, 12,* 367–85 (HG1)

Hoff-Ginsberg, E. 1986. Function and structure in maternal speech: their relation to the child's development of syntax. *Developmental Psychology, 22,* 155–63 (HG2)

Hoff-Ginsberg, E. n.d. Unpublished coding manual, University of Wisconsin-Parkside

Hoff-Ginsberg, E., & Shatz, M. 1982. Linguistic input and the acquisition of language. *Psychological Bulletin, 92,* 3–26

Hollander, M., & Wolfe, D. A. 1973. *Nonparametric statistical methods.* New York: Wiley

Howe, C. J. 1980. Learning language from mother's replies. *First Language, 1,* 83–97

Howe, C. J. 1981. *Acquiring language in a conversational context.* London: Academic Press

Hudson, R. A. 1975. The meaning of questions. *Language, 51,* 1–31

Joos, M. 1964. *The English verb: form and meanings.* Madison and Milwaukee: University of Wisconsin Press

Jordan, C. M., & Robinson, W. P. 1972. The grammar of working and middle class children using elicited imitations. *Language and Speech, 15,* 122–40

Kavanaugh, R. D., & Jen, M. 1981. Some relationships between parental speech and children's object language development. *First Language, 2,* 103–15

Kaye, K., & Charney, R. 1981. Conversational asymmetry between mothers and children. *Journal of Child Language, 8,* 35–49

Klima, E., & Bellugi, U. 1966. Syntactic regularities in the speech of children. In J. Lyons & R. J. Wales (eds.), *Psycholinguistics Papers.* Edinburgh: Edinburgh University Press

Kuczaj, S. 1976. Arguments against Hurford's 'Aux Copying Rule'. *Journal of Child Language, 3,* 423–7

Kuczaj, S. 1977. The acquisition of regular and irregular past tense forms. *Journal of Verbal Learning and Verbal Behaviour, 16,* 589–600

Kuczaj, S. 1979a. Influence of contractibility on the acquisition of *Be*: substantial, meager, or unknown? *Journal of Psycholinguistic Research, 8,* 1–11

Kuczaj, S. 1979b. Evidence for a language learning strategy: on the relative ease of acquisition of prefixes and suffixes. *Child Development, 50,* 1–13

Kuczaj, S. 1981a. More on children's initial failure to relate specific acquisitions. *Journal of Child Language, 8,* 485–7

Kuczaj, S. 1981b. The acquisition of copula and auxiliary *be* forms. In *Papers and Reports on Child Language Development* (no. 20). Stanford: Stanford University

Kuczaj, S. 1982a. On the nature of syntactic development. In S. Kuczaj (ed.), *Language development* (vol. 1: Syntax and semantics). Hillsdale, NJ: Erlbaum

Kuczaj, S. 1982b. Old and new forms, old and new meanings: the form-function hypothesis revisited. *First Language*, *3*, 55–61

Kuczaj, S., & Brannick, N. 1979. Children's use of the Wh question modal auxiliary placement rule. *Journal of Experimental Child Psychology*, *28*, 43–67

Kuczaj, S., & Maratsos, M. 1975. What a child CAN say before he WILL. *Merrill-Palmer Quarterly*, *21*, 89–111

Kuczaj, S., & Maratsos, M. 1983. Initial verbs of yes-no questions: a different kind of general grammatical category. *Developmental Psychology*, *19*, 440–4

Kypriotaki, L. 1974. The acquisition of Aux. In *Papers and reports on child language development* (No. 8). Stanford: Stanford University

Lakoff, R. 1969. *A syntactic argument for negative transportation*. Papers from the fifth annual conference of the Chicago Linguistic Society

Lakoff, R. 1972. Language in context. *Language*, *48*, 907–27

Lakoff, R. 1973. Language and woman's place. *Language in Society*, *2*, 45–80

Landau, B., & Gleitman, L. R. 1985. *Language and experience. Evidence from the blind child*. Cambridge, Mass.: Harvard University Press

Langendoen, D. T. 1970. *Essentials of English grammar*. New York: Holt, Rinehart and Winston

Leech, G. N. 1969 *Towards a semantic description of English*. London: Longman

Leech, G. N. 1976. *Meaning and the English verb*. Harlow: Longman

Leech, G. N., & Coates, J. 1980. Semantic indeterminacy and the modals. In S. Greenbaum, G. Leech & J. Svartvik (eds.), *Studies in English linguistics for Randolph Quirk*. London: Longman

Leopold, W. F. 1949a. *Speech development of a bilingual child: a linguist's record, vol. III: Grammar and general problems in the first two years*. Evanston, Ill.: Northwestern University Press

Leopold, W. F. 1949b. *Speech development of a bilingual child: a linguist's record, vol. IV: Diary from age 2*. Evanston, Ill.: Northwestern University Press

Lieven, E. V. M. 1982. Context, process and progress in young children's speech. In M. Beveridge (ed.), *Children thinking through language*. London: Arnold

Lyons, J. 1977. *Semantics* (vol. 2). Cambridge: Cambridge University Press

McDonald, L., & Pien, D. 1982. Mother conversational behaviours as a function of interactional intent. *Journal of Child Language*, *9*, 337–58

McNeill, D. 1966. Developmental psycholinguistics. In G. A. Miller & F. Smith (eds.), *The genesis of language*. Cambridge, Mass.: MIT Press

MacWhinney, B. 1982. Basic syntactic processes. In S. Kuczaj (ed.), *Language development* (vol. 1: Syntax and semantics). Hillsdale, NJ: Erlbaum

Major, D. 1974. *The acquisition of modal auxiliaries in the language of children*. The Hague: Mouton

Malan, K. 1983. *Maternal speech style and language development. An investigation of yes/no question forms and verbal auxiliary growth in a mother-child pair*. Unpublished M.A. project report, University of Reading

Maratsos, M. 1982. Construction of grammatical categories. In E. Wanner & L. R. Gleitman (eds.), *Language acquisition: the state of the art.* Cambridge: Cambridge University Press

Maratsos, M. P., & Chalkley, M. A. 1980. The internal language of children's syntax: the ontogenesis and representation of syntactic categories. In K. E. Nelson (ed.), *Children's language* (vol. 2). New York: Gardner Press

Maratsos, M., & Kuczaj, S. 1978. Against the transformationalist account: a simpler analysis of auxiliary overmarkings. *Journal of Child Language, 5,* 337–45

Menyuk, P. 1969. *Sentences children use.* Cambridge, Mass.: MIT Press

Menyuk, P. 1971. *The acquisition and development of language.* Cambridge, Mass.: MIT Press

Miller, W. R. 1973. The acquisition of grammatical rules in English. In C. A. Ferguson & D. I. Slobin (eds.), *Studies of child language development.* New York: Holt, Rinehart and Winston

Mills, A. E. 1981. It's easier in German isn't it? The acquisition of tag questions in a bilingual child. *Journal of Child Language, 8,* 641–7

Mills, A. E. 1985. Acquisition of German. In D. I. Slobin (ed.), *The crosslinguistic study of language acquisition* (vol. 1: The data). Hillsdale, NJ: Erlbaum

Moores, D. F. 1970. An investigation of the psycholinguistic functioning of deaf adolescents. *Exceptional Children, 36,* 645–52

Morgan, J. L., & Newport, E. L. 1981. The role of constituent structure in the induction of an artificial language. *Journal of Verbal Learning and Verbal Behaviour, 20,* 67–85

Nelson, K. 1973. Structure and strategy in learning to talk. *Monographs of the Society for Research in Child Development, 38* (1–2, serial no. 149).

Nelson, K. 1985. *Making sense: the acquisition of shared meaning.* Orlando, Fla.: Academic Press

Nelson, K. E. 1977. Facilitating children's syntax acquisition. *Developmental Psychology, 13,* 101–7

Nelson, K. E. 1980. Theories of the child's acquisition of syntax: a look at rare events and at necessary, catalytic and irrelevant components of mother–child conversation. *Annals of the New York Academy of Sciences, 345,* 45–67

Nelson, K. E. 1981. Toward a rare-event cognitive comparison theory of syntax acquisition. In P. S. Dale & D. Ingram (eds.), *Child language: an international perspective.* Baltimore: University Park Press

Nelson, K. E. 1983. Keynote address to the 1982 Child Language Seminar, University of London. *First Language, 4,* 51–4

Nelson, K. E., & Bonvillian, J. D. 1978. Early language development: conceptual growth and related processes between 2 and 4½ years of age. In K. E. Nelson (ed.), *Children's language* (vol. 1). New York: Gardner Press

Nelson, K. E., Carskaddon, G., & Bonvillian, J. 1973. Syntax acquisition: impact of experimental variation in adult verbal interaction with the child. *Child Development, 44,* 497–504

Nelson, K. E., Denninger, M. M., Bonvillian, J. D., Kaplan, B. J., & Baker, N. D. 1984. Maternal input adjustments and non-adjustments as related to children's linguistic advances and to language acquisition theories. In A. D. Pellegrini &

T. D. Yawkey (eds.), *The development of oral and written languages: readings in developmental and applied linguistics*. New York: Ablex (NDBKB)

Newport, E. L. 1977. Motherese: the speech of mothers to young children. In N. J. Castellan, D. B. Pisoni & G. R. Potts (eds.), *Cognitive theory* (vol. 2). Hillsdale, NJ: Erlbaum

Newport, E. L., Gleitman, H., & Gleitman, L. R. 1977. Mother I'd rather do it myself: some effects and non-effects of maternal speech style. In C. Snow & C. Ferguson (eds.), *Talking to children: language input and acquisition*. Cambridge: Cambridge University Press (NGG)

O'Connor, E. F. 1972. Extending classical test theory to the measurement of change. *Review of Educational Research*, *42*, 73–97

Page, E. B. 1963. Ordered hypotheses for multiple treatments: a significance test for linear ranks. *Journal of the American Statistical Association*, *58*, 26–30

Palmer, F. R. 1965. *A linguistic study of the English verb*. London: Longman

Palmer, F. R. 1979. *Modality and the English modals*. New York: Longman

Park, T.-Z. 1971. *The acquisition of German verb auxiliary* (Working Paper of the Psychological Institute). Unpublished manuscript, University of Bern, Switzerland

Park, T.-Z. 1981. The development of syntax in the child with special reference to German. *Innsbrucker Beiträge zur Kulturwissenschaft*, Sonderheft 45

Perkins, M. R. 1983a. *Modal expressions in English*. London: Pinter

Perkins, M. R. 1983b. *The acquisition of modal expressions*. Paper presented at the annual meeting of the British Association of Applied Linguists, Leicester University, September 1983

Perkins, M. R. 1984. Review of Haegeman (1983) and Coates (1983). *Journal of Linguistics*, *20*, 384–90

Peters, A. M. 1977. Language learning strategies: does the whole equal the sum of the parts? *Language*, *53*, 560–73

Peters, A. M. 1983. *The units of language acquisition*. Cambridge: Cambridge University Press

Peters, A. M. 1986. Early syntax. In P. Fletcher & M. Garman (eds.), *Language acquisition: studies in first language development* (2nd edn). Cambridge: Cambridge University Press

Pinker, S. 1981. On the acquisition of grammatical morphemes. *Journal of Child Language*, *8*, 477–84

Pinker, S. 1984. *Language learnability and language development*. Cambridge, Mass.: Harvard University Press.

Plomin, R., & DeFries, J. C. 1985. *Origins of individual differences in infancy*. Orlando, Fla.: Academic Press

Pullum, G., & Wilson, D. 1977. Autonomous syntax and the analysis of auxiliaries. *Language*, *53*, 741–88

Quirk, R., Greenbaum, S., Leech, G., & Svartvik, J. 1972. *A grammar of contemporary English*. London: Longman

Quirk, R., Greenbaum, S., Leech, G., & Svartvik, J. 1985. *A comprehensive grammar of the English Language*. London: Longman

Raban, B. 1988. *The spoken vocabulary of five-year-old children*. Reading: The Reading and Language Information Centre, University of Reading

Ramer, A. L. H. 1976. Syntactic styles in emerging language. *Journal of Child Language*, *3*, 49–62

Richards, B. J. 1986. YES/NO questions in input and their relationship with rate of auxiliary verb development in young children. In *Proceedings of the Child Language Seminar*. Durham: University of Durham

Richards, B. J. 1987a. *Individual differences and the development of the auxiliary verb system in young children*. Unpublished Ph.D. dissertation, University of Bristol

Richards, B. J. 1987b. Type/token ratios: what do they really tell us? *Journal of Child Language*, *14*, 201–9

Richards, B. J. 1987c. The role of imitation. *Cahiers de l'Institut de Linguistique de Louvain*, *12.3–4*: Langage enfantin, 257–74

Richards, B. J. 1988. 'Not wee-wee had he?': Individual differences and the development of tag questions in two- and three-year-olds. In *Proceedings of the Child Language Seminar*. Warwick: University of Warwick

Robinson, W. P. 1972. *Language and social behaviour*. Harmondsworth: Penguin

Scarborough, H., & Wyckoff, J. 1986. Mother I'd still rather do it myself: some further non-effects of 'motherese'. *Journal of Child Language*, *13*, 431–7 (SW)

Schachter, P. 1983. Explaining auxiliary order. In F. Heny & B. Richards (eds.), *Linguistic categories: auxiliaries and related puzzles* (vol. 2: The scope, order, and distribution of English auxiliary verbs). Dordrecht, Holland: D. Reidel

Schwartz, R. G., & Camarata, S. 1985. Examining relationships between input and language development: some statistical issues. *Journal of Child Language*, *12*, 199–207

Shatz, M. 1978. Children's comprehension of their mothers' question-directives. *Journal of Child Language*, *5*, 39–46

Shatz, M., & Gelman, R. 1977. Beyond syntax: the influence of conversational constraints on speech modifications. In C. Snow & C. Ferguson (eds), *Talking to children: language input and acquisition*. Cambridge: Cambridge University Press

Shatz, M., Hoff-Ginsberg, E., & MacIver, D. 1989. Induction and the acquisition of English auxiliaries: the effects of differentially enriched input. *Journal of Child Language*, *16*, 141–60

Shields, M. M. 1974. The development of the modal auxiliary verb system. *Birmingham Educational Review*, *26*, 180–200

Siegel, S. 1956. *Non-parametric statistics for the behavioural sciences*. New York: McGraw-Hill

Slobin, D. I. 1979. *Psycholinguistics*. Glenview, Ill.: Scott, Foresman and Co.

Slobin, D. I. 1982. Universal and particular in the acquisition of language. In E. Wanner & L. R. Gleitman (eds.), *Language acquisition: the state of the art*. Cambridge: Cambridge University Press

Slobin, D. I., & Welsh, C. A. 1973. Elicited imitation as a research tool in developmental psycholinguistics. In C. Ferguson & D. I. Slobin (eds.), *Studies of child language development*. New York: Holt, Rinehart and Winston

Smolak, L., & Weinraub, M. 1983. Maternal speech: strategy or response. *Journal of Child Language*, *10*, 369–80

Snow, C., & Ferguson, C. A. (eds.) 1977. *Talking to children: language input and acquisition*. Cambridge: Cambridge University Press

Stephany, U. 1986. Modality. In P. Fletcher & M. Garman (eds.), *Language acquisition: studies in first language development* (2nd edn). Cambridge: Cambridge University Press

Todd, P. 1982. Tagging after red herrings: evidence against the processing capacity explanation in child language. *Journal of Child Language*, 9, 99–114

Treder Barr-Smith, D. S. 1980. *Sentence imitation by children from 1 to 5*. Unpublished M.Ed. dissertation, University of Bristol

Twadell, W. F. 1960. *The English verb auxiliaries*. Providence: Brown University Press

Weeks, T. E. 1974. *The slow language development of a bright child*. Lexington, Mass.: Lexington Books

Wells, C. G. 1975. *Coding manual for the description of child speech* (2nd edn). Bristol: University of Bristol

Wells, C. G. 1978. What makes for successful language development? In R. Campbell & P. Smith (eds.), *Recent advances in the psychology of language* (vol. 3). New York: Plenum

Wells, C. G. 1979a. Learning and using the auxiliary verb in English. In V. Lee (ed.), *Language development*. London: Croom Helm

Wells, C. G. 1979b. *Coding categories for the analysis of adult speech*. Unpublished manuscript, University of Bristol

Wells, C. G. 1980a. Adjustments in adult–child conversation: some effects of interaction. In H. Giles, W. P. Robinson & P. M. Smith (eds.), *Language: social-psychological perspectives*. Oxford: Pergamon

Wells, C. G. 1980b. Apprenticeship in meaning. In K. E. Nelson (ed.), *Children's Language* (vol. 2). New York: Gardner Press

Wells, C. G. 1980c. *The language experience of five-year-old children at home and at school*. Unpublished coding manual, Bristol University

Wells, C. G. 1981. *Learning through interaction*. Cambridge: Cambridge University Press

Wells, C. G. 1982. Review of J. McShane. Learning to talk. Cambridge: Cambridge University Press, 1980. *Journal of Child Language*, 9, 264–8

Wells, C. G. 1985. *Language development in the pre-school years*. Cambridge: Cambridge University Press

Wells, C. G. 1986. Variation in child language. In P. Fletcher & M. Garman (eds.), *Language acquisition: studies in first language development* (2nd edn). Cambridge: Cambridge University Press

Wells, C. G., & Gutfreund, M. 1984. *Coding manual for the description of conversation*. Unpublished manuscript, University of Bristol

Wells, C. G., MacLure, M., & Montgomery, M. M. 1980. Some strategies for sustaining conversation. In W. C. McCormack & H. J. Izzo (eds.), *The Sixth LACUS Forum, 1979*. Columbia, S. Ca.: Hornbeam Press

Wells, C. G., Montgomery, M. M., & MacLure, M. 1979. Adult–child discourse: outline of a model of analysis. *Journal of Pragmatics*, 3, 337–80

Wells, C. G., & Robinson, W. P. 1982. The role of adult speech in language development. In C. Fraser & K. Scherer (eds.), *The social psychology of language*. Cambridge: Cambridge University Press

Wexler, K. 1982. A principle theory for acquisition. In E. Wanner & L. R. Gleitman (eds.), *Language acquisition: the state of the art*. Cambridge: Cambridge University Press

Wexler, K., & Culicover, P. W. 1980. *Formal principles of language acquisition*. Cambridge, Mass.: MIT Press

Woisetschlaeger, E. F. 1985. *A semantic theory of the English auxiliary system*. New York: Garland

Wong Fillmore, L. 1979. Individual differences in second language acquisition. In C. J. Fillmore, D. Kempler & S.-Y. Wang (eds.), *Individual differences in language ability and language behaviour*. New York: Academic Press

Yoder, P. J., & Kaiser, A. P. 1989. Alternative explanations for the relationship between maternal verbal interaction style and child language development. *Journal of Child Language, 16*, 141–60 (YK)

Index